W9-CMJ-235

Gramley Library
Salem College
Winston-Salem, NC 27108

REORIENTATIONS

PN
81
.R375
1990

REORIENTATIONS

Critical Theories and Pedagogies

Edited by

BRUCE HENRICKSEN

and

THAÏS E. MORGAN

UNIVERSITY OF ILLINOIS PRESS
Urbana and Chicago

Gramley Library
Salem College
Winston-Salem, NC 27108

© 1990 by the Board of Trustees of the University of Illinois
Manufactured in the United States of America
1 2 3 4 5 C P 5 4 3 2 1

This book is printed on acid-free paper.

Library of Congress Cataloging-in-Publication Data

Reorientations : critical theories and pedagogies / edited by Bruce
Henricksen and Thaïs E. Morgan.
   p.   cm.
   ISBN 0-252-01688-2 (cloth : alk. paper). — ISBN 0-252-06109-8 (paper :
alk. paper)
   1. Criticism.   2. Critical theory.   3. Literature—Study and
teaching.   I. Henricksen, Bruce.   II. Morgan, Thaïs E.
PN81.R375   1990
801'.95—dc20   89-37853
                                                          CIP

"Aunt Jennifer's Tigers" is reprinted from *The Fact of a Doorframe:
Poems Selected and New, 1950-1984*, by Adrienne Rich, by permission
of the author and W. W. Norton & Company, Inc. © 1984 by Adrienne Rich. © 1975, 1978 by W. W. Norton & Company, Inc. ©
1981 by Adrienne Rich.

CONTENTS

ACKNOWLEDGMENTS

The editors are grateful to Loyola University of New Orleans for defraying costs relating to this project. William T. Cotton and Carol Siegel provided helpful advice, and G. Douglas Atkins offered invaluable assistance in his capacity as referee reader. We also appreciate the support of Ann Lowry Weir and the excellent staff at the University of Illinois Press.

PREFACE

Thaïs Morgan and I met a few years ago when she interviewed for a position at Loyola University of New Orleans, where I was then the chair of the English Department. Her decisions took her elsewhere—she is presently at Arizona State University in Tempe—but she has become a valued colleague and friend. At the time of our meeting we were each, in separate ways, seeking to absorb and come to terms with the burgeoning of "theory" that characterized the 1970s.

It was tempting (and perhaps I should speak only for myself) to find in the textuality produced by semiotics, deconstruction, and post-structuralism a new and exciting game. The rules were different—wholeness and unity were out, aporia and indeterminacy were in. More seriously, the opposition between left-wing and right-wing deconstruction prompted one to see beyond textual theories to their larger social and political implications. But how theory might actually influence pedagogical practice was, for a time at least, an inconvenient question to many of our leading theorists.

Thaïs has worked out her solutions to the problem of a newly grounded pedagogy in a large state university and among graduate students as well as undergraduates. I have remained at a smaller Catholic university where I teach undergraduates exclusively. Both of us believe that to teach literature and writing is to be involved in a social and institutional critique, and that the intense theoretical activity of recent years (maligned by the likes of Allan Bloom and William Bennett) has contributed greatly to this project. This volume was planned with the purpose of presenting a variety of theoretical views and pedagogical practices, from a variety of institutional sites, that are unified by that same belief.

The views offered in this volume, ranging from opinions on broad issues, such as curricula and canonicity, to specific suggestions for teaching individual texts, are ideas for our time and our immediate future. If, as we believe, teaching is a historically situated and social act, then, as Paulo Freire has said, there is no timeless and unchanging role for the teacher. Nor is this a single-issue book. Instead, the reader will encounter essays written from within various, but not incompatible, concerns—the concerns of the feminist, of the historicist, of those who speak of empowerment through writing, and so on. Each essay addresses questions of our classroom practice or our institutional identity in terms of a vision of what the present moment demands.

Our ideal reader is someone who, while not seeking to bury all the canonized touchstones of the past, is aware of how traditional forms of knowledge have served the interests of some at the expense of others. This reader, believing that change in American higher education can help to bring about positive change in the larger society, is open to a future that will not simply repeat the past.

Bruce Henricksen

INTRODUCTIONS

THAÏS E. MORGAN

Reorientations

The collection of essays on critical theories and pedagogical practices
that you are about to read has been in the making for several years.
From the perspective of 1990 the 1980s look like a time of great ferment
in American society and culture; we cannot know now, but perhaps
our thirteen essays are part of what a future generation of historians
and culture critics will call (if they are still practicing anything resem-
bling a Foucauldian archaeology) an "epistemological break."[1] The heterogeneity of the thirteen essays in this book marks the heterogeneity
of our times of writing—sometime in the late '80s; the heterogeneity
of our geographies—somewhere in the United States at a state, religious, or private college or university; and the heterogeneity of our
identities along a variety of spectrums, including, but not limited to,
gender, social class, and political alignment. Consequently, readers can
expect to find a variety of ways of interrelating a wide range of critical
theories with pedagogical practices in *Reorientations*.

"Posties," or theorists and teachers working within the horizon of
postmodernism, poststructuralism, post-Marxism, postphenomenology,
posthumanism, and postpedagogy,[2] no longer share the comforting
humanist vision of a Wayne Booth or an M. H. Abrams, the latter of
whom, in 1977, could still convincingly assert that pluralism was the
best, most liberating, most democratic, and most tolerant position that
a teacher could adopt.[3] In contrast, Cary Nelson opened a 1986 collection of essays on theory and pedagogy with a series of questions,
thereby showing his awareness of the postmodern critique of "truth"
or certainty about knowledge and values. At crucial points in their
argument all of the essays in *Reorientations* carry the postmodern critique of knowledge from the domain of theory into the domain of
pedagogical practice. All of the theorist-teachers represented here are

3

actively engaged in trying out new directions for understanding cultural texts—literary, scientific, visual, philosophical, historical, theoretical. In the process of these reorientations, disciplinary boundaries are crossed and new fields of critical inquiry are proposed.

Shifting Canons

"How long should interpretations continue to have influence? Does it matter?"

"Is interpretation preeminently a form of knowledge?"[4]

In Part 1 of *Reorientations* Barbara Ewell, Reed Dasenbrock, and R. A. Shoaf focus on "shifting canons," or the relation of literature, interpretation, and knowledge. Their shared concern with the literary canon and the act of interpretation grows out of three reorientations in theory and pedagogy: Ewell focuses on the contributions of feminism, Dasenbrock on the problems posed by nationalism, and Shoaf on understanding the many dimensions of temporality. All three writers discuss an issue that has become increasingly urgent not only in departments of language and literature, but also across the disciplines in the 1980s: "canonicity," or who defines a canon of cultural texts, when, why, and for whom.

As Barbara Herrnstein Smith observes in an article on the contingencies of value in the criticism of literature and in aesthetics: "One of the major effects of prohibiting or inhibiting explicit evaluation is to forestall the exhibition and obviate the possible acknowledgement of divergent systems of value and thus to ratify, by default, established evaluative authority" and its institutionalization of a canon.[5] Ewell and Dasenbrock's essays take up the challenge of making explicit the implicit assumptions that authorize the literary canon as it is transmitted to and by thousands of teachers and students when they read "authorized" anthologies and "great" authors or "the classics." Ewell explains the ways in which feminists have critiqued the notion of "universality" and exposed the predominantly white, middle-class, masculinist bias of the literary canon as it has traditionally been understood. Dasenbrock argues that while literature by minorities should be taught, it cannot be simply added to the existing canon; instead, a thorough revaluation of the canon must take place.

Adrienne Rich has suggested: "To think like a woman in a man's world means thinking critically, refusing to accept the givens, making connections between facts and ideas which men have have left unconnected."[6] Ewell argues that feminist theories and pedagogies help us make connections that extend beyond the situations and writings of women. For example, one of the connections left unexplored until relatively recently by theorists, critics, and teachers of literature is the link between gender, race, and class that recurs throughout history and that is reproduced in all kinds of texts. In a 1981 article that emphasizes the complex relations between literature and the "world," Gayatri Spivak calls for an activist "pedagogy that would constantly seek to undo the opposition between the verbal and the social text."[7] The "world," or the social construction of "reality," includes not only ideologies of gender but also ideologies of race and class. Spivak asks teachers to intervene in the world, as she herself does, by making explicit and calling into question these ideologies and the ways in which they are implicated in one another. In a later article on "Imperialism and Sexual Difference," Spivak demonstrates how, often unwittingly, the post-modern teacher may successfully support feminist goals in the class-room but may at the same time reinforce "certain imperialist ideological structures even as [she/he] deconstructs the tropological error of mas-culism."[8] The implication is that today's teacher not only needs critical theories to "teach well" in an ethical sense, but also that he or she must be prepared to rethink and reorient personal values and alle-giances, not just the ideological formations found in literary and other cultural texts.

Similarly concerned with the impact of theory on the world both inside and outside the classroom, Dasenbrock explores the problems attendant upon the current movement toward opening up the canon to the literature of women, peoples of color, and the working classes, all of whom tend not to write in the genres or on the topics prescribed by the canon and its male, white, middle-class guardians. The attempt to open up the canon in the 1980s seems to have in common with the pluralism recommended in the 1970s the notion that "more is better" and the liberal belief (itself middle-class) that all interests can be ac-commodated—somehow—within the study of literature. The attrac-tiveness of this ideal notwithstanding, Dasenbrock argues that in fact the canon can't open to the literatures of all the interest groups—each with legitimate concerns—now competing for a place at the center of academic discourse. An example of this quandary of liberalism is the student demand for change in the content of a required world literature course at Stanford University in 1988, for instance, substituting Toni Morrison for Homer, Naguib Mahfouz for William Faulkner.[9] If the "classics" are cast out and the literatures of women, blacks, Hispanics, and "third-world" writers are put in, is this not a simple reversal of the hierarchy of "power/knowledge" without a change in the motives that ground canon formation in the first place?[10] Is not one hegemony being exchanged for another?

What, then, does literary theory have to offer women's studies, Native American studies, African-American studies, Hispanic studies, Asian studies, and parallel studies of socioeconomically, ethnically, or racially marginalized groups that are still marked as "other" within most American college and university curricula in the 1980s? Although theories like deconstruction have served to raise useful questions about race, gender, and class, what practical solutions to the problem of what to teach next semester do these theories provide? Should we teach "the" canon or something "other"? Dasenbrock gives no easy answers to such questions but suggests a risky "new recentering," a "new essentialism," that does not hesitate to make texts written by hitherto marginalized groups central and to create a new canon, even a new hierarchy, out of them. Significantly, Ewell encounters a similar quandary and offers a similar solution as she considers the impact of feminism on the teaching of literature. While women's studies "has produced otherwise unavailable insights into the nature of women's writing," she concedes that emphasis on women's biographies has made prominent their differences as members of various, sometimes competing or hostile, races, ethnic groups, nationalities, and classes (48). The result for pedagogical practice here again seems to be a reorientation in which texts are taught, a reorientation that dialogizes the canon and the student's experience through the diversity of women's voices and interests.

Shoaf highlights the problem of national differences in relation to temporal differences when late twentieth-century readers encounter literary texts that are written in languages other than modern English and that appear at various times in the distant past. While Dasenbrock proposes teaching courses in world literature based on the English language as an international language community—in which the voices of Chinese, Hispanic, Native American, and black African writers speak to us as forcefully as white American, white British, or white South African writers do—Shoaf proposes to study the international community of the Middle Ages—itself stratified into a hegemonic Latin language/literature (comparable to English) and various competing vernacular groups—as a site for rediscovering our own differences from each other and from the peoples of the past. Practicing a revisionist historicism in his classroom, Shoaf finds poststructuralist literary theories to be especially useful in trying to understand both his students' and his own need to know the past in terms of the present, or to "translate" the Middle Ages into contemporary concerns, and thus in some sense to forget it as well as to preserve it. For Shoaf, teaching medieval literatures in English translation is a sort of paradigm for teaching any literature and even for the process of communication itself: "typically, though we may only intermittently be conscious of it, we botch each other's words up fit to our own thoughts, even when we are only 'translating' within the same language" (78).

Shoaf's consciousness of his difference(s) from his students and the collective difference(s) of both teacher and students from past writers and cultures exemplifies the postmodern situation of *"différance"*[11] in gender, race, ethnicity, nationality, religion, class. To each of us, everyone else may appear to be a Grendel or radically Other, as Shoaf suggests: "Perhaps Grendel in *Beowulf* is the embodiment of the problem of translation. Grendel does *not* translate, nor can he be translated" (86). In response to this challenge of otherness, as formulated in contemporary critical theories ranging from feminism to psychoanalysis to deconstruction, two nearly opposite pedagogical reorientations emerge from Part 1 of this book: collaborative learning and conflictual learning.[12]

Feminist pedagogy, here outlined by Ewell, takes the direction of collaborative learning in its exploration of literature and issues of gender. Significantly, this direction has also proved useful to teachers of composition, as the several articles on collaborative learning in *College English* during the 1980s attest. For instance, in "Collaborative Learning and the 'Conversation of Mankind,' " Kenneth Bruffee reexamines the link between the pedagogical practice of "class discussion" and the teacher's authority as possessor of and spokesperson for "knowledge."[13] Despite announced intentions to the contrary, he observes, teachers usually do most of the "discussing," turning what was initially offered to the students as an "open" forum into a "closed" lecture. This slippage from the dialogical into the monological is not entirely innocent: a function of his or her training as a "professional" academic, the teacher's monologue also represents the unspoken belief that "knowledge"—literary or otherwise—is "something we acquire and wield as individuals" and not "something we generate and maintain in company with and in dependency upon each other" (645).[14] Referring to the postmodern redefinition of knowledge as "a social artifact" or "construction," Bruffee looks forward to a new pedagogy based on the concept of knowledge as "continual negotiation or conversation" in which a heterogeneity of values and interests is entertained without any underlying expectation that one superior "truth" will be determined at the end of the process (646-47). Bruce Henricksen offers a critical overview of various theories and pedagogies based on the conversation model in his introduction to *Reorientations*.

Ewell's call for personal involvement and intimacy in any pedagogy of feminist orientation parallels Bruffee's definition of a collaborative pedagogy oriented toward poststructuralist theories of subjectivity, knowledge, and power. "Like race and sexual orientation," Ewell says, "one can hardly discuss the topic [of gender] without engaging student emotions—and attention" (54). Through the issue of gender, alterity and textuality can be reconsidered in relation to each other and to the structures of our knowledge as members of various groups within society. In this reevaluation the teacher is as involved as the student, and everyone takes risks in reexamining questions of identity, belief, and action. Foucault's theories of discourse, knowledge, and power, for instance, provide one way of rethinking the Cartesian notion of the masterful, masculinist "self," now seen as a multiply situated, multi-faceted "subject" who is, through his or her very ability to act and speak within several discursive horizons or social groups at once, "sub-jected" to a variety of constraints and rules on what can be said and known.[15] Thus, as Frances Maher suggests in "Classroom Pedagogy and the New Scholarship on Women": "Central to this inclusion of the self as subject . . . is the teacher's acknowledgement of his or her perspective as, of necessity, a partial one as well." Instead of presenting a course in literature as "objective truth," or knowledge with a capital *K*, "the teacher must be explicit about his or her rationale behind the choice of readings, issues and so on."[16]

At this point, however, remembering my own experiences with trying to be honest about my assumptions and agenda as a teacher of literature and critical theory, the problem of conflict between teacher and student and conflict among students arises. But is conflict itself necessarily a problem? As feminists, both Maher and Ewell consider conflict a pos-itive factor in the scene of collaborative learning. Like Shoaf, Maher sees pedagogy as a translative activity in which the teacher "translates" literature and other cultural texts and contexts for the student while he or she "explains the rationale for" these "translating activities" (44). However, Maher cautions, this "stance does not, and should not, min-imize conflict or disagreement" in the classroom. At the same time, Ewell points out, the teacher, if a feminist, must endure an ongoing inner conflict, since she or he is "at once a representative of hierarchy and a visible challenge to it" (55). From another angle, Shoaf regards the activity of reading and "translating" the literatures of the past into our own languages and values as "aggressive, contending, 'contestual,' mutually assimilative." The postmodern reader is analogous to Beowulf in his confrontation with Grendel or the Other; as in John Gardner's novel *Grendel*, Beowulf represents the self-glorifying present over and against Grendel who stands for the misunderstood past. Applying Derrida's theory of the violence of all textualization or writing to teaching *The Norton Anthology of English Literature* makes sense here, too, for, as a freshman class asked me recently, "aren't all these guys dead, anyway?"[17]

The overlapping of collaborative pedagogies (never without conflicts) and conflictual pedagogies (never without collaboration) is perhaps an unexpected and paradoxical consequence of the application of critical theories to teaching. However, the heterogeneity of the theories and pedagogies represented in *Reorientations* may well be a response to the growing heterogeneity of our students', our institutions', and, in many cases, our own personal goals. In his preface to *Criticism in the University*, Gerald Graff reflects on the new importance of the interdisciplinary field called "cultural studies," itself simultaneously a producer and a product of the heterogeneous values and interests that constitute "America" in the '80s.[18] According to Graff, "The university does not have a unified cultural tradition to impart but rather a set of *cultural conflicts*—including conflicts over what the cultural tradition is and has been thought to be" (12, my emphasis). Graff's position here is implicitly opposed to the teaching of any canon at all. In an essay in the same book, he further claims that "the broad consensus which underlay traditional liberal education no longer exists, and that reestablishing coherence is now necessarily a matter of dramatizing exemplary conflicts and controversies rather than expounding the received great books, ideas and traditions" (80). Yet, I would suggest, this new positive-conflict model of literary studies is not necessarily a guarantee of freedom for all concerned: who decides on the "exemplary" (synonymous with "canonical") conflicts that will be discussed and valorized as such? And for what reason(s)? In other words, who ends up with the textual power?

Rethinking Texts

"Why do we interpret? Can we speak of a will to interpret, a need to interpret, a desire to interpret, a fear of interpreting?"

"Do interpreters seek power over the objects they interpret? Over their interpreters?"[19]

Part 2 of *Reorientations* focuses on the challenge of rethinking texts and includes three different proposals for changing the way we teach through insights gained from contemporary textual theories. *Text* is a theoretical concept that spans the twentieth century; emerging with Russian Formalism and American New Criticism, although already defined differently by these early modern movements, *text* at first designated any utterance (typically written) that can be studied through linguistic methods. After the 1960s *text* came to include all sorts of cultural "discourse" and modes of representation, regardless of media or academic disciplinary classification.[20] Partly in response to what has always been the interdisciplinary situation of English studies—as evidenced by the references to social history, iconography, and other extratextual factors in the footnotes in any *Norton Anthology*—and partly in response to the peculiarly postmodern reconception of all kinds of knowledge as necessarily heterogeneous in form and content (termed a "crisis" by some), theorists working in language, literature, and composition began in the 1980s to call for a renovation of curricula and pedagogical practices.[21] For instance, in a 1984 article that addresses the profession of English at large, Gerald Prince urges us to rethink the long-standing assumption that "interpretation is the real business of literary study" and to join social scientists in investigating the wider cultural implications of "symbolic behavior as manifested by the literary." Theory, Prince asserts, "is presupposed by practice," suggesting that the debates in the 1970s and early 1980s over theory versus practice were fundamentally misguided.[22] As the essays by Robert Scholes, Gregory Ulmer, and George Landow in Part 2 of *Reorientations* show, various recent theories of text or textuality are proving highly useful in changing both teachers' and students' assumptions about literature and its many links with other cultural and social phenomena. In Part 2, then, the reader can expect to find pedagogies based on theories of textuality that are cross-disciplinary in scope and that apply the ideas of Roland Barthes (semiotics), Jacques Lacan (psychoanalysis), Michel Foucault (social history), and Jacques Derrida (deconstruction), among others.

If the reorientations proposed by Scholes, Ulmer, and Landow are any indication, "English" in the 1990s is going to look less and less like English, traditionally defined as the study of the literary canon that constitutes part of the cultural heritage of Great Britian and the United States. Instead, "English" is going to look more and more like what in the past has been called "humanities" (an interdisciplinary program based on literary and other aesthetic texts, approached through qualitative rather than quantitative methods), or what is presently being called "cultural studies."[23] Thus, in "Toward a Curriculum in Textual Studies," Scholes outlines a fourfold plan that shifts "from a curriculum oriented to a literary canon toward a curriculum in textual studies" based on contemporary critical theories of "text."[24] Addressing all members of "this troubled discipline called 'English,' " Scholes offers textual studies as a solution to the often acrimonious debates within English departments over the priority of literature versus composition, English versus American literatures, theory versus literature, "coverage" versus "close reading," and so on (95-96). Rather than assign blame for the presumed crisis in English studies, Scholes, like Ulmer and Landow, views the current situation of change and heterogeneity as a positive opportunity for innovation on the part of English teachers at all levels of the education system.

Extending the arguments made in his book *Textual Power*, Scholes describes the practice of textuality within textual studies as "the actual production or composition of texts" by the students themselves (99). Instead of remaining passive consumers of novels or television programs or billboard advertisements, students are encouraged to recognize that they are already active producers of certain texts, such as oral narratives, and that they are capable of producing other types of texts as well, such as irreverent parodies of canonical literature. In proposing that teachers "shar[e] the powers and pleasures" of speaking, writing, and thinking in English with their students, Scholes draws on Barthes's semiotics as well as on the classical poetics of Horace, who exhorted would-be writers to move and to please their audience if they wanted to teach them anything (*docere, movere et placere*). Thus, textual studies includes not only "the two macro-structures of persuasion and narration, with their accompanying theories of rhetoric and narratology" — or the ancient and the modern — but also a postmodern focus on the fundamental "figurativity" of all language and knowledge, and on "subjectivity" as the discursive socialization of each person by his or her very participation in linguistic and other representations of a culture (106). In this way, Scholes's pedagogy of textual power entails both theory and practice, the production of one's own texts as well as the critical analysis of others' texts. Referring to Foucault's critique of the circulation of power through language and various forms of textuality, Scholes ultimately implies that teaching is always a political activity. Just as the traditional study of the canon tends to produce a "docile" subject "whose very writing is a kind of reading" and reverence for authority, so the new textual studies signal the emergence of a new kind of "subject" who will be a critical reader as well as a critical writer (96-97).

Although his proposal for a curriculum in textual studies parallels the radical or oppositional pedagogy discussed by Robert Con Davis

Gramley Library
Salem College
Winston-Salem, NC 27108

in Part 4 of *Reorientations,* Scholes recognizes the constraints on his hopes for students: in the "real world," new pedagogical goals based on new critical theories "must also be translated" or "institutionalized, departmentalized, and curriculized" according to existing "codes" within academe (98). At the same time, Scholes recognizes that the textual power offered to students by the practice of text production and textual critique "can be exercised only the price of [their] being subjected to the rules and limits established by . . . discourse" (109). Is there a potential contradiction here between the student's empowerment and his or her disempowerment through the study of language, literature, and other modes of textuality? Stanley Fish seems to think so. In "Anti-Foundationalism, Theory Hope, and the Teaching of Composition," Fish argues that "theory hope," or "the promise that theory seems to offer" for distributing power and knowledge differently in our society through the teaching of English, is doomed to fail because its "foundations" or theoretical principles are "from the very first implicated in everything it claims to transcend."[25] Fish further maintains that the "self-conscious knowledge" or critical consciousness currently valorized by postmodern theories and pedagogies is actually a tried-and-true, rather Arnoldian "assumption of liberal thought—that the only knowledge worth having is . . . achieved disinterestedly" (71). Consequently, Fish says, radical or oppositional pedagogy—which informs several of the essays in *Reorientations*—is internally contradictory, being both foundationalist and antifoundationalist at once: "it is curious to have an argument that begins by denying the possibility of a knowledge that is independent of our beliefs and practices end by claiming . . . the achieving of just such an independence." In conclusion, Fish declares: "Here the advice is, if all knowledge is situational, then let's teach situations" (74).

Yet whether Fish likes it or not, in the world of the late 1980s, as the liberal, middle-class, white, masculinist consensus confronts the demands of the many different groups, values, and needs that make up "America," our common ground or "foundation" is increasingly becoming just that: discursive "situations." What teachers in textual studies and many other programs that combine literature with theory are trying to do is nothing less than prepare students to deal with the language- and image-mediated "situations" that they encounter in their daily social lives. Moreover, as the essays by Scholes, Ulmer, and Landow here demonstrate, the goal of textual studies, textshop, or hypertext, respectively, is in fact not, in Fish's phrase, "the achieving of an independence" from all the ideologies active in our knowledge, but quite the reverse: a critical recognition of our subjectivity, its ideological grounds, and its alignments. Finally, Fish's resistance to the self-consciousness of theories of discourse, knowledge, and power and to the new pedagogies emerging from them is exemplary of the change (or "crisis") that the profession of English is undergoing. For instance, historically, nearly all present teachers of English in the United States have been professionalized into New Critical humanism, a system of beliefs that holds that we all have a unique, individual identity; that the literary author has a unique, individual intention discernible to the critic using the "right" methods (i.e., exegesis or close reading); and that literature offers the universal "truth" about all human experience.[26] It is understandably difficult, then, for many modern humanists who believe in the unique value of the "self" to accept postmodern critical theories that redefine the "self" in terms of a sort of personal text that is as readable and as (ex)changeable as other kinds of texts to which it is related in form as well as in content.

Furthermore, one need only look at the range of student work resulting from Ulmer's textshop in Part 2 of *Reorientations* to realize that theory has already become more than just a hope for the future. As described by Ulmer, the writings, readymade sculptures, and other experimental texts produced by his students working from current critical theories as well as from avant-garde art manifestoes and scientific models surprised even their own producers, who gained a sense of power, a new subjectivity, from learning how they, too—not just canonical authors or famous artists and scientists—could articulate knowledge and (re)shape ideology.

In his proposal for "an experimental humanities," Ulmer argues that "modern experimental arts and theory have . . . shown us how to make the language and literature disciplines equal partners with the other divisions of knowledge in the university" (113). Like Scholes's program for textual studies, Ulmer's textshop is broadly interdisciplinary: it makes connections between physical science and literature as well as between popular and high culture and between mass media and literature. Ulmer, Scholes, and Landow share the democratic goal of making the student less a consumer and more a coproducer of texts. For Ulmer, knowledge is a continual activity of critical inquiry and imaginative invention rather than a static set of information to be transmitted from teacher to student. Thus, he sees the modern avant-garde in art and literature as "the humanities equivalent of pure research" in the physical sciences, just as he sees the skill of imagining or imaging as the aesthetic equivalent of rational creativity in the laboratory. What the student in a textshop learns is twofold: "the epistemological assumptions at work in culture and in one's own thinking" (117) and how thinking itself has worked for others and might work for us now. "The point," here as in Scholes's textual studies, "is to produce a person capable not only of reciting the history of invention but of inventing something oneself" (117).

Interestingly, Ulmer's idea for a textshop that bridges the gap between humanities and sciences draws on psychoanalysis as much as on semiotics. In an article on psychoanalysis and education, Shoshana Felman suggests that "psychoanalysis has opened up unprecedented teaching possibilities" by reenvisioning pedagogy in terms of the analyst and the analysand, and in terms of the complex psychological processes of transference and identification.[27] Perhaps most challenging is the application of the psychoanalytical notion of the unconscious to understanding what transpires, through verbal language and through body language, between the teacher and the student and among the students in any classroom. "What," Felman asks, "is the unconscious, if not a kind of *unmeant knowledge* which escapes intentionality and meaning" (28) and language itself? Since neither the teacher nor the student can ever fully "know" or be in control of what he or she is saying or doing due to the play of the unconscious across language and the body, teaching can no longer be regarded simply as the authoritative transmission of information; instead, teaching becomes "the creation of a new *condition* of knowledge" in which both "I" and "the Other"—teacher and student or student and student—exchange knowledge (conscious) in ignorance (unconscious) (33).

Ulmer's experimental pedagogy puts these insights from psychoanalytic theory into practice. For instance, students are asked to think about the joint role of emotion and reason in the process of invention. Sigmund Freud himself provides a good example of how knowledge is built up out of cognition and affect, scientific fact and literary creation, simultaneously. "Let us think about Freud's invention for a moment," suggests Ulmer, referring to Freud's theory of the unconscious in *The Interpretation of Dreams*. "It consists of the generalization of his peculiar personal, familial circumstances, mediated through a major work of world literature (*Oedipus Rex*), into the discourse of medical science" (130). In a textshop students analyze this complex process of invention with the twofold aim of finding a model for understanding how their own thoughts and feelings (conscious and unconscious) work and for deciding how to generate their own text production. It is important to note that the goal of the textshop is not the same as a traditional, Platonic pedagogy in which students memorize and imitate the ideal knowledge of their teacher; rather, the goal is to discover a "personal cognitive style" and its relation to the configuration of various types of knowledge.

The mutual mapping of imagination and cognition also takes place when students use hypertext—or a multimedia computer program that can revolutionize the way literature and literary history are taught in English departments. By enabling a student at any level to move rapidly and easily around in a complex web of written and visual information, Landow explains, hypertext effectively reorients and widens attention. Through using hypertext, the student can move beyond a linear, print-bound book such as *The Norton Anthology* and explore "an infinitely re-centerable system whose provisional point of focus depends upon the reader, who becomes truly a user of knowledge" (135). In this way, hypertext realizes the dream of every English teacher who ever dragged a slide projector, a record player, and a large-scale map into his or her classroom for Survey of Literature. Through hypertext, explains Landow, both teacher and student are "freed" from the monological focus of an anthology to "discover" unsuspected connections between authors or events through computer links and to "make choices" about which relations between texts to pursue (137). Likewise, both teacher and student develop materials to add to the hypertextual system, thus becoming equals in the creation of knowledge.

Significantly, all three teachers in Part 2 of *Reorientations* have found theories of intertextuality useful for their innovative programs. "The principle of *intertextuality* is absolutely crucial to the development of a curriculum based on textual theory and practice" (104), states Scholes, who is especially interested in showing students "how new texts are in fact made out of old ones" and thus demystifying the idea of "originality" (104). Because they read intertextually, or in the recognition that all texts are interrelated formally and historically, Scholes's students feel able to produce their own texts, "to play irreverently with the texts of others" as well as to appreciate how others' texts work (105). Similarly, Ulmer's students analyze aesthetic texts on the same par with scientific texts to see how knowledge is created out of intertextual images and analogies that cross discplinary boundaries. Finally, as the very names of the computer program components ("InterVal" and "InterText") and as the collaborative nature of Landow's project show, hypertext is fundamentally based on the theory of intertextuality, or the necessary relatedness of all texts (oral, written, visual, and so on) in any culture or horizon of knowledge.

Moreover, as Landow notes, hypertext, precisely because it is developed out of theories of intertextuality, is unlike previous educational computer software in not promoting any "primary axis of organization" or "center" (149). To the postmodernist teacher, this decentering offers a new way of approaching the pedagogical problem of authority in the classroom, for in the hypertext laboratory the student is as likely to make a connection between the materials in the system as the teacher is. At the same time, the teacher's personal biases may figure less strongly in the learning process. "As the capacity of hypertext systems to be infinitely recenterable suggests, they have the corollary characteristic of being antihierarchical and democratic" (150). In a reversal of the exegetical focus of English studies, hypertext facilitates "the disappearance of boundaries between author and reader" (150), teacher and student; student users of hypertext "accept some responsibility" (151) as they construct materials to be inserted into the system: "students thus establish a community of learning, demonstrating to themselves that a large part of any investigation rests on the work of others"—perhaps one of the most important social lessons of intertextuality (151).

Landow's debate with Walter Ong on whether intertextuality or orality is representative of the new orientation of our postmodern culture implicitly raises the question of literacy, a subject of much controversy in the 1980s. Richard Ohmann, in an article entitled "Literacy, Technology, and Monopoly Capital," has argued against the introduction of computers into the teaching of language and literature on the grounds that "the computer and its software are . . . carrying forward the deskilling and controlling of labor . . . that has been a main project of monopoly capital."[28] Computer illiteracy will soon replace print-media illiteracy, Ohmann predicts, and today's class structure of elite readers versus working-class nonreaders will be replaced by an opposition between computer literates who work at Merrill Lynch versus computer illiterates who work at Wendy's (682-83). Ultimately, Ohmann grimly concludes, our "work for literacy is not in itself intrinsically liberating" (688). As the reader will find, the essays in Part 3 of *Reorientations* offer strong, practical refutations of Ohmann's position.

Reading and Writing Otherwise

> "Does interpretative writing differ from the kind of interpretation we do continually in the rest of our lives?"
>
> "How is difference (sexual, racial, class, national identity) inscribed in interpretation?"[29]

Ohmann's objections to the use of new computer technology in the teaching of reading and writing are met not only by the democratization of knowledge that Landow's program for hypertext offers, but also by

Lori Lefkovitz's demonstration that teaching the skills of literacy in tandem with critical theory does in fact liberate otherwise disenfranchised groups and does in fact succeed in sharing the textual power that literacy grants in our society today. Fully cognizant of the discursive constraints on what reading and writing skills enable anyone to do, Lefkovitz argues against so-called remedial writing and the marginalization of both composition teachers and their nonwhite, non-English-speaking, low-income students through the hierarchical organization of writing courses typical of most English departments. Instead of dividing composition from literature and both from theory, Lefkovitz shows how students seeking to enter the mainstream of American society and its economy by becoming fully literate can be empowered to do so as critically conscious citizens rather than remaining the semi-literate, socioeconomically marginalized underclass that Ohmann fears.

Undoubtedly the most convincing example of the textual power that Lefkovitz's composition pedagogy offers is the story of the Chinese woman student. After reading and writing about theory and literature focused on oppositions between nature and culture, as summed up in the phenomenon of the "wild child"—and after thinking about her own ambiguous position between American and Chinese discourses and ideologies—this student of English composition concluded: " 'I am a lazy student, and because I am lazy I am hurting my mother. If I were like other American teenagers, I would have written that I am hurting myself. I wish that I were home in China. Here, I am the wild child' " (174). Rather than disempowering, Lefkovitz sees this moment in her student's self-critical entrance into English in America as empowering: "To recognize how one's own discourse would differ from a dominant discourse involves reading, writing, and acting from a position of seized authority" (174). In the context of composition courses for marginalized social groups, then, Foucault's claim that the subject's entry into the intertextual discourse of his or her (native or adopted) culture is also a moment of subjection and resistance makes a good deal of sense. The English teacher, Lefkovitz urges, must work with the tension between literacy/centeredness/power and illiteracy/marginalization/powerlessness to make writing classes more than just a repetition of exclusions on the basis of gender, race, nationality, or class—exclusions that many students already encounter elsewhere in our society.

The essays by Lori Lefkovitz, Nancy Comley, and Elizabeth Flynn that form Part 3 of *Reorientations* are primarily concerned with writing and reading otherwise, or with the reshaping of composition pedagogies through various critical theories regarding the ways in which societies define hierarchies of power/knowledge according to race, nationality, class, and gender. Thus, while Lefkovitz considers the marginalizing effects of nationality and socioeconomic status, Comley examines the system of gender as it operates in English composition and literature courses. Applying insights from reader-response theory and feminism, Comley discusses how the ideology of gender marks student responses to Ernest Hemingway's short story, "Hills like White Elephants." The woman reader represents a particularly complex case of otherness, as both Ewell and Comley point out, because woman is pervasively defined as man's "other" or inferior in being different from man, female students both read and write "otherwise" than male students do. Specifically, Comley observes, female readers and writers are taught at school to read and write as men do. As a result, since Hemingway is usually presented as a "great" canonical author, the female reader who does not accept the portrayal of unequal power relations between the "girl" and the "man" in "Hills like White Elephants" is pedagogically forced to conclude that she herself is wrong, not Hemingway. Comley analyzes this typical situation: "To identify against oneself is to devalue one's experience, and to place oneself—if one is a woman—on the margins of (privileged) experience" (179). Furthermore, when students are taught to use the impersonal (in fact, male-gendered) pronouns *one* and *we* in writing papers and exams, the woman writer, like the woman reader, is again kept outside the text, in this case, even outside the very text that she herself has written.

Perhaps the most fascinating point in Comley's essay is her discussion of the way in which Hemingway hides the masculinist bias of his story behind the neutralizing pronoun *it* and the ways in which male and female students have responded to this strategy in their rewritings of the story. Comley's combination of reader-response theory and feminism also sheds light on the resistance of several male readers to the role of masculine "boon companion" that Hemingway writes into "Hills like White Elephants." Since the gendered subject is just as much a social construction as the racial or ethnic subject, these male students are manifesting the changes that sex and gender roles have been undergoing in the 1980s through their hesitation to adopt a "macho" identity in conformity with Hemingway's main male character in the story or with Hemingway's ideal male reader. A student named Michael, for example, chose to write a parody of the stereotypical sexist point of view, thereby attempting to become other to that ideology despite our culture's idealization of the male term in the formula of sexual difference. Another move toward understanding otherness was made by Keith, who rewrote Hemingway's story from what he thought a woman's viewpoint would be, thereby joining "great" authors like John Updike in the contemporary movement toward reorienting genders.

A quite different application of reader-response theories to English composition and literature is made by Flynn, who contrasts David Bleich's subjective approach with Louise Rosenblatt's transactional approach to the relation between reader and text. Flynn's and Lefkovitz's experiences with the application of criticism and theory in the composition classroom are particularly interesting because both teachers work with students who are not being professionalized as English majors and who, therefore, arguably might have no interest either in literature or in literary theory. With this in mind, Flynn describes her composition students as "preprofessional undergraduates" who plan to go into jobs in business, industry, government, law, or medicine, and then asks: "How much literary theory do these students need? Why do they need it?" (194, 195). Her answer is itself informed by critical theories of discourse, power, and the social construction of knowledge: "Students . . . need to learn how to identify their own . . . assumptions and those of others with whom they are agreeing or contending" (195).

With Ewell, Shoaf, and Lefkovitz, Flynn believes that the pedagogical situation involves conflict, just as daily social interactions do. As Flynn shows, a composition course reoriented through critical theories on language and ideology can enable preprofessional students "to become aware of their own interpretative strategies and the strategies of others" who are competing with them in the world (196). Indeed, the dominant ideology of success is an important factor in all composition courses and not only in those attended by preprofessionals, as Nicholas Coles and Susan Wall discuss in their article, "Conflict and Power in the Reader-Responses of Adult Basic Writers."[30] "Success" can be defined in terms of advancing along in a profession or in terms of gaining the basic literacy skills that will give one access to preprofessional training in the first place: "What has changed . . . is . . . not the motive for achieving advanced literacy, but the understanding of what such literacy entails" (309). Citing Lois Weis's study of black urban students, for instance, Coles and Wall emphasize that the English composition classroom tends to bring together people representing social groups with very divergent interests. Instead of homogenizing these different voices into one dominant discourse on "how to read and write," and instead of (once again) marginalizing black, Hispanic, or immigrant students, Coles and Wall suggest that "The more enabling path lies . . . through intensified engagement and even partisanship with the facts, experiences, and viewpoints represented 'in' books" (303). By recognizing the other so that he or she, too, may speak, Coles and Wall, like Flynn, find reader-response theory useful. Through an interaction with literary texts, otherwise marginalized readers, such as the Chinese woman in Lefkovitz's essay, can "supply the contexts of experience, memory, and concern within which knowledge is produced and its power released" (303).

At the same time as conflict takes place in the postmodern "noisy classroom," cooperation and a sense of community emerge too. For instance, Flynn uses student-written and "publicly shared" journals to "stimulate conversation" among students with different goals and backgrounds (205). These journals are discussed through reader-response theory not only as specimens of personal feelings, but also as "indications of differences that result from affiliation with social groups" (205). In a further step, as Michael Holzman argues in "The Social Context of Literacy Education," the English teacher can actually use the heterogeneous identities and interests of composition and literature students to construct a community.[31] This kind of pedagogy can be especially effective when the students participating have already been categorized by American society as other—racially, ethnically, linguistically, nationally. "Resistance to the institutions of the dominant society" may be the one goal that the members of an English class share, yet this in itself "is a form of group identification" that can generate increased fluency in conversation and the motivation to read and to write for, to, and against others (32). In such a heteroglossic situation, as in Lefkovitz's classroom, the margins become the center: oppositional pedagogy replaces the unquestioning routines of professionalization and cultural critique replaces simple literacy.

Teaching Reorientations

> "Are interpretative positions and conclusions historically and culturally specific? Are they historically, sociologically, and politically determined?"
>
> "Do interpretations always have political consequences?"[32]

As the title of this collection suggests, English has been and continues to be in flux throughout the latter half of the twentieth century, or the postmodern era. The thirteen teachers represented here see this mobility and heterogeneity as a positive opportunity more than as a crisis or a decadence. In Part 4 of *Reorientations* Brook Thomas and Robert Con Davis offer two different perspectives on the history of the intersections of literature and critical theory in the teaching of English. Significantly, although Thomas's call for a return to history and Davis's call for a revolution through theory might seem to be moving in opposite directions, their analyses of the institutional framework of English and their proposals for new pedagogies both depend on the notion of *ideology*, or the complex connection between knowledge and power that dynamizes our culture and hence the educational or acculturation process itself. At the same time Thomas and Davis share with the other contributors to *Reorientations* and with activist culture critics like Edward Said the belief that teachers and students of literature "are subject to and producers of circumstances, which are felt regardless of . . . the critic's methods. . . . The point is that texts . . . are always enmeshed in circumstance, time, place, and society—in short, they are in the world, and hence worldly."[33]

As described and practiced by the teachers in *Reorientations*, feminism, reader-response theory, new historicism, deconstruction, intertextual theory, and new Marxism are all means of reconceptualizing literature in terms of a "network of often colliding forces." Consequently, the activity of interpreting literature is treated as an opportunity for a critical rethinking of each reader's own situation in the world as well as of the social situations represented in diverse texts (Said 33). In a pragmatic consideration of the purposes of the general education course in literature required at most American universities, Thomas discusses students' "inability to encounter the otherness of a text from the past" and the historical "amnesia" that postmodern American culture is fostering in its citizens (219). Although he urges us to inform our teaching of literature with a new historical awareness that is critically alert to the way ideology works in society and in texts at all times, Thomas does not hold out any utopian hope that "changing the way we teach literature will drastically alter the historical conditions" (220). Rather, Thomas offers a beginning for change through linking historical and interdisciplinary analysis; such a pedagogical strategy is aimed at improving students' ability to figure out and respond responsibly to the multiple connections between socioeconomic and political conditions in the world today as those conditions have emerged from various past interactions.

Thomas is not alone in his emphasis on the importance of history, no longer viewed as a set of facts to be memorized but as a range of differences to be rethought. With Shoaf, for example, Thomas uses historical inquiry into literature as a way of challenging the current and widespread tendency to assume that the present is all we know and all we need to know. As historical subjects, each one of us confronts the problem of translating the past into terms that are meaningful for us now but that also recognize the otherness of the past. For Thomas, history is a way of realizing the interconnectedness of everything that we do, including the way in which we produce knowledge and distribute power, and this is one reason why he urges the integration of history and other kinds of studies into general education literature courses. In a move that parallels Dasenbrock's call for a "new essentialism," or a new canon of literature written by hitherto marginalized groups, Thomas favors a new focus on history and a turn away from the postmodern focus on the text promoted by, for example, semiotics and deconstruction. Specifically, Thomas takes issue with Scholes's "emphasis on training critical skills" rather than historical perspectives, an emphasis that, Thomas implies, characterizes all textual studies (222).

Yet do textual studies exclude historical studies, and does a focus on history necessarily preclude a focus on textuality in the same English course? Several essays here suggest that one of the most crucial new directions that has come out of combining literature and theory is precisely the historicizing of literature through theory. Thus, Shoaf uses Derrida's theory of *différance* to reinvigorate students' interest in medieval literatures, and Landow has used various theories of intertextuality to construct a computer program that is both historically rigorous and interdisciplinarily oriented in the connections it encourages students to make between events, texts, and images. Similarly, Ulmer's experimental textshop shows students how inventions and discoveries in arts and sciences have historical contexts in a specific time and place, just as the students' own texts have. Finally, in applying reader-response theories in composition classes, Comley and Flynn carry out textual analysis not as an end in itself but as a means toward a greater sociohistorical awareness for their students. Thus if, as Jerome McGann observes, "referentiality" appeared as " 'a problem' in formalist and text-centered studies" like Russian Formalism and American New Criticism, referentiality rethought through feminism or Foucault is less of a problem than a compelling interest to teachers and theorists in the 1980s.[34]

In "Toward a New History in Literary Study," Herbert Lindenberger argues that "the new history" entails a refusal to separate "social and aesthetic forms" on the grounds that "the older history . . . all too often refused to recognize the cultural biases and the interpretative conventions built into its method."[35] Lindenberger also connects textual studies with new historicism and both with interdisciplinary theories and pedagogies as interdependent means of achieving a critical "self-consciousness" about our involvement with literature in particular and our contribution to society in general (20). Above all, he points out, new historicism "has inherited from contemporary theory" a marked attitude of "suspiciousness toward established authority... which finds its embodiment in the strong social concerns within the new history" (21). This attitude or stance is a major factor in "oppositional pedagogy," as Robert Con Davis explains. Moreover, it is historically significant that all of the teachers writing in the present collection, regardless of the specific theories they espouse, participate in this postmodern mo(ve)ment through the critical or political awareness they seek to exemplify for and share with their students.

Feminism, semiotics, deconstruction, and Marxism provide most of the basic principles that inform oppositional pedagogy, which Davis defines as a "body of . . . thought that deliberately challenges dominant cultural and political orders with ideologically subversive" theories and practices (248). Like Thomas, however, Davis is wary of romanticizing the newness or revolutionary promise of the pedagogical reorientations he discusses. In pointing out the institutional constraints on the textual power he believes a curriculum in textual studies would afford students, Scholes in his essay here exemplifies what Davis describes as the typical dilemma of the oppositional critic-teacher who is "dependent on the social function of bourgeois institutions and yet committed to far-reaching change within and beyond them." Lefkovitz, too, problematizes her position as a white middle-class instructor in a composition class attended by immigrants and other marginalized groups, as does Ewell, who sees the feminist teacher as deeply divided between loyalty to the profession of English and a commitment to exposing that profession's gender biases.

The position of the oppositional critic-teacher can be seen as either marginal or mediatory.[36] In either case the oppositional teacher acts neither inside nor outside the educational system, because he or she neither wholly accepts nor wholly rejects the institutional and wider cultural framework in which and through which he or she works. In *Marxism and Deconstruction* Michael Ryan argues that the traditional humanist distinction between the "ivory tower" (inside) and "the world" (outside) has become tenuous at best, suspect at worst. "The university is a historical product," Ryan says; it "reproduces social stratification by rationing [and rationalizing] knowledge according to class . . . ; it trains social agents in the norms and mores of the dominant culture."[37] Given the inevitable complicity of all university and college teachers in the reproduction of the hegemonic system of power/knowledge, which is white, middle-class, and masculinist, Ryan claims, the outside of the university "is always already internal to the university" politically, economically, and socially speaking (142-43). As Davis suggests, therefore, one of the most urgent problems for oppositional teachers today is to decide on their position in the political spectrum and to determine exactly how to effect radical changes that enact their radical theories. Should we work for change in ideology and practice from outside the academy, with the French theorists and teachers of GRIP, or should we work for change from inside the academy, as Michael Ryan and Gerald Graff propose?[38] And in any institutional context, is there any valid historical sense in which an English teacher can "just teach literature" without taking a stand on the issues and values of his or her time and place in respect to the texts he or she is teaching?

After considering the challenges and difficulties of an oppositional pedagogy, Davis concludes: "There is, in sum, no such thing as 'pedagogy' " if we mean by that "a transcendental practice for the appropriation of 'truth' existing outside of history and socially derived conditions, but there is the practice of what has been [and is being] actually taught" (264). As an editor of *Reorientations,* I see all of our essays on theory and pedagogy as part of an ongoing social practice called "teaching English," which is very much involved in the oppositional movements Davis discusses. The heterogeneity and dynamism that characterize the title of this book—as well as its section titles— "Shifting Canons," "Rethinking Texts," "Reading and Writing Otherwise," "Teaching Reorientations"—and even the two editors' introductions fairly represent our attempts to understand our responsibilities as teachers of a historically situated network of knowledges through a cultural practice that interrelates theory, pedagogy, and the world. In an important sense, then, the essays in *Reorientations* mark both a return and a revolution: our theories and practices are continuations of past English studies as much as emergences of something as yet unthought and untaught.

NOTES

1. For a discussion and application of the idea of "epistemological break" or "epistemological rupture" (*"coupure épistemologique"*), see Michel Foucault, *The Order of Things: An Archaeology of the Human Sciences* (New York: Pantheon, 1970).

2. The term *postie* is suggested by Richard Rorty in a review of Jürgen Habermas's work. See "Posties," *London Review of Books* 9, no. 15 (3 Sept. 1987): 11-12.

3. Thus, in a well-known controversy with J. Hillis Miller, M. H. Abrams proposed a conciliatory pluralism: "insofar as we set ourselves, in the old-

fashioned way, to make out what the other means by what he says, I am confident that we shall come to a better mutual understanding" (p. 438). See "The Deconstructive Angel," in Robert Con Davis, ed., *Contemporary Literary Theory*, 1st ed. (New York: Longman, 1986), pp. 428-38.

4. Cary Nelson, "Problematizing Interpretation: Some Opening Questions," in his edited volume, *Theory in the Classroom* (Urbana: University of Illinois Press, 1986), pp. 7, 5. For another important collection of essays on contemporary theory and pedagogy, see G. Douglas Atkins and Michael L. Johnson, eds., *Writing and Reading Differently: Deconstruction and the Teaching of Composition and Literature* (Lawrence: University Press of Kansas, 1985).

5. Barbara Herrnstein Smith, "Contingencies of Value," in Robert von Hallberg, ed., *Canons* (Chicago: University of Chicago Press, 1984), p. 11.

6. Adrienne Rich, "Taking Women Students Seriously," in Margo Culley and Catherine Portuges, eds., *Gendered Subjects: The Dynamics of Feminist Teaching* (Boston: Routledge and Kegan Paul, 1985), p. 28.

7. Gayatri C. Spivak, "Reading the World: Literary Studies in the '80s," *College English* 43, no. 7 (Nov. 1981): 671. For an interesting example of the urgent linkage between teaching third-world literatures and taking political action, see Susan R. Benda and Morton H. Halperin, "Forbidden Writers — The Foreign Threat in Literary Garb," *College English* 47, no. 7 (Nov. 1985): 690-97.

8. Gayatri C. Spivak, "Imperialism and Sexual Difference," in Clayton Koelb and Virgil Lokke, eds., *The Current in Criticism: Essays on the Present and Future of Literary Theory* (West Lafayette, Ind.: Purdue University Press, 1987), p. 320.

9. See James Atlas, "The Battle of the Books," *New York Times Magazine*, June 5, 1988, sect. 6, pp. 24-27, 72-75, 94.

10. For an explanation of the term and concept of *power/knowledge*, see Michel Foucault, *Power/Knowledge: Selected Interviews and Other Writings, 1972-1977*, ed. Colin Gordon (New York: Pantheon, 1980).

11. For a brief description of Derrida's theory of *différance*, see Christopher Norris, *Deconstruction: Theory and Practice* (London: Methuen, 1982), pp. 46-48.

12. The problem of "otherness" is central to recent theories of gender, psychoanalysis, and race. On the Other in psychoanalysis, see the two special issues on "Psychoanalysis and Pedagogy," ed. Robert Con Davis, *College English* 49, nos. 6-7 (1987). For an application of theories of deconstruction to racial otherness, see Henry Louis Gates, Jr., ed., *"Race," Writing, and Difference* (Chicago: University of Chicago Press, 1986). The masculinist definition of Woman as Other is a pervasive issue in women's and gender studies.

13. Kenneth A. Bruffee, "Collaborative Learning and the 'Conversation of Mankind,' " *College English* 46, no. 7 (Nov. 1984): 635-52.

14. For the notions of *monologism* and *dialogism*, see M. M. Bakhtin, "Discourse in the Novel," in *The Dialogic Imagination: Four Essays*, ed. Michael Holquist (Austin: University of Texas Press, 1981), pp. 259-422. For the related term *heteroglossia*, see esp. pp. 301ff.

15. See Michel Foucault, "The Discourse on Language," in *The Archaeology of Knowledge*, trans. Alan Sheridan (London: Tavistock, 1974), pp. 215-37.

16. Frances Maher, "Classroom Pedagogy and the New Scholarship on Women," in Culley and Portuges, eds., *Gendered Subjects*, p. 41.

17. Derrida asks, "What links writing to violence?" at the beginning of "The Violence of the Letter: From Lévi-Strauss to Rousseau," in *Of Grammatology*, trans. Gayatri C. Spivak (Baltimore: Johns Hopkins University Press, 1976), pp. 101-40.

18. Graff's "Seven Propositions for Teaching" is the concluding section of his preface to Gerald Graff and Reginald Gibbons, eds., *Criticism in the University* (Evanston: Northwestern University Press, 1985), pp. 7-12.

19. Nelson, ed., *Theory in the Classroom*, p. 3.

20. For a definition of *text*, see A. J. Greimas and J. Courtés, *Semiotics and Language: An Analytical Dictionary*, trans. Larry Crist et al. (Bloomington: Indiana University Press, 1982), pp. 340-41. For a definition of *discourse*, see pp. 81-85.

21. For an exemplary early polemic on the "crisis" in English studies, see Eugene Goodheart, *The Failure of Criticism* (Cambridge, Mass: Harvard University Press, 1978). "Humanist criticism, which has as its object the quality of life as well as works of art, no longer has authority" (p. 8).

22. Gerald Prince, "Literary Theory and the Undergraduate Curriculum," *Profession 84* (New York: Modern Language Association, 1984), pp. 37, 40.

23. For a consideration of cultural studies and third-world literature that addresses Dasenbrock's concerns as well, see Fredric Jameson, "World Literature in an Age of Multinational Capitalism," in Koelb and Lokke, eds., *The Current in Criticism*, pp. 139-58.

24. Robert Scholes, *Textual Power: Literary Theory and the Teaching of English* (New Haven: Yale University Press, 1985), p. x. For a contemporaneous explanation of the field of cultural studies, see Jeffrey M. Peck, "Advanced Literary Study as Cultural Study: A Redefinition of the Discipline," in *Profession 85* (New York: Modern Language Association, 1985), pp. 49-54.

25. Stanley Fish, "Anti-Foundationalism, Theory Hope, and the Teaching of Composition," in Koelb and Lokke, eds., *The Current in Criticism*, pp. 65, 68.

26. For an influential oppositional critique of humanism in English studies, see Gerald Graff, *Literature against Itself: Literary Ideas in Modern Society* (Chicago: University of Chicago Press, 1979).

27. Shoshana Felman, "Psychoanalysis and Education: Teaching Terminable and Interminable," *Yale French Studies* 63 (1982): 22. On transference and identification as central problems for a psychoanalytically based pedagogy, see Gregory S. Jay, "The Subject of Pedagogy: Lessons in Psychoanalysis and Politics," *College English* 49, no. 7 (Nov. 1987): 785-800.

28. Richard Ohmann, "Literacy, Technology, and Monopoly Capital," *College English* 47, no. 7 (Nov. 1985): 683. For a more recent critique of computer-assisted English studies, see Andrew Sledd, "Readin' not Riotin': The Politics

of Literacy," *College English* 50, no. 5 (Sept. 1988): 495-508. Sledd fears that "schemes to educate young people in the latest technology of communication, the computer, are not intended to enlighten or empower them all in its use. Rather the plan is to produce a few experts in the service of established power" (p. 499).

29. Nelson, ed., *Theory in the Classroom*, pp. 3, 5.

30. Nicholas Coles and Susan V. Wall, "Conflict and Power in the Reader-Responses of Adult Basic Writers," *College English* 49, no. 3 (Mar. 1987): 298-314.

31. Michael Holzman, "The Social Context of Literacy Education," *College English* 48, no. 1 (Jan. 1986): 31.

32. Nelson, ed., *Theory in the Classroom*, pp. 7, 6.

33. Edward W. Said, *The World, the Text, and the Critic* (Cambridge, Mass: Harvard University Press, 1983), p. 35.

34. Jerome J. McGann, ed., *Historical Studies and Literary Criticism* (Madison: University of Wisconsin Press, 1985), p. 3.

35. Herbert Lindenberger, "Toward a New History in Literary Study," *Profession 84*, p. 20.

36. Carl Freedman, "Marxist Theory, Radical Pedagogy, and the Reification of Thought," *College English* 49, no. 1 (Jan. 1987): 70-82. "The class position of the academic teacher . . . is an ambiguous one. A teacher in a purely private university . . . would be a productive worker in the strict Marxist sense. . . . On the other hand, a teacher in a purely public or foundation-sponsored university . . . would be a member of . . . a subsumed class: that is, a class that neither creates nor extracts surplus-value, but that helps to produce the social circumstances in which such creation and extraction can take place" (p. 79).

37. Michael Ryan, *Marxism and Deconstruction: A Critical Articulation* (Baltimore: Johns Hopkins University Press, 1982), p. 136.

38. For a contrast between the oppositional pedagogies developed by GRIP and by Gerald Graff, see the essay by Robert Con Davis here. For a discussion of deconstructionist theories and the politics of oppositional pedagogy, see Gregory L. Ulmer, *Applied Grammatology: Post(e)-Pedagogy from Jacques Derrida to Joseph Beuys* (Baltimore: Johns Hopkins University Press, 1985), esp. pp. 157-88.

BRUCE HENRICKSEN

Teaching
against the Grain

> Ruling culture does not define the whole of culture, though it tries
> to, and it is the task of the oppositional critic to re-read culture so
> as to amplify and strategically position the marginalized voices of
> the ruled, exploited, oppressed, and excluded.
>
> Frank Lentricchia

Most of us do not teach in universities simply to reproduce society's divisions of labor, its class and patriarchal structures, and its ethnocentric values. Yet we were all trained and socialized to a profession in which such structures and biases were deeply rooted, and even the most oppositionally minded teachers will almost certainly, at times, reproduce what they would oppose. This is especially true since, as Jim Merod, Terry Eagleton, and others have argued, twentieth-century literary criticism and pedagogy have developed a conservative ideology of reading that separates the text from the social conditions of its production and that requires all readers to conform to a single identity implied by concepts such as "the" informed or competent reader.

The reproduction of existing social conditions and an opposing impetus to change them mingle in complex ways in the university, and it is often difficult to see clearly the extent to which one's own academic work is determined by the dominant ideology and the economy. Despite the internalization of society's more dismally eloquent voices within our institutions and curricula, the essays in this volume were written in the belief that teachers and critics can operate with a degree of autonomy sufficient to provide an oppositional force for change. Culture, then, is not conceived here—as it is in the common caricature of Marxist analysis—as simply a product of the economic "base" or of the "state apparatus." While culture, including our system of higher education, is certainly dialogically inhabited by these other voices, it possesses a degree of independence, allowing it to function as an arena of opposition and contestation.[1]

As teachers of writing, we often promote our "product" with claims of its economic value, telling students that writing well will get them ahead in the outside world. In this way the teaching of writing is directly implicated in the economic reproduction of class relations. As teachers of literature, we are usually less direct about the role a literary and cultural education plays as a marker of membership in an elite social class. Paul DiMaggio and Michael Useem remind us that "by offering a convenient yardstick for assessing the merit and cultivation of persons, culture can help in sustaining class continuity" (182). If our graduates cannot sell their literary knowledge as directly as they supposedly can sell their writing skills, literary training nonetheless accomplishes a cultural reproduction of class relations by providing students with a kind of symbolic capital.[2]

And yet much of what has occurred in literary theory in the past two decades has revealed the political complicities and subtexts not only in specific works and in canon formations, but also in various methods of interpretation and teaching.[3] This process of revelation is what Allan Bloom sees as *The Closing of the American Mind*. Bloom to the contrary, Marxism, feminism, and deconstruction now give us the means to redirect the force of literary education by encouraging students to question dominant hierarchies and received codes.

Gerald Graff's *Professing Literature: An Institutional History* narrates the evolution of the American university from an avowedly hegemonic institution existing to reproduce class interests, to the more open and democratic institution of today. And yet, influenced perhaps by formalist descriptions of literary change, Graff describes our pedagogical changes almost entirely in terms of internal dynamics, and he has little to say about how the institution was influenced by forces in the external social and political landscape.[4] Therefore, like T. S. Eliot's version of the literary tradition, Graff's history is oddly ahistorical and discontinuous with the larger society. Although he certainly is not on the side of those who think teaching should simply reproduce society's self-congratulatory myths, the oppositional model with which he concludes his study is limited by his refusal to position it within a social matrix. This limitation inheres in his definition of conversation in the academic setting.

One sign of our changing professional practice is the metaphor of the conversation, which has emerged as the enabling figure in a new, pragmatic understanding of the nature and aims of academic work.[5] Abandoning the search for a consensus based on universally grounded principles of knowledge, Richard Rorty argues in *The Consequences of Pragmatism* that "what matters is that the conversation be continuous and undistorted" (218). Taking his cue from Rorty, and also from Mikhail Bakhtin, Don H. Bialostosky calls for a "dialogic criticism," one which "will not try to decide among . . . competing claims or to synthesize . . . opposing theses but will try to imagine and enter their unrealized conversations" (792). Moving the dialogic model from the journals to the classroom, Graff concludes his history by advocating a curriculum designed to reveal and foreground the debates and disagreements our present curricular structures, often to the students' confusion, attempt with only partial success to conceal. "The pedagogical implication of dialogics seems to be that the unit of study should cease to be the isolated text (or author) and become the virtual space or cultural conversation that the text presupposes" (257).

Graff's argument offers a strong corrective to the tendency of departments to be dominated by a single critical or scholarly viewpoint and to recruit new faculty in terms of their theoretical, or antitheoretical, loyalties. Furthermore, any significant change that we make in the way knowledge is created, organized, and transmitted is likely to have social consequences, and Graff's is a model that can only encourage democratization. If his dialogic curriculum can help literature students see beyond the doctrines of specific professors, it might have the more significant consequence of prompting them to see beyond other ideologies.

But Graff is uncritical of the extent to which existing institutional structures produce the debate his students would hear. Jean-François Lyotard reminds us that

> an institution differs from a conversation in that it always requires supplementary constraints for statements to be declared admissible within its bounds. The constraints function to filter discursive potentials, interrupting possible connections in the communication networks: there are things that should not be said. They also privilege certain classes of statements (sometimes only one) whose predominance characterizes the discourse of the particular institution: there are things that should be said, and there are ways of saying them. (17)

While Graff's proposals would have a reorganizing effect on the level that is most visible to students, other aspects of institutional organization remain unexamined—the hierarchy of administration and faculty; the stratification of faculty into tenured, untenured, and part-time; salary differentials; the politics of publication and advancement;

and the relationships between knowledge and funding, to name just a few.

Graff is certainly aware of such factors, but he is overly sanguine about the possibilty of overcoming them so as to create free and unconstrained debate. All of these factors work to produce the knowledge, or the dialogue, the students will encounter, and they should become aspects of what is studied. Although an "ideal" dialogue might assume a situation of equality and justice among speakers, in real social situations exchanges are influenced by unequal distributions of power. Graff only begins to formulate a self-referential curriculum, and he does not consider what is distorted or repressed in the illusion of "free" and unconstrained dialogue.

What is wanted is something like a Bakhtinian analysis of how academic languages constitute a view of the world and its social relations. Such an analysis might try to reveal the rules that shape educational dialogue and identify the specific features of language that send messages about how knowledge should be defined and structured, how disagreements should be resolved, and what constitutes reason and authority. The ultimate goal of such analysis would be to reveal the mechanisms that form students as subjects.

So, while a curriculum that foregrounds debate is clearly preferable to one structured on a party line, Graff does not have enough to say about the implications of his argument for the student, for whom education (whether one thinks of "disinterested contemplation" as a real possibility or merely a way of masking social interests) is a device for acquiring social status and economic and political power. He does not, in other words, contextualize his model within the problematic of education as a class and power-allocating activity.

If, as theorists such as Mikhail Bakhtin have suggested, the literary signifier (be it the dialogic word or the larger text) is an arena of class struggle, the same is true of the pedagogical signifiers we create in our classrooms and with our curricula. Yet Graff (and here many of the essays in this volume implicitly depart from him) retains much from an older, monologic model. Graff's "dialogue" is a one-way hookup between faculty and student; it is only professors who speak, and their words remain uncontaminated either by the voice of the student or by social discourses originating outside the academy. Such hermetically encapsulated "dialogue" is actually monologue. While Frank Lentricchia calls for the academic intellectual to "retrieve his outsider's experience" (8) as a way of keeping channels open between the academy and the world, Graff's dialogue is strictly for insiders. Furthermore, it pays no attention to that other, "hidden" dialogue that structures the student's experiences.

An analysis of this hidden dialogue might begin with an examination of the exchange systems we perpetuate or initiate. Do we offer knowledge in exchange for respect or in exchange for measurable labor? Do we promise future success in exchange for present obedience? Does the exchange system tend to prefer and reward students of certain class, cultural, ethnic, or religious backgrounds? Is the exchange system gender biased? Which type of student decides the exchanges are not worthwhile and why? What are the agreements by which cultural difference becomes encoded as cultural deprivation?[6] Such questions must continually be reexamined as the composition of the student population becomes more diverse. As Rachel Sharp argues, the classroom is itself a site of social contradictions that must be revealed and exploited, and one way to do this would be to move the hidden dialogue into the open (85). This is to suggest that literary theory should not be taught in isolation from the social and institutional conditions of its production and transmission.

Graff speaks of the hidden socializing function of education when he says that the difficulty of organizing literature in the American academy had to do with creating "as a curriculum under more or less democratic conditions something that had previously been part of the socialization of a particular class" (2). But the dialogic model he describes retains traces of the old hidden curriculum of socialization. It is only a slight exaggeration to say that it is democratic only for the professors, and therefore it runs the risk of merely reinscribing whatever interests inform their self-perpetuating practices. In fact, "students" to Graff are those few students who are themselves about to enter the profession of literature.

Certainly Graff has every right to limit his analysis to the kind of curriculum most appropriate for this special class of students, but these people will in turn educate other students with more diverse backgrounds and futures. Tomorrow's educators who are today's graduate students are the survivors of a long process that has helped to reinforce class differences and to exclude the working class from intellectual work. The theoretical preparation of these future teachers must take their social functions seriously, and it could do this by offering them a socially contextualized curriculum in which they themselves are part of what is studied.

Graff is more inclined to open such lines of analysis in his discussion of the early American university than he is in the presentation of his own curriculum. He says that the function of the American university in its early days was normative, "the transmission of humanism and cultural tradition in the Matthew Arnold sense" (3). His study concludes by substituting the competing voices of the current theoretical scene for the older humanism, but with no particular end in view other than the apparent assumption that society needs to know what literary theorists are arguing about. It is difficult to see how his model will produce antihegemonic contestation outside the academy—how, for instance, it will empower working-class intellectuals. Only the most reactionary critics of education would not agree that some level of contestation is necessary in a university, and the conversational model provides contestation in a manner convenient to the encompassing reproductive functions of the institution.

Furthermore, while Graff is aware of the way "literature" has functioned as an elitist category, his dialogic pedagogy takes this category for granted. Marxist critics have argued that the category of the literary serves to extract certain texts from the historical conditions of their production, substituting an idealist theory of their origins by which literature reflects some Platonic realm of universal (and therefore ahistorical) "truths." The concept of the literary in the hands of conservative New Critics worked to minimize the explanatory power of historical and social realities. As Tony Bennett says, the very question "What is literature?" is ideologically freighted, calling for idealist responses (105). There runs, then, throughout Graff's discussion, which treats both literature and the theoretical dialogue as somehow existing beyond ideology, a strain of idealism that has a depoliticizing influence on his analysis.

A new pedagogy must reestablish the connections between literature and history, culture and society. It must ask, for instance, how the student, particularly the undergraduate who is an outsider temporarily visiting our small world, is improved and enriched by studying our professional debates as they are so often conducted. Will the world become a more just place by teaching students that many professors today cannot decide if texts have definite meanings and have elevated their indecision to a marker of professional status? While the stakes involved in decisionmaking in the larger world become increasingly high, the best of the new theorists often argue, with a triumphant sense of having found the final irony, that what is undecidable is the question of undecidability itself. This is why at the end of *The World, the Text, the Critic*, Edward Said expresses concern over the emergence of a new form of "religious" academic, donning again the vestments of mystery and priestly authority, genuflecting, perhaps, at the shrines of absence, aporia, and the undecidable. If their denial of foundations has robbed criticism of a place to stand as a form of social action, the relativism implicit in the dialogic model does not restore our footing.

The resurgence of one or more forms of relativism is a salient feature of late twentieth-century life. Historical relativism is found in the notion that truth claims are generated by "discursive formations" (Michel Foucault) or paradigms (Thomas Kuhn) that are subject to cataclysmic historical change. Cognitive relativism is found in Rorty's pragmatic escape from truth. Cultural and cognitive relativism are found in the privileging of "little stories" over master narratives (Jean-François Lyotard) and in the belief that interpretations are "correct" only in relation to the interpretive conventions of specific communities of interpretation (Stanley Fish). Individual relativism is found in psychoanalytically oriented reader-response theories (Norman Holland and David Bleich). Various relativisms converge in assaults on "presence," the stable center, the hierarchies of the dominant discourse, and so on.

Since relativism, in its denial of absolute standards by which rival claims may be negotiated, can discourage committed belief and action, it is entirely appropriate to see these assaults on absolutes as a legitimation crisis.[7] Relativism corrects a reactionary authoritarianism that presented its claims, under the pretense of objectivity, as depoliticized "truths." But it can also be simply another move in the game of depoliticizing intellectual work. The freshman's belief that a poem can mean whatever one decides it means is the carefully nurtured product of a consumer society for which the individual ego is the first article of faith; the performative model the freshman's professors are adopting is hardly different.[8] Observing a connection between J. L. Austin and IBM, Terry Eagleton says that in either case "the goal is no longer truth but performativity, no longer reason but power" (AG, 134). Therefore advocates of the conversational model should decide in what specific areas they will settle for Rorty's notion that they write or teach merely to keep the conversation going.

Although it is beyond the scope of this introduction to analyze in detail the interests served by the conversational paradigm, it might be noted in passing that this pragmatic paradigm is internally convenient to a profession that thrives on a multiplicity of viewpoints and must, to insure its survival, continually produce fresh illumination. To believe in radical epistemological breaks, and that we live in the midst of one, can function for academics the way the planned obsolescence of the light bulb does for GE. And a paradigm that encourages us to hold our views with something less than total commitment is also, like Arnold's notion of the "disinterestedness" of culture, convenient to an external power structure that does not want to be bothered by meddling

professors. One may believe, therefore, that certain theoretical disputes—for instance, the question of whether meaning is in the text or
in the reader—can never be settled in ultimate terms. But it is crucial
to examine, in terms of the present historical moment, the social interests served by teaching this or any other theoretical belief.

The older, quasi-religious academic model (many of our colleges and
universities began as training institutions for clerics) assumed, with
Orwell's George Winston, that there was truth and there was untruth.
The professor's hegemonic discourse descended upon docile students.
From the perspective of this practice, a dialogic model may seem to
reduce the university to something like a perpetual motion machine
for empty signifiers. On the other hand, many have come to see the
older truth claims as, in Barthes's term, "alibis" (M, 123) for particular
interests and power arrangements. Especially important in this regard
are the analyses of the objective paradigm in literary studies offered
by Eagleton in *Literary Theory: An Introduction* and by Paul A. Bové in
Intellectuals in Power: A Genealogy of Critical Humanism. At its worst
the traditional academy, as Said describes it, served "as an agent of
closure, shutting off human investigation, criticism, and effort in de-
ference to the authority of the more-than-human, the supernatural,
the other worldly" (290).

The conversational model resists the "power" of a single, hegemonic
discourse and in this regard is liberating. It offers, however, no firm
ground on which to stand—nothing to believe in but the conversation
itself. The older model tells you firmly where to stand, but offers no
acknowledgment of its own political, authoritarian nature. What is
needed, it would seem, is some mediation between the two models, a
pedagogy that is critical of the various centrisms that have paraded as
truth but that does not deny the possibility of belief and of meaningful
social action (as opposed to mere academic performance). For Lentricchia, society itself is the necessary mediating factor.

> If we put "society" back into Rorty's analysis, we will quickly see that
> the conversation is not and never has been as free as he might wish;
> that the conversation of culture has been involved as a moving force in
> the inauguration, maintenance, and perpetuation of society; that the
> conversation of culture, in other words, displays some stubbornly per-
> sistent patterns. . . . It is hard to get into; harder still to speak on your
> own once you do get in; tougher yet to move the conversation in any
> particular direction that you might desire. For this conversation has been
> propelled and constrained mainly by collective voices, sociohistorical
> subjects, not private ones, not by "autonomous" intellectuals. The in-
> volvement of cultural conversation in the social has always borne pur-

pose, but the rhetoric is generally masked and the telos (the exercising— channeling, influencing, distributing, imposing—of a form of social power) is generally invisible. (16-17)

To believe in the social construction of knowledge may itself involve a kind of relativism, but as Sharp says while describing the work of Michael Young, we must, by virtue of a sort of existential wager, behave as though it does not.⁹ Pedagogy that wagers for human betterment can acknowledge the social constraints upon the conversation but nonetheless behave as though what one says matters.

This pedagogy, however, exists today as a minority effort—a third-party alternative to the traditional hegemony and to the more recent relativisms. Furthermore, our universities, emphasizing specialization and departmentalization, cling to older structures. Thus we have a gap between our most recent thinking about how knowledge is created and the more traditional manner in which it is still transmitted. In *The Postmodern Condition* Lyotard says that the closing of this gap will sound "the knell of the age of the Professor" (53), and to think seriously about the problematic of power/knowledge is to redefine one's role as a teacher. Accordingly, many of the essays in this volume, in particular those by Robert Scholes, Gregory Ulmer, and George Landow, involve a radical reorientation of the concept of the teaching self.

Meanwhile, paradoxically, to oppose existing structures and systems of authority, one must first gain authority. And this too often commits us to a self-perpetuating and trivialized political microcosm, a theme park of leftists, rightists, anarchists, and special interest groups, all safely competing at conferences, in journals, and in committee meetings. Derrida need not have looked back to Descartes to discover folly within reason. As Said writes, "A visitor from another world would surely be perplexed were he to overhear a so-called old critic calling the new critics dangerous. What, this visitor would ask, are they dangerous to? The state? The mind? Authority?"(160). The fact is that most of what occurs in the world today occurs without reference to, or knowledge of, the issues that are such precious items of exchange to academics and such play money to others. And some professors seem to prefer it that way. We need a pedagogy that criticizes more meaningfully the dominant ideologies and their disguises.

Gregory S. Jay, in an article demonstrating that deconstruction is a values-oriented discourse, writes: "None of the debates of late over the crisis of the university will carry us far unless they recognize the inherent nihilism of that vocationalism which today threatens to transform education into a personnel training-center for specific intellectual, corporate, economic, and social interests. The human sciences will complete their suicide should they pursue the goal of learning how better to service the desires of such interests" (189). No single collection of essays could map a definitive course for the unmasking of the myths that reinforce today's power arrangements, or for redirecting the university's drift toward complicity with them. But this volume does, we hope, offer a useful exchange concerning the reorientation of our pedagogy, both in terms of general principles and specific classroom practices.

NOTES

1. The idea that culture is determined and therefore largely reproductive is seen in Fredric Jameson's *The Political Unconscious*. Jameson uncovers the hegemonic or reactionary subtexts in the works he studies, thus demonstrating how culture is inhabited by the voices of the economy and the state. But a companion study could perhaps attempt the inverse, to find oppositional subtexts in apparently conformist texts.

2. See Apple, "Reproduction and Contradiction in Education," on economic and cultural reproduction. DiMaggio and Useem, in the same volume, discuss the role of the arts in corporate America and the screening mechanism by which acquaintance with the arts constitutes a "cultural capital" with which one purchases entry into the upper levels of society.

3. Two excellent collections of essays on literary and composition theory in the university classroom are Atkins and Johnson, eds., *Writing and Reading Differently*; and Nelson, ed., *Theory in the Classroom*.

4. In contrast, see Bowles and Gintis, *Schooling in Capitalist America*. Although their focus is more upon pre-university education, their methods could apply to a study of universities as well. They establish connections between the economy and education, analyzing how the logic of ownership and accumulation in capitalism influences educational structures and practices. They examine structural relations between work and education and historical parallels between the growth of capitalism and the growth of the educational system. See also Hogan's "Education and Class Formation: The Peculiarities of the Americans."

5. Just a few years ago Geoffrey Hartman spoke of the metaphor of the conversation as implying an antitheoretical position (42-45). Today it seems more appropriate to see this metaphor as itself central to theory.

6. Most of these questions are posed by David Hogan in his discussion of the work of Paul Willis (59).

7. On the other hand, relativists or pragmatists such as Rorty see their position as enabling action by releasing it from the shackles of "truth." It is action thus liberated that he theorizes in what he calls "edifying philosophy" (as opposed to systematic philosophy). But, as Lentricchia says, in its "reactive,

goal-less character," it is hard to see why anyone would need such edification (17).

8. Consider Stanley Fish's "Demonstration vs. Persuasion: Two Models of Critical Activity" in *Is There a Text in This Class?*

9. Sharp, *Knowledge, Ideology and the Politics of Schooling*, 82. This book, commencing with discussions of Thorstein Veblen, Max Weber, Emile Durkheim, and Karl Mannheim, is an excellent introduction to twentieth-century work in the sociology of education.

WORKS CITED

Apple, Michael W., ed. *Cultural and Economic Reproduction in Education: Essays on Class, Ideology, and the State*. Boston: Routledge and Kegan Paul, 1982.
———. "Reproduction and Contradiction in Education: An Introduction." In Apple, ed., *Cultural and Economic Reproduction*. 1-31.
Atkins, G. Douglas, and Michael L. Johnson, eds. *Writing and Reading Differently*. Lawrence: University Press of Kansas, 1985.
Barthes, Roland. *Image, Music, Text*. Trans. Stephen Heath. New York: Hill and Wang, 1977.
———. *Mythologies*. Trans. Annette Lavers. New York: Hill and Wang 1972.
Bennett, Tony. *Formalism and Marxism*. London: Methuen, 1979.
Bialostosky, Don H. "Dialogics as an Art of Discourse in Literary Criticism." *PMLA* 101 (1986): 788-96.
Bloom, Allan. *The Closing of the American Mind*. New York: Simon and Schuster, 1987.
Bové, Paul A. *Intellectuals in Power: A Genealogy of Critical Humanism*. New York: Columbia University Press, 1986.
Bowles, S., and H. Gintis. *Schooling in Capitalist America*. New York: Basic Books, 1976.
DiMaggio, Paul, and Michael Useem. "The Arts in Class Reproduction." In Apple, ed., *Cultural and Economic Reproduction*. 181-201.
Eagleton, Terry. *Against the Grain*. London: Verso, 1986.
———. *Literary Theory: An Introduction*. Minneapolis: University of Minnesota Press, 1983.
Eliot, T. S. "Tradition and the Individual Talent." In *Critical Theory since Plato*. Ed. Hazard Adams. New York: Harcourt Brace Jovanovich, 1971: 784-87.
Fish, Stanley. *Is There a Text in This Class? The Authority of Interpretive Communities*. Cambridge: Harvard University Press, 1980.
Graff, Gerald. *Professing Literature: An Institutional History*. Chicago: University of Chicago Press, 1987.
Hartman, Geoffrey H. "Tea and Totality: The Demand of Theory on Critical Style." In *After Strange Texts: The Role of Theory in the Study of Literature*. Ed. Gregory S. Jay and David L. Miller. University: University of Alabama Press, 1985: 29-45.

Hogan, David. "Education and Class Formation: The Peculiarities of the Amernicans." In Apple, ed., *Cultural and Economic Reproduction*. 32-78.

Jameson, Fredric. *The Political Unconscious: Narrative as a Socially Symbolic Act*. Ithaca: Cornell University Press, 1981.

Jay, Gregory S. "Values and Deconstructions: Derrida, Saussure, Marx." *Cultural Critique* 8 (Winter 1987-88): 153-96.

Lentricchia, Frank. *Criticism and Social Change*. Chicago: University of Chicago Press, 1983.

Lyotard, Jean-François. *The Postmodern Condition*. Trans. Geoff Bennington and Brian Massumi. Minneapolis: University of Minnesota Press, 1984.

Nelson, Cary, ed. *Theory in the Classroom*. Urbana: University of Illinois Press, 1986.

Rorty, Richard. *The Consequences of Pragmatism*. Minneapolis: University of Minnesota Press, 1982.

Said, Edward. *The Word, the Text, and the Critic*. Cambridge: Harvard University Press, 1983.

Sharp, Rachel. *Knowledge, Ideology and the Politics of Schooling: Towards a Marxist Analysis of Education*. London: Routledge and Kegan Paul, 1980.

PART ONE

Shifting Canons

BARBARA C. EWELL

Empowering Otherness:
Feminist Criticism and the Academy

Feminist criticism, rooted in the civic and intellectual unrest of the
1960s, poses a radical challenge to the liberal arts academy, perhaps
the most radical since Petrarch and his "umanista" insisted that the
"trivia"—the disciplines of manner and value (rhetoric, logic, and
grammar)—should take educational precedence over the quadri-
vium—the quantitative abstractions of geometry, arithmetic, astron-
omy, and music. Petrarch's humanistic education, of course, ushered
in an unparalleled revolution, not only in the academy, but throughout
the white Western world. Indeed, the worldview it generated remains,
despite some wear and tear, essentially intact today. But more than six
hundred years in roughly the same track inevitably produces ruts. The
rigidity and abstraction, the quantitative, technical emphasis at the
expense of moral value and meaning in education that so frustrated
Petrarch in the fourteenth century appear anew as the academic malaise
of the twentieth. Only this time humanism itself, promising eternal
value and universal truth and insisting on its own dispassionate objectivity, has become disconcertingly sterile, without confidence or a
clear vision of itself, unable to recall where the path is headed and
increasingly, uncomfortably aware that its bedrock looks and feels more
like quicksand. At the risk of undoing the metaphor altogether, what
is needed—and what, I would argue, feminist criticism offers—is
another, serious look at the terrain. Maybe linear paths aren't the point,
after all.[1]

One of Petrarch's worthiest successors, John Henry Cardinal Newman, aptly described the guiding tenet of the modern university as
"intellectual excellence." In Newman's view, the liberal arts university
modestly proposed "to have mapped the Universe" (187) and thus to
be in the business of imparting to individuals the "clear, calm accurate

vision and comprehension of all things" (203). Twentieth-century science and experience have seriously undermined any such reification of knowledge and the humanists' presumption that their pursuit of truth has been dispassionate or objective. The current excitement in critical theory, for example, is generated precisely from this recognition of the illusoriness of objectivity and its attendant presumptions of authority. Structuralism, reader-response theory, deconstruction, psychoanalytic theory, Marxism, and their sundry variations all attest to the current search for another perspective, other principles by which "meaning" and "knowing," specifically with respect to a literary text, can be understood. But it is the particular charisma of contemporary feminist criticism (which has drawn productively from all these approaches) to make visible and intensely personal the deepest assumption of Newman's project by exposing the profound pretense underlying it. The university (and the society whose values it both shapes and expresses) has not produced an accurate or "universal" map at all. Where, feminists have simply and tellingly asked, are the women? Isn't all this talk of "objective reality" and "rigorously tested observations about human behavior" merely—in Adrienne Rich's words—"what man, above all white men, in their male subjectivity, have decided [is] important" ("Claiming" 232)?

The deadliness of feminism's challenge to objectivity is its accuracy in exposing male privilege as the primary assumption of the claim to universality.[2] Men (that is, white, upper-class, Western men) have presumed their social predominance to be coextensive with reality, and thus their "clear, calm accurate vision and comprehension of all things" the definitive perspective, the sole measure of reality. "Objectivity" as a method depends upon this unacknowledged masculinist bias, and the university, as its chief stronghold, embodies that bias not only in its intellectual ends but in its institutional means. As Basil Bernstein observes, the institutionalization of public knowledge specifically reflects "both the distribution of power and the principles of social control" (47). Thus, as in the society it serves, every dimension of the academy's organization assumes the priority and priorities of men: from the cluster of mostly male administrators and faculty at the top to the mostly female students and clerical and janitorial workers at the bottom; from the fragmentation of knowledge into discrete disciplines to the favoring of researchers—and particular kinds of research—over teachers—and particular styles of teaching; from the hierarchies of rank and tenure to the professional societies and our impaneled pronouncements; from the lecterns and podia in front of orderly rows of student desks to the promotion and protection of organized competition as sport. Ironically, the grounding of this organization—impartial "objectivity"—has been steadily undermined by science itself, both in its empirical formulations of indeterminacy and relativity and (perhaps more influentially) in its reflexive consideration of the nature of scientific paradigms.[3] It has remained for feminism to expose the specific male bias that has empowered and informed the foundations of that "objectivity."

The intimacy of this exposure is particularly threatening. We are no longer discussing interesting theoretical alternatives to objectivity, but confronting concrete social and personal realities. The feminist assertion that eternal truths and objective standards are no more than distorted and partial views is understandably disturbing. But when such an assertion deliberately implicates one's wife or personal secretary, we can hardly be surprised if the defense of the status quo begins to resemble Custer's last stand. Such personal relevance is precisely what the institutions of liberal knowledge have sought to exclude—to our peril. Confining our grasp of truth to a single perspective and ignoring its partiality creates nothing short of a one-dimensional and dangerously misleading mirage obscuring the complexity of human reality.

The construction of an "other" perspective, based on the notion that gender is socially constituted in a subjective (not the objective) world, lies at the heart of the feminist critique of the academy and the culture it legitimates. Ironically, those same self-consciously liberal standards of objectivity that are being impugned have also permitted feminist criticism, like other radical critiques, to achieve a tentative and marginal status within academic institutions. But pluralism is itself a subtle legitimation of the status quo; an apparently well-meaning inclusion also insures control and promotes co-optation.[4] Fortunately, other more tangible and pragmatic factors have also encouraged the inclusion of feminist criticism within the academy and have allowed it to develop more cogently its challenge within and to the institution.

The 1960s and 1970s, for example, were decades of expansion for the academy; open admissions, returning adult students, and proliferating junior college systems generated an unprecedented access to higher education. Encouraged by the women's movement to seek wider economic and social opportunities, women appeared on campuses (as in the work force) in ever greater numbers. By the first half of the 1980s, women were a numerical majority at many institutions, and women's education became "literally central to the post-secondary enterprise" (Hall and Sandler 1). Among the anomalies these new women students encountered on campus was a system in which only a quarter of their professors were female, clustered in the lower ranks and earning 20 percent less than their male colleagues (Astin and Snyder 29). But while these proportions remained steady throughout the decade, women scholars constituted a critical mass for changing that system. Inspired, like their students, by the energy of the women's movement, they forged a new discipline that would question and threaten to transform the entire university: women's studies.

As yet, however, the resistance to such transformations has been understandably powerful.[5] Women's studies remains marginalized within most institutions, occasionally buttressed by mainstreaming projects that propose to integrate the expanding scholarship on women into traditional curricula and classes. But if the impact of women's studies seems limited in the university as a whole, its challenge has not been insignificant, particularly within disciplines. Recently even the president of the Modern Language Association declared the effects of feminist criticism on literary study to have been "tremendous and irreversible" (J. Hillis Miller 286), revising the terms of fundamental debates within the profession. In the remainder of this essay, I propose to examine two such affected aspects of literary study—its canon and its pedagogy—to explore some implications of a feminist critique for the disciplines and thus for the academy as a whole.

The literary canon was an early target of feminist criticism. Encouraged by their political experiences in the women's movement, women in the academy focused first on the literary texts that constituted the base of their profession. In the process, they came to question not only the sources of literary authority, but the nature and function of literature as a discipline. Two facts emerged. First, with very few exceptions, women writers had been excluded from the culture's vision of itself as expressed in its literature; and second, the images of women projected by the canonized writers of both sexes were disturbingly narrow, indicating a corresponding narrowness in the culture at large. The "role of woman"—that tired chestnut of exam and term paper topics—could no longer be assumed. Its use as a question had itself to be questioned, since the answers it required so patently served the biases of its origins. Indeed, the discipline that condoned such a question had to be subjected to analysis.

With this recognition came a sense of profound betrayal by a trusted and revered source—the masterworks, the classics, that we, as ardently as our male colleagues, had learned to love and admire and read. They did not mirror absolutes tested by time and intellect and embodying unchanging, universal truths. Rather, instructed by the angry visions of Kate Millett and Mary Ellmann, we understood that these absolutes had been constructed by a culture that inscribes gender as well as tests.

And that inscription, for women at least, defined a very limited range of behaviors and postures. The mutability of the canon, changes in literary tastes, and the relative place of texts in the mysterious hierarchy of greatness were not the issue, but rather canonicity itself. Obviously, there were other possibilities for women than those represented by Helen, Beatrice, Cordelia, or Molly Bloom. We simply had not been allowed to imagine them as canonical, approved, or valid. In recognizing that the boundaries of our imaginings were not our own, we became "other" to what we had trustingly—naively—thought was "our" tradition, too.

This new perception of the canon generated what Adrienne Rich calls "Re-vision—the act of looking back, of seeing with fresh eyes, of entering an old text from a new critical direction" ("When" 35). This re-vision became the nascent act of feminist criticism and an important tool in redefining both the canon and the discipline as a whole. New readings of newly recovered writers and new interpretations of familiar ones were tried out in classrooms, gradually appeared on panels and in the journals, and more gradually affected the shape of literary histories and anthologies. This process, in turn, mobilized the acknowledged, if determinedly informal, means of canon-formation: critical discussion. Insofar as these new readings exposed the sexist ideologies that shaped women characters or explored the relationships among culture, character, and gender, they altered and continued to alter our sense of the power relations girding our belief in critical absolutes.

But the acceptance of these reevaluations has been slow. How slow is documented by the authors of *Feminist Scholarship: Kindling in the Groves of Academe*, who find, for example, "that the total proportion of work on women is far less in literature than one would anticipate in these central, gatekeeper journals," despite some "marks of a feminist consciousness working within the field" (DuBois et al. 176). Their surprise at their findings confirms, among other things, the hidden power of the pluralist mask as a defender of the literary status quo. As Laurie Finke warns, the pluralism of the critical free market remains an ideological myth that deftly conceals the masculinist assumptions that actually govern the rates of exchange (257). Feminist readings and re-visions remain obstinately marginal, admitted and admissible only insofar as they reconfirm the centrality of the prevailing vision that adopts them to its measure. A feminist reading becomes acceptable when it appears in a "major" journal or press, is affiliated with a "leading" research institution, or addresses a "master" work. In no way are such revisions allowed to revise the power structures that automatically reduce any serious challenge to an intellectual exercise.

More effective in challenging the canon, its limited concept of women, and its disciplinary foundations (and certainly more visible in its consequences for research) have been the search for women writers and the corollary tracing of a female literary tradition. The recovery and reevaluation of the hundreds of women writers that has taken place in the last twenty years is certainly, to date, the most substantial achievement of feminist critics. Directly responding to the informal canon-keepers who insisted that women weren't there because there weren't any women, this painstaking bibliographical, textual, and critical work has established a firm empirical base for much of the theoretical and curricular revision that feminist criticism proposes. Moreover, the recovery of writers like Kate Chopin, Zora Neale Hurston, Susan Glaspell, and Meridel Le Sueur suggests not only the fallibility of canonical criteria in identifying value, but also alternative versions of the literary tradition. Onto the pages left blank by the canon, women writers can be seen to project other images of women, images that ineluctably modify those inscribed in the culture.

Those alternative images, not surprisingly, emerge most clearly in the isolation of an exclusively female tradition of writing: if women writers are going to be "other" anyway, then they can best be "other" all by themselves. A number of major studies, notably Elaine Showalter's *A Literature of Their Own,* Ellen Moers's *Literary Women,* and most recently and tangibly, Sandra Gilbert and Susan Gubar's *Norton Anthology of Literature by Women,* have sought, or at least proposed, versions of that tradition. Like any more conventional grouping of writers—on the basis of nationality ("American Literature") or time period ("Renaissance Literature"), or ethnicity ("African-American Literature"), or aesthetic practice ("The Modernists")—the isolation of a female tradition has produced otherwise unavailable insights into the nature of women's writing. All of the studies named above, for example, emphasize the connections among women writers and their reliance on their foremothers, who, as Virginia Woolf first pointed out, were most relevant to them in finding their own distinctively female voices. The examination of such influences richly complicates, if not dissolves, the standard conceptions of women writers, like Elizabeth Barrett Browning or Emily Dickinson, as merely shadows of male authors or anomalies of genius. Other patterns have also emerged: characteristic themes and concerns, common aesthetic issues, generic likenesses. But such similarities have, more significantly, highlighted internal differences as well: of race, of class, of sexuality, of ethnicity—in addition to the temporal and national distinctions that literary historians have always acknowledged. The recognition of these differences and the critical effort to allow them—not to reduce "women writers" to the same monolith that has characterized "writers"—has been an at once painful and creative consequence of defining a women's tradition of literature and, implicitly, of redefining the literary discipline as a whole.[6]

With the reflexivity common to postmodernist criticism, the perception that complex relationships inhere within the paradigm of a women's literary tradition has precipitated some key recognitions about the nature and goals of feminist criticism itself. As Lillian Robinson observes, the "difference of gender is not the only one that subsists among writers . . . [and it] may not always be the major one. Women differ from one another by race, by ethnicity, by sexual orientation, and by class" (146). She further observes that each of these differences "contributes its historic specificity to social conditions and to the destiny and consciousness of individual women" (146). That these are not primarily individual attributes but "social definitions" emphasizes the intersecting commonalities that women share with one another, as well as with—perhaps primarily with—men. The recognition of these constantly shifting relationships clarifies the grounds for delineating black women's literature, lesbian writing, or a Hispanic women's tradition. But by encouraging a reexamination of the assumptions of a separate women's tradition of writing, it also foregrounds an issue central to feminist criticism: the undermining of unstated, totalizing perspectives that uncritically accept partial truths as wholes. In addition, this internal critique challenges the continuing prominence of "white and middle-to-upper class" as an unspoken norm for the limited inclusion of women that does occur in the prevailing canon. That narrow inclusion highlights the underlying hierarchicalism that fosters racial and heterosexist prejudice, exposing anew the power structures that permit only superficial incorporation of any challenge to their hegemony.

A related consequence of this search for a women's tradition of literature has been a broadening of the notions of what constitutes a literary text and a corresponding expansion of the critical tools necessary to evaluate them. Recognizing that women, like working-class men, were usually denied both access to the publishing world and, more tellingly, the leisure and cultural encouragement that public writing demands, feminist critics expanded their definitions of literature to include such nontraditional forms as diaries, journals, autobiographies, and private poetry. At the same time, they began a corresponding reassessment of domestic and popular fiction—much of it written by and for women, and all of it rejected from the canon as presumably failing to meet its aesthetic criteria.

While these new genres often yield exactly the self-conscious voices and images we expect from literature, conventional means of literary assessment have proven insufficient in appraising their worth. Diaries and letters, for example, are clearly susceptible to critical categories like persona, imagery, syntactical patterns, style, narrative strategies and structures, even mythic design (Hoffmann 4-6). But the analytical sum of these elements does not adequately name the power of, say, Maimie Pinzer's stark epistolary accounts of working-class life or even the complex and coy self-revelations of Anaïs Nin's diary. Several borrowed critical strategies have turned out to be useful, such as Marxist social and ideological analysis, psychoanalytic patterns of gender relations, and deconstructionist descriptions of difference. But like these approaches, feminist criticism has also turned to other disciplines altogether in order to appraise these new texts appropriately. As Marilyn Williamson explains, an understanding of the sociohistorical and ideological contexts of a text—the prevailing sexual ideology, the language assigned to genders and classes, as well as social, economic, and historic conditions—is critical to analysis, opening up nontraditional texts, in particular, to a judicious assessment of their "intrinsic merit" and "historical significance" (145).

This fluency in other disciplinary methodologies is basic to the feminist critique of the established disciplines. Eschewing their fragmented analysis, feminist criticism seeks a more holistic and contextual methodology. Such a multidimensional approach encourages an awareness of the multiple pressures on any discourse, the inability to isolate meaning and value from perspective, the tangle of ideology in language—all factors in determining the function of gender in culture as well as in texts. This exchange of disciplinary method and material in women's studies is also redefining disciplinary boundaries. Represented in the university as departments, such boundaries are basically nineteeth-century expressions of the modern failure of coherence, the fragmentation that Descartes's masculinist rationalism bequeathed to science as a model of inquiry (Bordo 440). Women's studies proposed in its stead a more inclusive and coherent view of reality, one that specifically includes the "others" excluded by the dominant model of truth. This incorporation of materials and methods other to literary study thus fosters an openness, not only to new kinds of texts, new processes of evaluation, new writers and new literature, but also to a new understanding of the purposes of our discipline in illuminating meaning in the texts of our lives.

That this reshaping of literary study is but dimly reflected in the canon more than twenty years later, however, only reconfirms the persistence and power of the structures it represents. One need only glance at a few of the classroom anthologies that render our canon most concretely or, even more tellingly, at the syllabi of a few survey courses to discover a continuing disproportion of any others: women, ethnic or racial minorities, homosexuals. There may be one or other, or even one of each, but the essential canon remains intact, its structures impervious to the challenge these additions represent. Indeed, the "add and stir" model still prevalent in the academy cannot expose the assumptions that inform literary value and thus affect the deep transformation of the structures of knowledge that feminist criticism proposes.[7]

But if the notion of canonicity retains a predominance of white, upper-class males as its best exemplars, it only accurately—if unfortunately and more and more dangerously—represents our culture. It is a measure of the radicalness of the reconceptualization that feminism proposes that so little actual change has occurred in the classroom. As Susan Hardy Aiken explains, there is clearly too much in the canon about "the territorial imperative and the various symbolic economies operant within it, patrilineal genealogy and . . . Judaeo-Christian theology" that many professors and readers still want retold in the metatextual narrative of our "Masterworks" (293). Cultural institutions and the self-images they reflect die difficult deaths. But if feminist criticism has not yet recreated the premises and contours of the one-sided story the canon tells—its metatext—then the exposure of the explicit partiality of its authority has at least signaled the inevitability of its demise.

In like fashion, feminist pedagogy has exposed the buried premises of our teaching practices. Much discredited but still prevalent, the current model of university instruction, not unlike the canon, echoes and enforces our cultural attachment to objectivity and a single Truth. Most of us have, at some point, perpetuated the scene ourselves: The professor, elevated by a podium and authorized to speak by his [sic] lectern, lectures to his receptive (or at least quiescent) students in their self-contained seats about the objective, incontrovertible truths of the discipline of which he is master. Everything in the academy, from registration practices that establish large lecture sessions, to the physical design of classrooms and desks, to grades and GPA's, to the prevalence of textbooks and mandatory syllabi and courses, assert this model of instruction. Indeed, most teachers have learned their disciplines within it, and many of us can conceive of no better way to profess them.

Though few of the assumptions underlying this pedagogy—objectivity, universal value, rationality, the autonomous self—remain unchallenged, even within the disciplines being lectured about, the pedagogy itself survives to reiterate those premises. Educational research and experience, of course, have long since demonstrated its deficiencies. As Paulo Freire noted two decades ago, this "banking concept" of instruction—the professor depositing knowledge into the student— only recapitulates the oppressive, singular paradigm of the dominant culture and actively discourages students, especially those of "other" classes or cultures, from making the connections between their lives and what they are "learning" (60). Though Freire never mentions women as such a group, they particularly have suffered from this model. Culturally inscribed as passive objects for the imprint of the male subject—taking men's names, bearing their children, conforming to their projections and expectations—women in the classroom have found that passivity doubly inforced (Maher 31). Since women are patently excluded from the content of the disciplines, their reception is expected to be unresisting. Professors call on women students less frequently, ask them less probing questions, and interrupt or ignore their comments more often. Moreover, the aggressive, competitive, "masculine" style of classroom exchange disadvantages the less acceptable, cooperative, contributive style culturally determined for women (Hall and Sandler 8).

Redressing women's absence in the content of the disciplines clearly implied revising the educational philosophy that likewise insured women's exclusion. As in other educational reforms with political roots, women's studies—"the academic arm of the women's movement"— drew upon its political experience in evolving more appropriate instructional paradigms for its radically new contents. Consciousness-raising, "CR," a primary tool of women's self-liberation, offered a ready model for the classroom integration of personal observation and experience with a collective (and empowering) understanding of its meaning—its theory. "Feminist method," as Catherine MacKinnon argues, "is consciousness raising": "the collective critical reconstitution of the meaning of women's social experience, as women live through it" (255). MacKinnon emphasizes the intrinsic relationships between theory and practice in feminist method: "Feminism turns theory itself—the pursuit of a true analysis of social life—into the pursuit of consciousness and turns an analysis of inequality into a critical embrace of its own [gendered] determinants" (255). This adaptation of feminism to the classroom, as to research, has not been unproblematic, but its results have contributed significantly to the overall educational reform that has remained painfully underway since the 1960s, as well as to the disciplinary and paradigmatic revisions that long-overdue reform implies.[8]

While the method of CR has determined the outlines of feminist pedagogy, the experience of the classroom has governed its dynamics. One element in those early women's studies classes, those first "Images of Women in Literature" courses, was the unfamiliarity of the terrain. Not only students, but teachers as well, plunged into an uncharted territory, compelled to create the maps as they went along. Teachers experienced a particular risk and exhilaration at finding themselves learning from students more immediately than any educational piety had ever predicted they would. There was a dearth of published primary material, virtually no critical explications to rely on, no canonical syllabi or graduate school lists of great works from which to plan a course— even texts had to be created and shared. The result in the classroom was a powerful collaboration between student and teacher, a breaking down of the barriers between the learned and the learners, and the replacement of the single right answer with cooperative conclusions about what is true. Students experienced for themselves the drama of research and of testing the validity of the intellectual frameworks they were being asked to understand. This collaborative spirit rapidly extended beyond the classroom, as professional networks emerged to share and learn from these teaching experiences. A widespread, informal distribution of experimental syllabi and reading lists developed, helping to formalize and disseminate these new feminist pedagogies.[9]

The personal involvement in one's own education that such collaboration invited was further enhanced by the course content itself and the dramatic shifts of perspective its examination fostered. The intimacy of the experience of seeing for the first time the partiality of a vision one had assumed to be whole, the discovery, for the first time, of the the authority of one's own experience, created, for students and teachers alike, the impact of a religious conversion: one's life changed and there was no going back. (See, for example, Gilbert 849-50 and Showalter, "Women's" 34-35.) In such a charged atmosphere, the relationship between literary texts and experience readily collapsed as literature became relevant to life in searing and unforgettable ways. It was no small matter, for instance, to find an experience as secret and silenced as menstruation appear for the first time in a fictional text, validated and explored in all its messy ambiguity; Stephen Dedalus's masturbatory fantasies never possessed such a disturbingly familiar resonance. Women's specific lives emerged with the clarity that only literature offers and that the partial angle of male authorial and critical perspectives had obscured and distorted. In the classroom this clarity redirected literary study from outside—the grasp of abstract concepts and alien, dissonant texts—to inside—the assimilation of exempla that directly illumined one's life and experience. Students' lives and their perceptions of their lives became, as Freire and others had urged, the real object of study.

The means by which feminist pedagogy sustains this convergence of concept and experience derives precisely from the immediacy of its focus on gender as a cardinal cultural inscription. Not only is gender theoretically fundamental to our cultural paradigms, but everybody has one, and the experience of gender is thus both determining and emotionally charged. Like race and sexual orientation, one can hardly discuss the topic without engaging student emotions—and attention. That engagement, volatile and potentially disrupting as it is, also generates the necessary context for relating intellectual frameworks to personal experience. It opens up, rather forcefully, the pathways that learning requires between idea and life, thought and action.

More important, the focus on gender foregrounds alterity. Dramatizing the determinacy of perspective, feminist criticism radically undermines the "objective" structures of knowledge. Exploring that otherness, difference, and its subversion of the sovereign subject is, of course, the poststructuralist project that has most directly engaged feminist adherents.[10] Feminist criticism shares with deconstruction an opposition to hierarchy, the decentering of the (male) subject, and the recognition of the determining force of culture and language in human experience. Moreover, feminist criticism shares the pedagogical aim that Robert Scholes and Jeffrey Peck, among others, have articulated of making literary study, as the study of textuality, a means of revealing "the epistemological structures that organize how we know, how our knowledge gets transmitted and accepted, and why and how students receive it" (Peck 51). The feminist classroom applies the peculiar immediacy of gender to these issues; they then materialize in the specific exploration of how a systematic opposition of gender shapes meaning and language, how the recognition of that hierarchical domination reveals the arbitrariness of the "inferiority" of one of the opposed terms, and thus how other perspectives and systems of value are possible.

Building on the inherent engagement of this content, feminist pedagogy has evolved a number of specific techniques, all of which are designed to channel and focus this convergence of concept and experience. Necessarily, their intermediate goal has been called the "one central strand" of feminist pedagogy, student participation (Schilb 216). Florence Howe, whose articulations of the aims and methods of women's studies have been particularly influential, singles out three such strategies that have characterized feminist teaching: small group collaboration, including discussion, group projects, and group grades (which deprivilege the single viewpoint and validate other perspectives); the action project, internships or research directly related to women's issues (which demonstrate the interaction of intellectual concepts and experience); and journal writing (which both legitimizes experience as a subject of analysis and encourages the personalizing of theory through the act of writing) (161-62). Each of these techniques, as Klein explains ("Dynamics" *passim*), attempts to empower students, to give them an active role in their own learning process, to provide them with access to their experience as subject to analysis, and thereby to enjoin them in the critique and deconstruction of the cultural determinations that shape all human experience, especially gender. Students of literature are thus enabled to participate in the undoing of the artificial hierarchies that language and culture impose, redefining, for example, "literature" and "canon" in the study of nontraditional or noncanonical texts. Or, in studying, for example, how the emergence of the "new woman" after World War I shaped Hemingway's portrayal of the American housewife, or how literary rapes echo the misogynist patterns of response in contemporary assault, they can better recognize the interconnections of context and authority. By seeing in journals and collaborative projects their own experience as texts and the contextuality of every text, they are encouraged to participate in their own empowerment both as subject and as other, part of a thick web of changing (and changeable) contingencies.

Paradox and conflict inevitably inhere both in such strategies and in the unsettling purposes they imply. Nowhere is that conflict more complex than in the feminist teacher—at once a representative of hierarchy and a visible challenge to it. Indeed, the feminist teacher epitomizes the pedagogical struggle to empower otherness—other points of view. A prevailing complaint and consequence of CR-derived methodology in the classroom is exactly the loss of authority, the threat of structurelessness.[11] Feminist classrooms often struggle against diffusion, degeneration into rap sessions, and the loss of critical thought. Evaluation becomes tangled in the mire of subjectivity: how can "standards" be applied when their distorted perspective has been deliberately exposed? How can the teacher exert authority when its deconstruction is in process? The female professor, moreover, only intensifies the dilemma. Often perceived by her students and conditioned by her culture to be a nurturer, supportive and forgiving, she is required by her chosen role to be a judge, evaluating and discriminating. As a woman, she participates in the category of other—passive, acted upon (sexual) object. As a professor, she is authority, agent (asexual) subject. As a feminist, however, she is engaged in undoing an authority that, on the one hand, she has never had, and on the other, she has—at the least—usurped. To her students—as often to herself—she inhabits a peculiar space, a space of self-deconstruction in the interest of creating another source of power—a power she already articulates in her explicit marginality. The power of this marginality is, of course, a function of the center it opposes: who is marginal is determined by who occupies the center. Female professors experience the dynamic of their opposition to the center in every dimension of their academic lives, as colleagues, administrators, researchers, writers, teachers. But they have also effectively used that dynamic to remain, often as tokens and exceptions, within the academy, even as they work to change it, to relocate the centers they oppose.

But where? In the thick contexts of the classroom and the academy, of gender, race, sexuality, religion, ethnicity, the positions of marginalities and centers are constantly shifting. Other contingencies, for example as a black or lesbian professor or as a male feminist, further redefine a feminist teacher's relation to authority, positioned at or apart from the center. What these complex relations reveal, however, is precisely the necessity for defining a location, for understanding our points of view, with their limitations as well as their strengths. As Adrienne Rich explains, such "locations" force us to risk whatever claims to the center we may have struggled to acquire, but they also keep us from asserting the exclusive authority we are trying to undo: "Recognizing our location, having to name the ground we're coming from, the conditions we have taken for granted—there is a confusion between our claims to the white and Western eye and the woman-seeing eye, fear of losing the centrality even as we claim the other. . . . Living in the climate of an enormous either/or, we absorb some of it unless we actively take heed" ("Notes" 219, 221).

In practical terms, what this means for feminist teachers is the articulation of a location for their own complex perspectives, the grounds of their authority. Elaine Marks describes her identification of such a self-location for her French literature students: "I spend a significant amount of time presenting myself, explaining my intellectual and political formation, and situating my ideology, by which I mean my unconscious assumptions and blind spots (I have figured some of them out) in a historical and socio-cultural context, insisting on the inevitable differences between students who are in the late teens and early twenties (there are exceptions) and myself. I present myself as strongly influenced . . ." (178).

Such self-conscious positioning of the point of view of authority is precisely the lesson we most want our students to learn: not simply, as Peter Elbow once affirmed, to encourage a student "to act on his [*sic*] own motivation" and "evaluate ideas and perceptions on their own merits and not in terms of who holds them" (79); but, indeed, to insist instead that the merits of ideas and perceptions must be evaluated in terms of who holds them and how and why, to make clear that no one speaks without partiality, that we are all subjects and objects of languages and cultures whose meanings we must comprehend, at once from within and without.

That contextualizing of authority illuminates the pivotal goal of feminist pedagogy and the central theme of feminist criticism's challenge to the academy: the connection of theory with action. In discussing the shortcomings of radical Marxist pedagogy, Carl Friedman notes a failure to respond to "the divided class identity that U.S. capitalism imposes upon academic teachers" (81). Academic radicalism, he suggests — unionizing, collective bargaining, and alliances with other members of the university system — would clarify that self-division and thus assist the revolutionary dissolution of "a great many academic myths" (80). In contrast, feminist criticism and pedagogy, which share Marxism's revolutionary intent and marginal status, are already closely linked with feminist praxis. Precisely in their ambiguous, articulated relationship with the institution they represent, feminist teachers act to disengage their power and discover their shared otherness. As a woman, the feminist teacher shares the student's (or the secretary's or the maid's) disenfranchisement, while as professor (or as white or heterosexual), she acknowledges her role in that oppression — seeking in the articulation of these locations to undo the power of their oppositions. Less semiotically, feminist criticism also retains direct and visible links to activism through the women's centers on many campuses. Featuring and often sponsoring feminist research, such centers are usually engaged in activist issues such as child care, rape prevention, rank and salary discrimination, and affirmative action. The closeness of these ties transfers to the classroom, making exemplary and direct the relationship of the political and the personal, the theoretical and the experienced.

In these ways, then, feminist pedagogy enacts and enables its theoretical concerns. Claiming no more (or less) than the fact of gender as its distinctive contribution to progressive education, feminist pedagogy makes explicit the passion, the commitment that constitutes all good teaching. Even the "objectivity" and safe emotional distance that continue to define much academic practice are, as Janice Raymond observes, merely "passion divorced from its depth. . . . For professors are never really neutral nor do they ever merely teach. . . . Facts always bear meaning, and professors in many subtle ways impart this meaning" (57). What feminist teachers do is articulate those hidden paradigms that organize facts and meanings, enunciate the partial perspectives that pose as "universal," disguising their biased authority, and expose at the same time their own "locations," thus helping to undo the hierarchies they imply. That revelation of location, of politics, has become—in the wake of objectivity's failure as a source of meaning and value—a hallmark of teaching integrity. For, as Florence Howe observes: "In the broadest context of that word, teaching is a political act; some person is choosing, for whatever reasons, to teach a set of values, ideas, assumptions and pieces of information, and in so doing to omit other values, ideas, assumptions and pieces of information. If all those choices form a pattern excluding half the human race, that is a political act one can hardly help noticing" (283).

Feminist criticism and pedagogy intend to make us notice. In its challenges to the canon, to the curriculum, to the disciplines, to administrative structures, to the design of our classrooms, and to the methodologies they imply, feminist criticism seeks to expose the partiality of the truths these academic institutions dubiously sustain and on which they unsteadily depend. The enterprise is as political as the structures themselves. But their reconstruction, already underway, haply promises another vision of the architecture of knowledge, one whose powers and dimensions we have, so far, only glimpsed.

NOTES

1. I am much indebted to Teresa Toulouse for her thoughtful reading and critique of this essay and to the Newcomb College Center for Research on Women for access to its excellent library.

2. This conclusion is central, for example, to Irigaray's discussion of Freud, Plato, and the Western philosophical tradition.

3. Kuhn's work has influenced a broad range of disciplines in their reflections on how the structures of knowledge are determined and how they change. For its application to women's studies, see Coyner 50ff. and Stanley and Wise 154ff.

4. Though Kolodny has argued for the pluralism of feminist criticism, see Armstrong and Finke on the theoretical implications of such a stance.

5. For a recent account of the various forms that resistance takes, see Aiken et al. See also the discussion of disciplinary resistance in DuBois et al. and a

schematic version of the phases of curriculum integration and its obstacles in MacIntosh.

6. See esp. the critiques of "white women's studies" by Hull and Smith, and of heterosexism by Zimmerman.

7. The ineffectiveness of this approach is noted throughout the literature assessing the effect of women's studies in the curriculum. See the essays in Schuster and Van Dyne; Spanier, Bloom, and Boroviak; and MacIntosh.

8. Several essays in Bowles and Klein specifically address the problem of creating a feminist methodology for research. Those with particular applicability to literary studies include Coyner, Klein "How," and Westkott. Stanley and Wise also provide a useful analysis of the dilemmas in reconciling the "subjectivity" of feminism with the "objectivity" of the academy, specifically in the social sciences.

9. An account of the dissemination of these early pedagogies is included in Boxer 664-66 and notes. See also Klein for other instances of this early collaborative experience in "Dynamics" 189.

10. See, for example, the discussion of these connections in Jardine, Jones, or Meese.

11. This theme was articulated early in the literature of feminist pedagogy and continues to be an issue. See Klein "Dynamics" 189 and notes. More recent discussions have examined the creative challenge of the "loss of authority" in the classroom: see Friedman, Culley, and Nancy Miller.

WORKS CITED

Aiken, Susan Hardy. "Women and the Question of Canonicity." *College English* 48 (March 1986): 288-301.

Aiken, Susan Hardy, et al. "Trying Transformation: Curriculum Integration and the Problem of Resistance." *Signs* 22 (Spring 1987): 255-75.

Armstrong, Paul B. "The Conflict of Interpretations and the Limits of Pluralism." *PMLA* 98 (May 1983): 341-52.

Astin, Alexander W., and Mary Beth Snyder. "Affirmative Action 1972-1982: A Decade of Response." *Change* 14, no. 5 (1982): 26-31, 59.

Benstock, Shari, ed. *Feminist Issues in Literary Scholarship*. Bloomington: Indiana University Press, 1987.

Bernstein, Basil. "On the Classification and Framing of Educational Knowledge." In Michael F. D. Young, ed., *Knowledge and Control*. London: Collier Macmillan, 1975. 47-69.

Bordo, Susan. "The Cartesian Masculinization of Thought." *Signs* 11 (Spring 1983): 439-56.

Bowles, Gloria, and Renate Duelli Klein, eds. *Theories of Women's Studies*. London: Routledge and Kegan Paul, 1983.

Boxer, Marilyn J. "For and about Women: The Theory and Practice of Women's Studies in the United States." *Signs* 7 (Spring 1982): 661-95.

Coyner, Sandra. "Women's Studies as an Academic Discipline: Why and How to Do It." In Bowles and Klein, eds., *Theories of Women's Studies*. 46-71.

Culley, Margo. "Anger and Authority in the Introductory Women's Studies Classroom." In Culley and Portuges, eds., *Gendered Subjects*. 209-18.

Culley, Margo, and Catherine Portuges, eds. *Gendered Subjects: The Dynamics of Feminist Teaching*. Boston: Routledge and Kegan Paul, 1985.

DuBois, Ellen Carol, et al. *Feminist Scholarship: Kindling in the Groves of Academe*. Urbana: University of Illinois Press, 1985.

Elbow, Peter. "Exploring My Teaching." *College English* 32 (April 1971): 743-53. Rpt. in *Embracing Contraries: Explorations in Learning and Teaching*. New York: Oxford University Press, 1986. 69-84.

Ellmann, Mary. *Thinking about Women*. New York: Harcourt Brace Jovanovich, 1968.

Finke, Laurie. "The Rhetoric of Marginality: Why I Do Feminist Theory." *Tulsa Studies in Women's Literature* 5 (Fall 1986): 251-72.

Freedman, Carl. "Marxist Theory, Radical Pedagogy and the Reification of Thought." *College English* 49 (Jan. 1987): 70-82.

Freire, Paulo. *Pedagogy of the Oppressed*. Trans. Myra Bergman Ramos. New York: Seabury Press, 1970.

Friedman, Susan Stanford. "Authority in the Feminist Classroom: A Contradiction in Terms." In Culley and Portuges, eds., *Gendered Subjects*. 203-8.

Gilbert, Sandra M. "Life Studies, or, Speech after Long Silence: Feminist Critics Today." *College English* 40 (April 1979): 849-63.

Gilbert, Sandra M., and Susan Gubar. *The Norton Anthology of Literature by Women*. New York: Norton, 1985.

Hall, Roberta M., and Bernice R. Sandler. "The Classroom Climate: A Chilly One for Women?" Washington, D.C.: Project on the Status and Education of Women, Association of American Colleges, 1982.

Hoffmann, Leonore. Introduction. In Leonore Hoffmann and Deborah Rosenfelt, eds. *Teaching Women's Literature from a Regional Perspective*. New York: Modern Language Association, 1982. 1-14.

Howe, Florence. *Myths of Co-education: Selected Essays 1964-1983*. Bloomington: Indiana University Press, 1984.

Hull, Gloria T., and Barbara Smith. "Introduction: The Politics of Black Women's Studies." In Gloria T. Hull, Patricia Bell Scott, and Barbara Smith, eds. *All the Women Are White, All the Blacks Are Men, But Some of Us Are Brave*. Old Westbury, N.Y.: Feminist Press, 1982. xvii-xxxii.

Irigaray, Luce. *Speculum of the Other Woman*. Trans. Gillian C. Gill. Ithaca, N.Y.: Cornell University Press, 1985.

Jardine, Alice A. *Gynesis: Configurations of Women and Modernity*. Ithaca: Cornell University Press, 1985.

Jones, Anne Rosalind. "Inscribing Femininity: French Theories of the Feminine." In Gayle Greene and Coppélia Kahn, eds. *Making a Difference: Feminist Literary Criticism*. London: Methuen, 1985. 80-112.

Klein, Renate D. "The Dynamics of the Women's Studies Classroom: A Review Essay of the Teaching Practice of Women's Studies in Higher Education." *Women's Studies International Forum* 10 (Spring 1987): 187-206.

————. "How to Do What We Want to Do: Thoughts about Feminist Methodology." In Bowles and Klein, eds., *Theories of Women's Studies.* 88-104.

Kolodny, Annette. "Dancing through the Minefield: Some Observations on the Theory, Practice, and Politics of a Feminist Literary Criticism." *Feminist Studies* 6 (Spring 1980): 1-25. Rpt. in Elaine Showalter, ed. *The New Feminist Criticism.* New York: Pantheon Books, 1985. 144-67.

Kuhn, Thomas S. *The Structure of Scientific Revolutions.* 2d ed. Chicago: University of Chicago Press, 1970.

MacIntosh, Peggy. "Interactive Phases of Curricular Re-Vision." In Bonnie Spanier, Alexander Bloom, and Darlene Boroviak, eds. *Toward a Balanced Curriculum: A Sourcebook for Initiating Gender Integration Projects.* Cambridge, Mass.: Schenkman, 1984. 25-34.

MacIntosh, Peggy, and Elizabeth Minnich. "Varieties of Women's Studies." *Women's Studies International Forum* 7 (Summer 1984): 139-48.

MacKinnon, Catherine A. "Feminism, Marxism, Method and the State: An Agenda for Theory." *Signs* 7 (Spring 1982): 515-44. Rpt. in Elizabeth Abel and Emily K. Abel, eds., *The Signs Reader: Women, Gender and Scholarship.* Chicago: University of Chicago Press, 1982. 227-56.

Maher, Frances. "Classroom Pedagogy and the New Scholarship on Women." In Culley and Portuges, eds., *Gendered Subjects.* 29-48.

Marks, Elaine. "Deconstructing in Women's Studies to Reconstructing the Humanities." In Schuster and Van Dyne, eds., *Women's Place in the Academy.* 172-87.

Meese, Elizabeth A. *Crossing the Double-Cross: The Practice of Feminist Criticism.* Chapel Hill: University of North Carolina Press, 1986.

Miller, J. Hillis. "Presidential Address 1986. The Triumph of Theory, the Resistance to Reading, and the Question of the Material Base." *PMLA* 102 (May 1987): 281-91.

Miller, Nancy K. "Mastery, Identity, and the Politics of Work: A Feminist Teacher in the Graduate Classroom." In Culley and Portuges, eds., *Gendered Subjects.* 195-200.

Millett, Kate. *Sexual Politics.* New York: Avon Books, 1970.

Moers, Ellen. *Literary Women: The Great Writers.* Garden City, N.J.: Doubleday, 1976.

Newman, Cardinal John Henry. *The Idea of a University.* In William E. Buckler, ed. *Prose of the Victorian Period.* Cambridge, Mass.: Riverside, 1958. 179-225.

Peck, Jeffrey M. "Advanced Literary Study as Cultural Study: A Redefinition of the Discipline." In *Profession 85.* New York: Modern Language Association, 1985. 49-54.

Raymond, Janice. "Women's Studies: A Knowledge of One's Own." In Culley and Portuges, eds., *Gendered Subjects.* 49-63.

Rich, Adrienne. "Claiming an Education." In *On Lies, Secrets and Silence.* 231-35.

————. "Notes toward a Politics of Location." In *Blood, Bread and Poetry: Selected Prose, 1979-85.* New York: Norton, 1986. 210-31.

———. *On Lies, Secrets and Silence: Selected Prose 1966-1978.* New York: Norton, 1979.

———. "When We Dead Awaken: Writing as Re-vision." In *On Lies, Secrets and Silence.* 32-49.

Robinson, Lillian S. "Feminist Criticism: How Do We Know When We've Won?" *Tulsa Studies in Women's Literature* 3 (Spring 1984): 143-51.

Schilb, John. "Transforming a Course in American Literary Realism." In Schuster and Van Dyne, eds., *Women's Place in the Academy.* 201-18.

Scholes, Robert. *Textual Power: Literary Theory and the Teaching of English.* New Haven, Conn.: Yale University Press, 1985.

Schuster, Marilyn R., and Susan Van Dyne, eds. *Women's Place in the Academy: Transforming the Liberal Arts Curriculum.* Totowa, N.J.: Rowman and Allanheld, 1985.

Showalter, Elaine. *A Literature of Their Own: British Women Novelists from Brontë to Lessing.* Princeton, N.J.: Princeton University Press, 1977.

———, ed. *The New Feminist Criticism: Essays on Women, Literature and Theory.* New York: Pantheon Books, 1985.

———. "Women's Time, Women's Space: Writing the History of Feminist Criticism." In Benstock, ed., *Feminist Issues in Literary Scholarship.* 30-44.

Spanier, Bonnie, Alexander Bloom, and Darlene Boroviak, eds. *Toward a Balanced Curriculum: A Sourcebook for Initiating Gender Integration Projects.* Cambridge, Mass.: Schenkman, 1984.

Stanley, Liz, and Sue Wise. *Breaking Out: Feminist Consciousness and Feminist Research.* London: Routledge and Kegan Paul, 1983.

Westkott, Marcia L. "Women's Studies as a Strategy for Change: Between Criticism and Vision." In Bowles and Klein, eds., *Theories of Women's Studies.* 210-18.

Williamson, Marilyn L. "Toward a Feminist Literary History." *Signs* 10 (Autumn 1984): 136-47.

Zimmerman, Bonnie. "What Has Never Been: An Overview of Lesbian Feminist Literary Criticism." *Feminist Studies* 7 (Fall 1981): 451-75. Rpt. in Showalter, ed., *The New Feminist Criticism.*

REED WAY DASENBROCK

What to Teach
When the Canon Closes Down:
Toward a New Essentialism

The most important development in the study of literature over the past few years is that once again pedagogy is no longer a dirty word. One of the things that made New Criticism genuinely new, at least from I. A. Richards's *Practical Criticism* to Brooks and Warren's *Understanding Poetry*, was its concern with teaching. How do we teach literature in the classroom? Richards's work was perhaps more important for posing the question than for any concrete answers, but Brooks and Warren felt they had an answer, an answer that because of its pedagogical effectiveness proved to be extremely influential. The theoretical disputes that over the past twenty years have dislodged New Criticism from its theoretical hegemony nonetheless tended, at least at first, to sidestep the question of teaching. And this led to the paradoxical situation in which New Criticism was simultaneously widely discredited as a theory and just as widely employed as a teaching method. This cognitive dissonance has more than a little to do with the strained tone in which literary theorists attacked the New Critical "dogma" they tended to employ in the classroom.

Things have changed, as this collection of essays should show. Some literary theorists have realized that the recent wave of theoretical inquiry has implications for teaching and that these implications should be pursued. It is acceptable once again to devote energy to thinking about what we do and should do in the classroom. And though I would maintain that the current wave of pedagogical reflection has yet to match the power of the pedagogical contributions of Richards or Brooks and Warren, nonetheless the movement as a whole is an admirable development. Most of us teach for a living, and our collective sense of who we are and what we do can only be sharpened by accepting that reality, but of course no one currently working in the field would argue that it is enough simply to come to terms with the reality of the teaching profession. We would all, I'm sure, wish to change that reality as well. And here I would argue that the reflection we have been engaged in hasn't gone far enough.

To simplify, two key issues are at stake: how do we teach and what do we teach? The thrust of my argument is that in asking what do we teach, we have focused too much on the choice of individual texts and not enough on the larger curricular categories in which we study those texts. To the question, what (texts) do we teach, I would like to add the question, what (courses) do we teach? We need to rethink course design as well as our choice of texts. Of the two, course design is arguably the more important; it is clearly the more neglected.

Inasmuch as the effort to change what we teach can be summarized, it can be summarized in the phrase *opening up the canon.* The established canon of English and American literature as received and taught has been seen to be a very partial representation, biased toward men from privileged classes and races. Advocates of literature by women and by marginalized social and economic groups have pressed to open up the canon, to move toward a more expansive, pluralistic view of literature with room for all sectors of society (see Fiedler and Baker). But there is a problem with this movement, or at least with the way it has been conceptualized: in a number of important senses, the canon can't open. There are demonstrable and important constraints on the number of writers, especially from the past, that we can study and teach.[1] The move to open up the canon has been primarily additive, adding works by women and minorities to the canon. One concrete result of this can be seen in the standard anthologies used in survey courses, especially anthologies of American literature, which keep getting longer and longer. But our courses aren't getting any longer, and I don't suspect that our students read more for their classes or outside of class, so an ever-growing percentage of these massive anthologies is going unread. This is not a trivial fact. Unless our students take more courses or do more reading in or beyond their courses, the amount of material they will encounter is a fixed quantity. As Marjorie Perloff has pointed out: "For every X that is added to a given syllabus or anthology, a Y must, after all, be withdrawn. The class that reads Chopin's *Awakening* will not, in all likelihood, have time for Henry James' *Portrait of a Lady.* I am not saying that this is necessarily a bad thing, but we should be under no illusion that we have replaced a 'closed' and narrow canon with an 'open' and flexible one" (128).

So the logical end result of "opening up the canon" may well be a contradiction. Scholars investigating our literature are finding more and more writers whom they urge upon our attention. Our collective sense of our literature is becoming more complex, more variegated, and much richer (this is particularly true in American literature, where the movement toward canon-revision has been strongest, but it is true elsewhere as well[2]). And I certainly welcome this development. Yet when we come to present this material to our students, our additive rhetoric of "opening up the canon" meets hard, subtractive logic. We can't teach the new literature in addition to the old canon: something has to give, substitutions have to be made, in the classroom the canon inexorably closes down.

The language of opening up the canon therefore needs rethinking. The new material being added to the canon as it opens up risks being left out of the canon as it closes back down, in just the way minorities newly hired under affirmative action programs tend to be fired first during layoffs because of their lack of seniority. Last in, first out may be the order of the day in curricula as well as in fire departments and police forces. The reason will be the same: seniority. When hard choices have to be made and justified, "central" figures will always win out over "marginal" figures. "These are the central texts our students need to know," so the argument will always run, and the figures perceived to be central are likely to be those who have long been considered central.

This can be seen clearly enough in the recent calls to teach a core (see the Bennett Report). Those concerned with opening up the canon have, of course, strongly opposed the contrasting call to return to a core and have pointed out that the core called for by the Bennett Report, for example, is almost exclusively a core of texts by European males;[3] it is, in short, the old canon we are trying to move away from. But the call to return to a core has been made more persuasive by the inability of the other side to contest the received vision of the core. "Opening up the canon" implies dilation without a reordering within the opened-up canon, and this failure to confront the issue of centrality head-on will, I think, prove costly in the confrontation over centrality that must necessarily follow the opening up of the canon. What will we teach when the canon closes down, as it must? What we feel to be central, of course. So if we wish to avoid returning to the older vision of the core of central texts that we have sought to move away from, we need to contest the older vision of centrality.

How might we do that? One of the sources of the current ferment of interest in pedagogy is the theoretical ferment of the 1970s, and contemporary literary theory, drawing on Derrida and Wittgenstein, has made the very concepts "central" and "marginal" susceptible to deconstruction. To say that certain writers, certain texts, form a given tradition that is central is to be guilty of a certain essentialism now thoroughly displaced, in theory at least, by Wittgenstein's notion of family resemblances and by Derrida's notion of the supplement. Hierarchies of major and minor, central and marginal, greater and lesser, need deconstruction so that we can see how we have been imprisoned within them.[4] This deconstructive assault on essentialism has come at the same time as the movement to open up the canon, and in their stress on decentering, these two movements closely resemble one another. But, this decentering once accomplished, where are we? After things are decentered, how do we organize them?

This is another way of asking about the political implications of deconstruction, and this is a controversial, indeed vexed, question that I can touch on only very quickly. One answer has always been that despite its radical tone and appearance, deconstruction is a fundamentally conservative movement that essentially leaves things as they are. To deconstruct a hierarchy is still to leave us imprisoned within it: "Derrida cannot relinquish the formal oppositions whose inadequacy he has intimated" (Law 162). And this position has been developed at length by Edward Said in his "Reflections on American 'Left' Criticism": "the oppositional manner of new New Criticism does not accurately represent its ideas and practice, which, after all is said and done, further solidify and guarantee the social structure and the culture that produced them. . . . A visitor from another world would surely be perplexed were he to overhear a so-called old critic calling the new critics dangerous. What, this visitor would ask, are they dangers to? The state? The mind? Authority?" (159-60). Deconstruction, in this view, leaves us within the central categories of male European culture, even though—or perhaps because—it puts those categories into question; in the same way, it leaves us within the central texts of that culture it has deconstructed. Even Jonathan Culler has conceded that "deconstructive criticism has concentrated on major authors of the canon" (280). And J. Hillis Miller has turned that into a credo: "I believe in the established canon of English and American literature and in the validity of the concept of privileged texts" (12). As Marjorie Perloff has noted, inasmuch as deconstructive critics replace that canon, they tend to replace it with "a rather narrowly drawn 'post-Structuralist' canon" of privileged theoreticians, who again turn out to be male Europeans (128). And Said is surely right to say that the war between deconstruction and the traditionalists can now be seen to have been largely shadowboxing, as deconstruction all along was operating from a position very close in values to that of the traditionalists who have so vehemently opposed it.

But this description of deconstruction could be redescribed as a description of the Yale School deconstruction of J. Hillis Miller, Geoffrey Hartman, and Paul de Man, for there is another, quite different characterization of deconstruction that would assign it a rather different role to play in the current debates over the canon and over centrality. This more avowedly political view would see the deconstructing of a hierarchy as itself a political gesture, and Derrida himself has gestured in this direction, arguing for instance that deconstruction is "a way of taking a position, in its work of analysis, concerning the political and institutional structures that make possible and govern our practices" (qtd. in Culler 156). This perspective of Derrida's has been echoed in the work of Gayatri Spivak and in attempts such as Michael Ryan's to align Marxism and deconstruction. But there isn't a Berlin Wall between these two schools of thought. Barbara Johnson begins her recent *A World of Difference* by criticizing her own earlier work for adhering to a Yale School conservatism and only considering white male writers; her new work employs deconstructive methodologies to discuss the writings of black female writers. So we are not likely to find a consensus on whether deconstruction is inherently radical or conservative or even whether it has helped open up the canon or has helped keep it from opening, as leading deconstructive critics can be found arguing on both sides of this issue.[5] And the conclusion I would draw is that whether one sees deconstruction as radical or conservative in its implications for the canon, neither characterization helps us with the current dilemma: what we do after the old essentialism has been deconstructed. Our task now is not to dislodge an old hierarchy but to keep it from relodging itself. I don't see that either conservative or radical deconstruction has much to offer in this situation, since both seem caught up in the moment of dislodging, valorizing that as the critical act par excellence.

What I would like to suggest is that to teach, to prescribe a curriculum, to assign one book for class as opposed to another, is ineluctably to call certain texts central, to create a canon, to create a hierarchy, in short, to be an essentialist. And the seemingly attractive argument made to the effect that we should move away from canon-formation toward canonical "heterodoxy" (Guillory 359) is simply a utopian notion that cannot be realized. We can't read everything, we can't teach everything, we can't study everything. And this means that there is no escaping the task of selection, no escaping the task of canon-formation, and no escaping essentialism. Deconstruction helped dislodge the old essentialism, but it can't give us what we need now. If we want to contest the old essentialism successfully, we need a vision of what we do that would valorize as central precisely what the old essentialism and the old canon marginalized and devalued. We need, not the by now familiar decentering, but a new recentering. We need, in short, a new essentialism. Without a new essentialism, our curriculum will continue to be shaped by the old. With a new essentialism, and only with a new essentialism, will the material recently added to the canon stay put, redefined as central, when the canon closes down.

By the end of this essay it should be clear what new essentialism (and new canon) I would put in place, but first we need to see the logic of the old canon. The determinate canon J. Hillis Miller believes in is the canon of English and American literature, and that phrase perfectly represents the map of English literature held by most professors of English and enshrined in all our institutions. The literature anthologies already referred to above serve a basic building block in the curriculum of virtually every English department: the lower-division surveys. The surveys divide literature into three parts: American, English, and World. World literature is in languages other than English, read in translation, and English and American literature are therefore understood to divide the world of literature in English between them. And though these anthologies and the courses they are designed to serve offer the most clear-cut example, literature in English is similarly divided between the English and the Americans in all our institutions and ways of representing literature (see my "English Department Geography"). This is true, somewhat surprisingly, even for most of those trying to open up the canon. This movement has been stronger in the study of American literature than anywhere else, but the effort has been to rethink the canon of American literature rather than to rethink the need for an organizing concept such as "American literature."

Why is this so? It certainly was not always so, for the origins of the study of literature were never narrowly nationalistic. Aristotle didn't refuse to comment on Homer even though Homer probably wasn't an Athenian; Longinus didn't ignore the Book of Genesis even though it was the product of an alien people and culture; Horace certainly didn't ignore the Greek poets, though he wrote in Latin. There has always been a tendency to consider literature in a given language as a cohesive unity, but that posits language communities—not nation-states—as the logical way to subdivide the world of literature. There is, moreover, a broad understanding in our era of the dysfunctional nature of nationalism, yet English professors hold onto the values of nationalism as stoutly as politicians calling for protectionist legislation, immigration controls, and preemptive strikes against nations whose systems of government they dislike. Unfortunately, this is also largely true of professors of other languages, who just as vehemently are professors of Italian or Peruvian or German literature. Even among scholars of comparative literature, the institutional antidote to nationalistic categories, it is the exception who doesn't say, "I do comparative work, but my real field is Italian or French or whatever." What has happened to the international impulse of Renaissance humanism in which Erasmus, More, Linacre, and others had a broadly shared international culture?

That was based on Latin, one response might run, and Latin disappeared as an international language a long time ago. True enough, but English has taken its place and now functions as a broad international language with, moreover, an important role inside nearly one-quarter of the world's countries. English is also an important international literary language, and English and American literature emphatically do not divide the world of English literature between them. Important writing in English is being done all over the world in more than thirty countries. This development is something those calling for a return to the old essentialism generally fail to recognize. J. Hillis Miller, for example, in the essay in which he develops his credo about English and American literature, seems to be arguing for a return to studying literature in English as opposed to work in other languages. But he states this as "English and American literature," seemingly unaware of any other literatures in the English language. Similarly, E. D. Hirsch's focus in *Cultural Literacy* is unabashedly on national cultures, as the subtitle of his book, *What Every American Needs to Know*, transparently reveals.[6] Hirsch, unlike Hillis Miller, at least recognizes that other countries, such as Australia and India, use English (17-18), but his stress is even more nationalistic than Hillis Miller's: "To teach the ways of one's own community has always been and still remains the essence of the education of our children, who enter neither a narrow tribal culture nor a transcendent world culture but a national literate culture" (18).

But that is not to say that simply expanding the number of national categories will solve the problem. The problem is our reliance upon nationalistic categories in the first place. Our nationalistic emphasis on English and American literature misses a lot because much of the most interesting writing being done in English today comes from outside England and America. But even if we move toward an awareness of the other national literatures in English, such as Nigerian literature in English (a country not found in Hirsch's list of nations using English

[78]), we are still going to miss a lot because national categories seem curiously blunt instruments for the representation of the international character of literature in English today. Once we use a category like "American literature," as any Derridean or Wittgensteinian would tell us, the temptation is to look for the essence of that category, to look for the truly American in American literature. (William Spengemann has acutely criticized this tendency in the study of American literature, which he calls the "exceptionalist claims" made for American literature [213].) What we do is divide the concept internally, privileging the pure case over the marginal or problematic. So William Carlos Williams is seen as more of an American writer than Ezra Pound or T. S. Eliot, since he stayed home while they went to Europe. Willa Cather is seen as a more American writer than Ole Rölvaag, since her descriptions of the settling of the Plains are in English, not Norwegian. And John Cheever is seen as a more American writer than Leslie Marmon Silko or Maxine Hong Kingston because he comes from a more mainstream community than Native or Chinese Americans. Comparably, Buchi Emecheta's *In the Ditch*, set in London, is the most striking portrayal of the Welfare State gone disastrously astray that I know, yet Emecheta's Nigerian origin tends to disqualify her from consideration as an English writer. These are precisely the kinds of exclusions and hierarchies that critics opening up the canon struggle against, but I would argue that as long as we organize our literature around value-laden terms such as "American" and "English," these exclusions and hierarchies are inescapable. To ask if something is part of American literature or not can never be a neutral act of description, and in the resulting struggle much of what is most interesting in American literature is not going to meet someone's criterion of "Americanness." Thus our reliance upon the national categories of English and American literature not only causes us to miss much that lies clearly outside English and American literature, but it also causes us to miss much that lies not so clearly inside.

There is a simple solution to this: we should declare that it is literature in English, not English and American literature, that we study; the language should be seen as the thread that holds us together. All professors of English teach in departments of English, after all, and we should understand a concern with the language as more fundamental than a concern with any given national categories.

Important consequences follow or would follow from this subtle shift in terminology and emphasis. The history of English is, of course, not a history of two discrete nation-states, England and America. The

United States of America has been an independent nation for just about half of its recorded history (even if one ignores everything prior to the European "discovery" and settlement), and England has not been a discrete nation-state for 385 years. The history of English is rather a history of a gradual expansion of the language beyond its home in England to encompass the entire world. A full history of this expansion would of course be the subject of a book, but it can be divided into four partially overlapping stages. In the first, encompassing the period up to the early seventeenth century, English became the dominant language of the British Isles, not just England, and the "Celtic periphery" was brought under (a somewhat unstable) English political and linguistic hegemony. The second phase can be roughly placed during the seventeenth and eighteenth centuries, the period of the "First British Empire," as it has been called, in which the British settlements in America flourished and then broke away. The third stage has been called the "Second British Empire," that far more imposing imperial edifice with India as its core that rose on the ruins of the first and lasted into the second half of this century. The fourth stage is the current stage of implosion, in which Britain has divested itself of its colonies but a dual legacy of empire remains in the worldwide spread of English and in the minorities from the former colonies who now live in Britain.

Each of these periods has left a political and social legacy that causes problems for anyone thinking of literature in English as a combination of English and American literature. The English domination of the Celtic periphery raises a host of problems in definition and categories: are Irish, Welsh, and Scottish literature part of English literature, or should they be considered independent entities? The argument for coherence is a powerful one, given the influence of English literature on Celtic writers, yet any specialist in the Celtic literatures will tell one, justly, that Celtic writers draw on their own heritage as well as that of the English and that they don't receive proper recognition in courses on English literature. And this is not an issue that has been faced squarely, particularly in the design of our curriculum. We tend to call our historical and survey courses "English literature," throwing in Sheridan, Scott, Yeats, and others without providing an adequate explanation of their differing cultural backgrounds and contexts. The lasting legacy of the first British Empire is, of course, the United States. The concept of American literature would seem to have handled that legacy well enough, but our habit of dichotomizing English and American literature causes problems as well as solves them: we have a hard time dealing with mixed cases, with English writers like Auden or Isherwood who came here or with American writers such as James or Eliot who moved to England. And William Spengemann has recently argued that we should abandon the very concept of American literature, given the amount of American literature we have misunderstood by "keeping it separate from the rest of the world, especially Britain" (237). Far more complexity was introduced by the second British Empire, during which English spread all over the world. Writers from the West Indies, Africa, Asia, and the Pacific are English rather than American in some trivial senses: they spell color with a *u*, and they play cricket rather than baseball. But their cultural and political frames of reference are far more variegated than that and can only be misread by dividing literature in English between the English and the Americans. The initial reaction to such complexity was simply to ignore the plethora of world writing in English, but this has been challenged most directly by the changing shape of writing coming from England, by the preeminence in English literature of writers originally from around the world such as V. S. Naipaul and Salman Rushdie. It has become impossible to continue to ignore the fact that English literature is no longer very English, at least by F. R. Leavis's standards. Comparable issues are raised in American literature by the increasingly powerful work of writers from marginalized immigrant or indigenous communities, such as Asian Americans, Native Americans, and Chicanos.

But if we say that the English language and its spread provides our thread of coherence, these marginal examples that threaten the coherence of English and American literature become just the opposite, central examples of the spread of English into new lands and communities. Each moment of expansion breaks or risks the coherence of the nation-based category, but that moment is central in a model based on the expansion of the language. Let me take the eighteenth century as a convenient example. Most traditional England-centered models of English literary history would define Fielding and Richardson as central figures in the novel, Pope as the central poet, and Johnson as the central poet-critic. It should be easy to see the parallel between this list of central figures and an England-centered notion of English literature. But if we make the expansion of English — not England itself — central to our conception of English literature, our sense of what is central changes. An astonishingly high percentage of the great writers and thinkers in English in the eighteenth century comes from the "Celtic periphery," preeminently from Scotland, though the Ireland that produced Berkeley, Goldsmith, Burke, and Sheridan and gave a home to Swift isn't to be ignored. The nonnationalistic model would see this not as a curious anomaly to be ignored, but as the beginning of a decisive shift in English-language culture away from England that should be emphasized. Moreover, there is at least an interesting homology between our sense of Fielding and Richardson as initiators of the tradition of the English novel and their role as initiators of the domestic novel, the novel about people staying at home, in England. Other novelists, including Defoe and Smollett, were intimately linked to the spread of English and wrote novels depicting that spread.[7] Though academics teach and write about Fielding and Richardson far more often than Defoe, it is Defoe who remains the central novelist of the century for world writers in English, as his narratives of the world outside England remain potent images, in many cases images to be struggled against. I cannot imagine a contemporary novelist rewriting *Joseph Andrews* or *Clarissa* in the way J. M. Coetzee grapples with *Robinson Crusoe* in his recent *Foe*. And of course, the cultural renaissance of the Celtic periphery and the spread of the empire are closely linked phenomena: the British Empire could almost be called the Scottish Empire, so important were the Scots in the expansion of the Empire. And this link finds its literal embodiment in Smollett's *Roderick Random*, as well as, more obliquely, in *Gulliver's Travels*.

So in place of the centripetal canon oriented toward the England of Pope, Fielding, Richardson, and Johnson, a centrifugal canon might focus on Swift, Defoe, Smollett, and Boswell.[8] This is a slight change, perhaps, as all these figures are recognized to be important and are placed in the canon somewhere. But as one moves closer and closer to the present, a centripetal, England-centered canon captures fewer and fewer of the important figures, whereas a centrifugal canon focused on the totality of writing in English has no difficulty at all in representing the panorama of world writing in English. The same is true within the study of American literature. It took considerable energy to get American literature recognized as a distinct entity in the first place, so powerful were the centripetal tendencies of the English tradition. But once established, the study of American literature has by and large replicated the same centripetal tendencies, privileging those at the defined center over the margins. This is the context in which it has been so difficult to open up the canon to work by minorities and women, since they have been perceived to be at the margins. But if we replace the category of nationalism with the category of language, just the opposite happens. And the now dynamically defined center is not England, but instead whatever new group is acquiring English or beginning to write in it at that moment.

This simple reversal of emphasis in redefining the center does everything we need, I think, to keep the canon from closing down in the wrong way. Much that was central in the old canon remains central in this one, but not always for the same reasons. By anyone's standards Spenser is a great poet, the greatest nondramatic poet of the Elizabethan era. But in a centrifugal history, he takes on renewed emphasis as someone involved in the expansion of the Empire, directly in Ireland and through his connection with Raleigh, and indirectly in a variety of ways in his poetry and poetics. *The Tempest* becomes a central play of Shakespeare's, central for its representation of colonization and discovery rather than for its return to the romance wellsprings of literature, as Northrop Frye—himself a child of empire—would have it. *The Tempest* just as much as *Robinson Crusoe* has been a text writers from once-colonized countries have reacted against and rewritten, as can be seen in George Lamming's *The Pleasures of Exile*. As great as they are, both Defoe's and Shakespeare's works stand revealed in this context as the voice of the colonizer depicting the colonized; we also need to find a place in what we teach for Caliban's response to Prospero and Friday's response to Crusoe. Only a centrifugal conception of literature in English that embraces Lamming and Coetzee as well as Shakespeare and Defoe can place all these works in the juxtapositions they deserve.

So opening up the canon, though important, is not enough. We also need to rethink the field in order to find a central—not marginal—place for the work added to the canon as it opens up. Until this is achieved, that work will remained marginalized and insufficiently appreciated, always in danger of losing its place as the canon closes down. In this essay, I have offered my sketch of how to rethink the field, and I offer it in an unabashedly essentialist mode of thought. For the only way to resist the essentializing move back to the "classics of English and American literature" is to redefine the essence of our concerns, from the literature of the English and the Americans to English literature in its entirety, from a nationalist conception of English literature to an acceptance of its internationalism.

NOTES

1. Joe Weixlmann has recently called attention to one of these constraints that I won't discuss here, which he calls "lethargy," though it might be more charitably called "inertia": "Finally, when I cite lethargy as a major inhibiting factor in the process of canon reformation, I do not mean to imply that English professors are wont to be lazy. The fact is that most have been trained to teach traditional literary figures within traditional subject areas and that, when they teach literature courses, they are inclined to put that training to use" (279).

The exigencies of publication constitute another important constraint: it involves a considerable investment to make a wide range of texts available, and so there are economic factors as well as institutional ones tending to narrow our representation of past literature.

2. For a recent portrait of canon revision in a traditional field of English literature, see Curran.

3. Scholes notes this almost in passing ("It would be easy to criticize this list upon all sorts of grounds" [115]), but he focuses his critique on the notion of a list rather than the particulars of Bennett's list.

4. Wheeler is particularly clear on this aspect of deconstruction, as he is on the relation between what he calls Wittgenstein's "conservative deconstruction" and the more radical deconstruction of Derrida.

5. The recent revelations that Paul de Man wrote for a pro-Nazi newspaper in occupied Belgium during World War II have sharpened and complicated this debate without resolving it. Obviously, those inclined to attack deconstruction or Yale School deconstruction as inherently conservative—even reactionary—have found new ammunition in these revelations; those inclined to defend deconstruction and Yale School deconstruction as responsibly conservative have a problem. But as no one ever presented de Man's work as favoring an open canon, these revelations leave the debate over the canon in basically the same place it was.

6. Hirsch has repeatedly denied that his notion of cultural literacy implies either a core or a canon (see "'Cultural Literacy' Does Not Mean 'Canon'" 118-19), and certainly his general point that literacy depends upon readers' knowledge and therefore upon cultural literacy—which I think is largely correct—doesn't necessarily link him to an essentialist or canonical view of what to teach. But his further, independent assumptions about the right kind of cultural literacy to teach—his focus on national cultures and his particularly narrow view of the culture of the United States—show him to be much closer in spirit to the Bennett Report and the calls for a core than his disclaimers would allow. This is altogether to be regretted, as the more technical side of Hirsch's argument could be taken in a diametrically opposed direction from Hirsch's myopic nationalism. True cultural literacy would be international in scope, as it has always been.

7. The distinction I am drawing here relies upon Martin Green's distinction between the domestic and the adventure novel (58), and Green's study is an important step toward freeing the study of literature in English from its centripetal Anglocentrism. The problem with Green's approach (aside from his ignoring the response of the colonized) is that he seems to have internalized the literary evaluations of the centripetal canon so thoroughly that he keeps apologizing unnecessarily for the inferior literary merit of the work he discusses.

8. Swift and Pope were good friends, of course, while Swift and Defoe were lifelong enemies (as Green points out 89-92); yet that is less important for my terms here than that Swift and Defoe were interested in the same

things, empire and exploration, even if Defoe was an apologist for and Swift a critic of these developments.

WORKS CITED

Bennett, William. "'To Reclaim a Legacy': Text of Report on Humanities in Education." *The Chronicle of Higher Education* (28 Nov. 1984): 16-21.

Culler, Jonathan. *On Deconstruction: Theory and Criticism after Structuralism.* Ithaca: Cornell University Press, 1982.

Curran, Stuart. "Altering the 'I': Women Poets and Romanticism." *ADE Bulletin* 88 (Winter 1987): 9-12.

Dasenbrock, Reed Way. "English Department Geography." *ADE Bulletin* 86 (Spring 1987): 16-23.

Fiedler, Leslie A., and Houston A. Baker, Jr., eds. *English Literature: Opening Up the Canon.* Baltimore: Johns Hopkins University Press, 1981.

Green, Martin. *Dreams of Adventure, Deeds of Empire.* New York: Basic, 1979.

Guillory, John. "The Ideology of Canon Formation: T. S. Eliot and Cleanth Brooks." In *Canons.* Ed. Robert von Hallberg. Chicago: University of Chicago Press, 1984: 337-62.

Hirsch, E. D., Jr. " 'Cultural Literacy' Does Not Mean 'Canon.' " *Salmagundi* 72 (Fall 1986): 118-24.

———. *Cultural Literacy: What Every American Needs to Know.* Boston: Houghton Mifflin, 1987.

Johnson, Barbara. *A World of Difference.* Baltimore: Johns Hopkins University Press, 1987.

Law, Jules. "Reading with Wittgenstein and Derrida." In *Redrawing the Lines: Analytic Philosophy, Deconstruction and Literary Theory.* Ed. Reed Way Dasenbrock. Minneapolis: University of Minnesota Press, 1989. 140-68.

Miller, J. Hillis. "The Function of Rhetorical Study at the Present Time." *ADE Bulletin* 62 (1979): 10-18.

Perloff, Marjorie. "An Intellectual Impasse." *Salmagundi* 72 (Fall 1986): 125-30.

Ryan, Michael. *Marxism and Deconstruction.* Baltimore: Johns Hopkins University Press, 1982.

Said, Edward. "Reflections on American 'Left' Criticism." In *The World, the Text, and the Critic.* Cambridge: Harvard University Press, 1983: 158-77.

Scholes, Robert. "Aiming a Canon at the Curriculum." *Salmagundi* 72 (Fall 1986): 101-17.

Spengemann, William C. "American Writers and English Literature." *ELH* 52, no. 1 (1985): 209-38.

Spivak, Gayatri Chakravorty. *In Other Worlds: Essays in Cultural Politics.* New York: Methuen, 1987.

Weixlmann, Joe. "Dealing with the Demands of an Expanding Literary Canon." *College English* 50, no. 3 (March 1988): 273-83.

Wheeler, Samuel C, III. "Wittgenstein as Conservative Deconstructor." *New Literary History* 18, no. 2 (Winter 1988): 239-58.

R. A. SHOAF

Literary Theory, Medieval Studies, and the Crisis of Difference

In Memoriam
Judson Boyce Allen

[N]o translation would be possible if in its ultimate essence it strove
for likeness to the original. For in its afterlife ... the original under-
goes a change. Even words with a fixed meaning can undergo a
maturing process.

Walter Benjamin

'And of myne olde servauntes thow mysseyest,
And hynderest hem with thy translacyoun....'
'what so myn auctour mente,
Algate, God wot, yt was myn entente
To forthre trouthe in love ...
... this was my menynge.'

Geoffrey Chaucer

Philosophical discourse cannot master a word meaning two things
at the same time and which therefore cannot be translated without
an essential loss.

Jacques Derrida

In the present climate of uneasy pluralism where the major authors of
the traditional canon must increasingly compete with film studies, wom-
en's studies, Jewish studies, cultural studies, African-American studies,
and a host of other new, exciting, and important disciplines, medievalists
have just cause for concern at declining enrollments and widening
incomprehension of what medieval literature is really like. Middle
English poetry, in particular, is especially vulnerable to declining enrollments or, the obverse of the dilemma, to translations as the only

way it can be taught; but Dante and Jean de Meun are hardly less vulnerable and increasingly can only be presented, at least to any large segment of student population, in translation. Given this predicament, responsible medievalists must appeal to literary theory for an epistemology and, indeed, an ontology of translation that can enable them to teach monuments of medieval European literature in translation without sacrificing all of the irreducible difference of their original languages and cultures.[1] In particular, literary theory can help them understand and communicate such problematics as punning, allusion, quotation, and voice as instances of the boundary or membrane between two languages and cultures, where difference is put in crisis and where, as a result, remembering the original becomes simultaneous with loss and forgetting of the original (Italian, French, German, etc.)— indeed, without a mature and potent body of theory, medievalists are in peril when it comes to justifying the presence in the canon of much of what is best in medieval literature.

The following remarks are a preface, as it were, to a manual of literary theory for the medievalist.[2] The manual would begin with an epigraph drawn from Shakespeare. In *Hamlet*, with typical poignancy, Shakespeare observes in the character of Ophelia the difficulty and pain of interpretation—her speech is nothing, yet her audience does and must make something of it:

> *Gentleman:* Her speech is nothing,
> Yet the unshapèd use of it doth move
> The hearers to collection—they yawn at it,
> And botch the words up fit to their own thoughts;
> Which, as her winks and nods and gestures yield them,
> Indeed would make one think there might be thought,
> Though nothing sure, yet much unhappily.[3]

Here, indeed, is almost a paradigm of human signification and its interpretation: typically, though we may only intermittently be conscious of it, we botch each other's words up fit to our own thoughts, even when we are only "translating" within the same language.[4] In the most extreme cases—such as Othello—a man can botch words, signs, symbols, symptoms up to fit his own thoughts to the point of his own madness; or worse: Iago, whose name is *I ago*, "I act, or perform, or play" (and just possibly also *I ego*—recall his declaration "I am not what I am"[5]) plays upon Othello's "unbookish jealousy" (4.1.101) not only to inscribe all around Othello the signs to be interpreted, but also to insinuate the very thoughts Othello will botch the signs up to fit. Iago's infinite cruelty is precisely his uncannily acute understanding of human understanding—"Demand me nothing. What you know, you know" (5.2.303). And if someone objects that Ophelia is mad as Iago is certainly insane—surely they provide no paradigm of human signification and its interpretation—then one can only reply, after reading Ophelia's later lyrics sung in response to Gertrude and Claudius: if this be madness, make the most of it—even as Shakespeare, though hardly approving of him, made the most of Iago's dramatology.

To make the most of this "madness"—that interpretation, really a form of translation, botches the words up fit to our own thoughts—let me comment on an example from Chaucer's *Troilus and Criseyde*.[6] In book 1, the narrator remarks of Troilus, after the latter has seen and fallen in love with Criseyde:

And over al this, yet muchel more he thoughte	*much*
What for to speke, and what to holden inne;	*speak*
And what to *arten* hire to love he soughte,	*direct*
And on a song anon-right to bygynne,	*immediately*
And gan loude on his sorwe for to wynne.[7]	*began*
	get the better of

Arten means *direct* or *urge on*,[8] but it is also a pun, *art-en*; and the pun plays havoc with the narrator's presumptions at this point in the narrative.[9] *Art* will induce (and seduce) Criseyde to love: she will succumb to such art as that of Troilus's *canticus*, which follows immediately upon this passage, as well as to that of Pandarus's mediation.[10] But it is just this *art*, the art of the go-between or the "Galeotto," that the narrator in the early part of the poem is pleased to think he is innocent of. He is no Pandarus, he is sure. For example, he goes on in the next stanza to exclaim:

And of his song naught only the sentence,	*not*
As writ myn auctour called Lollius,	*wrote*
But pleinly, save oure tonges difference,	
I dar wel seyn, in al, that Troilus	*say*
Seyde in his song, loo, every word right thus	
As I shal seyn.	

(1.393-98)

And yet he cannot except "oure tonges difference." "Oure tonges difference" is precisely what prevents the kind of naive transparency the narrator boasts here that he can provide. "Oure tonges difference," in fact, demands of the translator that he use art—that is, that he self-consciously transform the original so as to emphasize in his language what is distinctive about it in its language. Translation without transformation is a dream of fullness and presence hopelessly afflicted with nostalgia[11]—a nostalgia, moreover, that is corrupt, since it entices its victim to shirk authorial responsibility (as the narrator endeavors to do, for example, in the proem to book 2, lines 9-18).

Chaucer the poet positions the pun on *arten* in book 1 to subvert the narrator's presumption of innocent instrumentality, and in doing so, he provokes us to realize that the narrator is already saying more than he is aware of. Love is inseparable from art, language from desire, rhetoric from eros, and the narrator, we gradually perceive, has to (and does) learn the coincidence of language and desire in the course of "translating" the book of Lollius. He becomes ever more responsible for what he is saying and for what what he is saying is saying. Thus his motives change by poem's end, and art has had much to do with the change. The narrator at poem's end knows that he cannot circumscribe[12] *arten* in the way he presumed he could at poem's beginning; the narrator at the end knows and fears the price of such closure.[13]

To teach the pun in this passage (and in effect I have just taught it), I have had to be a better translator than the narrator. I have had to be more like the translator the narrator becomes at poem's end. I have had, in short, to read as if I were a writer translating the original into a different language (although not necessarily into a different tongue) and translating it with complete consciousness that I was transforming it in the process. I have had, in effect, to assume responsibility for the original as if it were mine (though, of course, it is not mine, strictly speaking). And this I could do, and did do, only with a theory of translation as the loss of fullness and presence. To have taught the text otherwise would have been to presume, as did the narrator, an innocent instrumentality and a transparency of history—it would have been, in effect, to be hopelessly naïve. But the teacher cannot afford such naivete (especially the modern teacher of medieval studies). Every reader, in fact, from the beginning student to the seasoned professional, is also a writer, or more accurately, a rewriter—and must be aware of that.[14]

If every reader is a writer or rewriter, translating the original into a new version (however provisionally), then the original must be indeed a mercurial (and hermeneutic) object—in fact, an object like the Cheshire cat not always "there," wherever that is, or "there" only always partly. This characteristic of the original and its crucial implications are especially well illustrated in canto 24 of Dante's *Inferno*. Here, in the first of the cantos of the thieves, Dante inscribes a vision of the evanescence of the text (how it is "stolen" and "steals away").[15] This vision provides a useful refinement for the manual of literary theory for the medievalist.

In *Inferno*, cantos 24 and 25, Dante confronts a crisis of convention; in effect, he has to begin the canticle all over again.[16] Twice he recalls his and Virgil's setting out on the journey in cantos 1 and 2. The first time, he explicitly directs the reader back to the beginning of the canticle:[17]

> ché, come noi venimmo al guasto ponte,
> lo duca a me si volse con quel piglio
> dolce ch'io vidi prima a piè del monte.
> (24.19-21 and cf. 1.76-81)

[for soon as we were on the broken ridge, / my guide turned back to me with that sweet manner / I first had seen along the mountain's base.]

The second time, he is less direct but no less evocative:

> Leva'mi allor, mostrandomi fornito
> meglio di lena ch'i' non mi sentia,
> e dissi: 'Va, ch'i' son forte e ardito.'
> (24.58-60)

[Then I arose and showed myself far better / equipped with breath than I had been before: / 'Go on, for I am strong and confident.']

Similarly, at the end of canto 2, the pilgrim says to Virgil:

> 'Tu m'hai con disiderio il cor disposto
> sì al venir con le parole tue,
> ch'i' son tornato nel primo proposto.
> Or va, ch'un sol volere è d'ambedue:
> tu duca, tu segnore e tu maestro.'
> (2.136-40)

['You, with your words, have so disposed my heart / to longing for this journey—I return / to what I was at first prepared to do. / Now go; a single will fills both of us: / you are my guide, my governor, my master.']

Both moments emphasize that here the poet, too, just like the pilgrim, "catches his breath," so as to continue the poem, even as the pilgrim continues the journey; this emphasis is further strengthened by the occurrences of *convenire*, strategically located as they are to insist that both pilgrim and poet must and do find new conventions to continue their labors.

The first two occurrences of *convenire* primarily denote "necessity," but clearly each can at the same time connote "convention":

'Omai *convien* che tu così ti spoltre,'
disse 'l maestro, 'ché, seggendo in piuma,
in fama non si vien, né sotto coltre;
   sanza la qual chi sua vita consuma,
cotal vestigio in terra di sé lascia,
qual fummo in aere e in acqua la schiuma.
   E però leva sù, vinci l'ambascia
con l'animo che vince ogne battaglia,
se col suo grave corpo non s'accascia.
   Più lunga scala convien che si saglia.'

(24.46-55, emphasis added)

['Now you must cast aside your laziness,' / my master said, 'for he who
rests on down / or under covers cannot come to fame; / and he who
spends his life without renown / leaves such a vestige of himself on
earth / as smoke bequeaths to air or foam to water. / Therefore, get
up; defeat your breathlessness / with spirit that can win all battles if /
the body's heaviness does not deter it. / A longer ladder still is to be
climbed.']

The second of these two occurrences of *convenire* is the more accessible
at first. It is necessary that a longer ladder be climbed, and it is also
convenient, for without the convenience of this ladder the pilgrim could
not ascend to God, just as, without the "convention" of this ladder—
ultimately the entire poem itself, a *lunga scala* indeed (not unlike Jacob's
ladder)—the poet could not transcribe the journey to God.

In effect, Virgil and Dante the poet announce the need for the poem
to discover anew the conventions that will lead to its culmination.
Hence we can see that Virgil also, in the first occurrence of *convenire*,
urges the pilgrim to be himself convenient to the duty before him ("not
lazy") so that he might, in effect, become his fame, for if he becomes
his fame, the traces or signs (*vestigio*) he leaves behind him will be
who he is. The poem is Dante, although Dante, doubtless, was more
than the poem.

Such reasoning helps us to understand the terzine immediately following:

Parlando andava per non parer fievole,
onde una voce uscì de l'altro fosso,
a parole formar *disconvenevole*.

     . . .

Io era vòlto in giù, ma li occhi vivi,
non poteano ire al fondo per lo scuro,
per ch'io: 'Maestro, fa che tu arrivi

da l'altro cinghio e dismontiam lo muro,
ché, com' i' odo quinci e non intendo,
così giù veggio e neente *affiguro.'*
    'Altra risposta,' disse, 'non ti rendo
se non lo far; ché la dimanda onesta
si de' seguir con l'opera tacendo.'

(24.64-78, emphasis added)

[I spoke as we went on, not to seem weak; / at this, a voice came from the ditch beyond— / a voice that was not suited to form words. / . . . / I had bent downward, but my living eyes / could not see to the bottom through that dark; / at which I said: 'O master, can we reach / the other belt? Let us descend the wall, / for as I hear and cannot understand, / so I see down but can distinguish nothing.' / 'The only answer I give to you / is doing it,' he said. 'A just request / is to be met in silence, by the act.']

Here *convenire* appears in *disconvenevole,* where this word extends the emphasis on the difficulty of going on with the poem since a voice "a parole formar disconvenevole" ("that was not suited to form words") must perforce, if it is not somehow translated, block and impede and ultimately terminate the poem. Once again, then, *convenire* (or a form thereof) has emerged at a moment of crisis in the text. Moreover, in this case, it is reinforced in its role of marking the crisis by the verb *affiguro*: not only can the pilgrim not "make out" when he looks into the depth, but the poet cannot "figure" either—cannot make the figures that would continue the poem. Virgil's response, finally, seals the emphasis on the crisis. His only response, he says, is to do what the pilgrim has asked, " 'ché la dimanda onesta / si de' seguir con l'opera tacendo' " (" 'A just request / is to be met in silence, by the act' "; 24.77-78). His silence, in short, is the space in which the words of the poem can be resumed or reconvened, for it is the context of the deed (*l'opera*) which is also the work/poem (*l'opera*).

From the perspective thus achieved, we can circle back to the opening of canto 24 and "translate" Dante's image of the evanescence of the text:

In quella parte del giovanetto anno
che 'l sole i crin sotto l'Aquario tempra
e già le notti al mezzo dì sen vanno,
    quando la brina in su la terra assempra
l'imagine di sua sorella bianca,
ma poco dura a la sua penna tempra,

lo villanello a cui la roba manca,
si leva, e guarda, e vede la campagna
biancheggiar tutta; ond'ei si batte l'anca,
  ritorna in casa, e qua e là si lagna,
come 'l tapin che non sa che si faccia;
poi riede, e la speranza ringavagna,
  veggendo 'l mondo aver cangiata faccia
in poco d'ora, e prende suo vincastro
e fuor le pecorelle a pascer caccia.

(24.1-15)

[In that part of the young year when the sun / begins to warm its locks beneath Aquarius / and nights grow shorter, equalling the days, / when hoarfrost mimes the image of his white / sister upon the ground—but not for long, / because the pen he uses is not sharp— / the farmer who is short of fodder rises / and looks and sees the fields all white, at which / he slaps his thigh, turns back into the house, / and here and there complains like some poor wretch / who doesn't know what can be done, and then / goes out again and gathers up new hope / on seeing that the world has changed its face / in so few hours, and he takes his staff / and hurries out his flock of sheep to pasture.]

We have here an extended trope of writing itself, its instability and evanescence. The frost makes an image of the snow: the verb *assempra*[18] not only insists on representation, but also on the inevitable temporality of representation, since within it is also heard, ironically, *sempr[e]*; the irony depends, of course, on the next line, which will subvert the *sempr[e]* with its radical insistence on mutability and evanescence— "ma poco dura a la sua penna tempra" ("because the pen he uses is not sharp"—literally: "because little while lasts the pen's temper"). The pretensions of writing to permanence are thus put in question. And primarily because writing is constantly subject to being botched by the reader—hence the "villanello," who botches the "brina" up fit to his own thought: he is the figure of all readers who interpret the text without allowing that the text may (and probably will) "change its face."

The "villanello" botches the text of the hoarfrost up to fit his pre-conception, his pre-script. When that text disappears, however, the "new" text that "replaces" it, though obviously more "stable" than the first, is not, even so, permanent or, especially, transcendent; it too is subject to change ("in poco d'ora," moreover), provoking more and different interpretations—it will be "there" only for a while ("poco dura"). And to hypostatize its "there," to reify it into an immutable presence, may be to rigorize the text beyond any possibility of subsequent translation, because its "there" does change from culture to culture, from time to time.[19] And the importance of a text for a later day may just be its changeable "there," inviting different readers at different times in different places to botch it up, rewrite it, in new and intriguing ways: even as in *arten* there is *art-en*, even as in *assempra*, there is *sempr[e]*, so in all texts, perhaps, if we are vigilant readers, there are other texts waiting to be written out through our translations.

And if medievalists would successfully meet the crisis of difference in the classroom, then one alternative they can consider is teaching translation as well as teaching various texts in translation. They can teach reading as translation along lines roughly similar to those I have described here in my sketch of a manual of literary theory for the medievalist. And in doing so, they will gain one other significant advantage: they will also be teaching one of the most fundamental characteristics of medieval culture — or, precisely, translation. For medieval poetry, especially later medieval poetry, is poetry forged in the crucible of translation, from Latin into the vernaculars and from one vernacular to another — think only of Deschamps's honorific for Chaucer, "grand translateur."[20] In fact, medieval poetry without translation is unthinkable, and teaching it without also teaching translation and, indeed, theories of translation should be equally unthinkable.

As this brief manual began with an epigraph, from Shakespeare's *Hamlet* (and also *Othello*), so it would end with a brief epilogue, from *Beowulf*. For some time now I have taught the episode of the building of Heorot (64a-85b) as analogous to and in some ways possibly dependent on the account in Genesis of the building of the Tower of Babel. I have based this argument, in part, on striking narrative similarities between the two moments:

> Porro Chus genuit Nemrod: ipse coepit esse potens in terra. . . . Erat autem terra labii unius, et sermonum eorumdem. Cumque profiscerentur de oriente, invenerunt campum in terra Sennaar, et habitaverunt in eo. Dixitque alter ad proximum suum: Venite, faciamus lateres . . . et dixerunt: Venite, faciamus nobis civitatem et turrim, cuius culmen pertingat ad caelum et celebremus nomen nostrum antequam dividamur in universas terras.

> Now Chus begot Nemrod: he began to be mighty on the earth. . . . And the earth was of one tongue and of the same speech. And when they removed from the east, they found a plain in the land of Sennaar and dwelt in it. And each one said to his neighbor: Come, let us make brick. . . . And they said: Come, let us make a city and a tower, the top whereof may reach to heaven: and let us make our name famous before we be scattered abroad into all lands.[21]

Þa wæs Hroðgare here-sped gyfen,
wiges weorð-mynd. . . .
                     Him on mod be-arn
Þæt heal-reced   hatan wolde,
medo-ærn micel   men gewyrcean,
Þone y*ldo be*arn   fre gefrunon,
                . . .
                     scop him Heort naman,
se Þe his wordes geweald wide hæfde.

[Then Hrothgar was given victory in battle, / such honor in war. . . . It came to his mind / that he would command a royal building, / a gabled mead-hall fashioned by craftsmen, / which the sons of men should hear of forever. . . . He, whose word / had power everywhere, said its name, 'Hart.']²²

Both accounts begin with a statement to the effect that the ruler has grown powerful in his land; both accounts then proceed to relate the decision to build an edifice that will memorialize and blazon the triumphs and the fame of the ruler and his people; in both accounts there is a suggestion that the motive behind this decision is at least in part pride, pride in achievement and pride of national or racial identity; finally, in both accounts the edifice constructed is immediately visited with punishments by powers beyond the conception of mortals.²³

Here the parallels, if there are any, would seem to end.²⁴ But perhaps not. Perhaps Grendel in *Beowulf* is the embodiment of the problem of translation. Grendel does not translate, nor can he be translated. He does not talk with people, he eats them—thus eliminating, radically, the need for translation.²⁵ If God punishes the Tower of Babel with babble, the confusion of tongues that necessitates translation, it is arguable that He punishes Hrothgar and Heorot with Grendel, the monster who proves the necessity of translation—where translation fails, cannibalism follows.

Grendel is the "mearc-stapa, se þe moras heold, / fen ond fæsten" (103a-104a), the keeper of the fen, the dweller at the edge, the monster not only on but also of the margin.²⁶ He is the radical and unappeasable incommunicableness begotten of the attempt at structure by human being; he is the implacable remainder, whom only superhuman strength can dispose of. All structure is exclusive, because partial and autotelic, but a structure that asserts its specialness or distinctiveness to the exclusion of all likeness with or repetition of any otherness will, experience suggests, become the victim of its difference: its specialness will cannibalize it or babble it (or, in terms of our own era, "nuke" it). Such internality, such exclusivity, cries out for translation—thus proving the necessity and usefulness of translation; and when Beowulf arrives at the Danish court to kill Grendel, he demonstrates that Heorot, Hrothgar's pride, is only human, a structure in need of translation.

In a sense, then, Beowulf is a translator: he speaks different languages. Beowulf is a killer, too, though. The lesson here is hard but useful. Every literary text is a Heorot of sorts, a structure positing a threshold or a margin that, like the orifices of the body, both invites and excludes, entices and threatens. All students approaching a literary text for the first time encounter the monster of the margin, the demon of the threshold, asserting that they must be consumed, lose themselves, before they may enter the world of the text and know its structure: interpretation is that difficult even in the students' own language—if the language is foreign to the student, then the jeopardy is double. Slaying the monster of the margin ultimately means that students take over the text, assume it as their own—botching it up fit to their own thoughts. Reading and translating are not passive and receptive, but aggressive, contending, contestual, mutually assimilative—students come eventually to speak the text and, as we say, speak it as their own. The text is still Joyce's or Chaucer's or Virgil's, or the *Beowulf* poet's, but only in the context and the contest of the student's translation, itself transacted in the context and the contest of the tradition of the text's translation.[27]

To teach students this is to teach them what *Beowulf* or *Hamlet* is really about. When Beowulf kills Grendel and eventually his mother, he makes discourse possible again in Heorot—conversation, song, boasts, greetings, and so on.[28] Similarly, in *Hamlet*, death after death is the necessary preface to discourse in the court of Denmark. And in *King Lear*, nothing less than multiple slaughter is necessary before Edgar can finally say: " 'The weight of this sad time we must obey, / *Speak what we feel*, not what we ought to say.' "[29] Again and again, the price of discourse proves to be blood. If at the best of times, we botch each other's words up fit to our own thoughts (because after all we do each resemble a text), if that is the best we can do with translation, then without translation we all too easily degenerate into cannibalism—if not actually ingesting each other's flesh, then, typically, indiscriminately sponging each other's words and thoughts.

We can then perhaps benefit from keeping Grendel and Heorot and Beowulf in mind: every scene of translation is also a scene of violence— and the violent shall bear it away. Because structure is exclusive and partial, we must train our students to reorient themselves toward the whole through translation and theories of translation, especially when they are reading literature "already" in "translation." If poetry is what gets lost in translation, then restitution will begin in, though never be completed by, recognizing that loss is the content (and discontent) of literature. Literature is about what, could literature say it, would make literature unnecessary. The content of literature is its discontent: that no structure is all-inclusive, no language universal.[30] In its struggle with this discontent, translation saves the content but, just so, perpetuates the discontent—even as Beowulf, in the end, meets Grendel again in the Dragon (the text has changed face). Translation, then, will always fall short, but translation is our only defender against Grendel. Whether reading in their own language or in a foreign language, but especially in the latter case, our students must be brave translators, prepared for their encounter with Grendel so that they too may dwell awhile in a "H(e)art" (my translation) not their own.

NOTES

1. See, further, Eugene Vance, *Mervelous Signals: Poetics and Sign Theory in the Middle Ages*, Regents Studies in Medieval Culture (Lincoln: University of Nebraska Press, 1986), chs. 8 and 10 esp.; see also Vance's review of Brian Stock's *The Implications of Literacy* in *Diacritics* 15, no. 3 (1985): 55-64, esp. p. 55; consider also my review of Vance's book in *Speculum* 63 (April 1988): 480-83.

2. As such, they draw freely on work I have published recently in which I try to develop a context of literary theory for medieval studies; see esp. "Notes toward Chaucer's Poetics of Translation," *Studies in the Age of Chaucer* 1 (1979): 55-66; "Dante's *Commedia* and Chaucer's Theory of Mediation: A Preliminary Sketch," in *New Perspectives in Chaucer Criticism*, ed. Donald M. Rose (Norman, Okla.: Pilgrim Books, 1982), pp. 83-103; *Dante, Chaucer, and the Currency of the Word: Money, Images, and Reference in Late Medieval Poetry* (Norman, Okla.: Pilgrim Books, 1983); *The Poem as Green Girdle: "Commercium" in "Sir Gawain and the Green Knight"* (Gainesville: University Presses of Florida, 1984); "Chaucer and Medusa: *The Franklin's Tale*," *Chaucer Review* 21 (1986): 274-90; "The Crisis of Convention in Cocytus," in *Allegoresis: The Craft and Meaning of Allegory*, ed. J. Stephen Russell (New York: Garland, 1988), pp. 235-54; "The 'Syngne of Surfet' and the Surfeit of Signs in *Sir Gawain and the Green Knight*," in *The Passing of Arthur: Loss and Renewal in Arthurian Tradition*, ed. Christopher Baswell and William C. Sharpe (New York: Garland, 1988), pp. 152-69; and "Medieval Studies after Derrida after Heidegger," in *Sign, Sentence, Discourse: Language in Medieval Thought and Literature*, ed. Julian N. Wasserman and Lois Y. Roney (Syracuse: Syracuse University Press, 1989), pp. 9-30.

Recently I have prepared an edition of *Troilus and Criseyde* (East Lansing, Mich.: Colleagues Press, 1989) designed primarily for undergraduate audiences, in which, by a combination of glosses and annotations, I seek a text that reads with the convenience of a translation but without the effacing of the original that a translation normally entails; the edition is, in one sense, a testing of the understanding of translation I am developing here—it produces a text in which the crisis of difference is always and everywhere visible.

3. *Hamlet* 4.5.7-13, in *The Riverside Shakespeare*, ed. G. Blakemore Evans (Boston: Houghton Mifflin, 1974). All references to Shakespeare are to this edition.

4. Cf. Jacques Derrida, "Roundtable on Translation," in *The Ear of the Other: Otobiography, Transference, Translation*, ed. Christie V. McDonald, trans. Peggy Kamuf (New York: Schocken Books, 1985), pp. 93-161, esp. pp. 95 and 131; see also Derrida, "Des Tours de Babel," trans. Joseph F. Graham, in *Difference in Translation*, ed. J. F. Graham (Ithaca: Cornell University Press, 1985), pp. 165-207.

5. *Othello* 1.1.69.

6. Here I draw from my article "The Play of Puns in Late Middle English Poetry: Concerning Juxtology" in *On Puns: The Foundation of Letters*, ed. Jonathan Culler (London: Blackwell, 1988), pp. 44-61.

7. *Troilus and Criseyde* 1.386-90 (emphasis added), ed. Stephen A. Barney, *The Riverside Chaucer*, based on *The Works of Geoffrey Chaucer*, ed. F. N. Robinson (Boston: Houghton Mifflin, 1987); all citations of Chaucer are from this edition.

8. See Norman Davis et al., *A Chaucer Glossary* (Oxford: Clarendon Press, 1979), p. 7.

9. Dante uses a similar pun, on Italian *arte*, in the *Purgatorio*, canto 1, line 126; for a discussion of it, see Shoaf, *Dante, Chaucer, and the Currency of the Word*, pp. 56-57. The text and translation of Dante's *Commedia* cited here and elsewhere is that of Allen Mandelbaum, *The Divine Comedy of Dante Alighieri* (New York: Bantam, 1982, 1984, 1986).

10. See *Troilus and Criseyde* 3.253-55 (emphasis added): " 'for the [Troilus] am I [Pandarus says] bicomen, / Bitwixen game and ernest, swich a *meene* / As maken wommen unto men to comen.' "

11. See Derrida, "Des Tours de Babel," pp. 174-75, 190-91. See also Walter Benjamin, "The Task of the Translator," in *Illuminations*, ed. Hannah Arendt, trans. Harry Zohn (New York: Schocken Books, 1969), pp. 69-82, esp. p. 73; helpful, if provocative, commentary on Benjamin is found in Paul de Man, "Conclusions: Walter Benjamin's 'The Task of the Translator,' " in *The Resistance to Theory* (Minneapolis: University of Minnesota Press, 1986), pp. 73-105; also useful, though different in approach, is W. Haas, "The Theory of Translation," *Philosophy* 37 (1962): 208-28, esp. pp. 223, 228. Finally, consult also H. Marshall Leicester, Jr., "Oure Tonges *Différance*: Textuality and Deconstruction in Chaucer," in *Medieval Texts and Contemporary Readers*, ed. Laurie A. Finke and Martin B. Schichtman (Ithaca: Cornell University Press, 1987), pp. 15-26.

12. See *Troilus and Criseyde* 5.1865.

13. See Shoaf, *Dante, Chaucer, and the Currency of the Word*, pp. 142-57.

14. This holds, I am claiming, even for beginning students who, in my experience, learn best by being trusted with the responsibility to read as rewriters. To their question, "what does this mean?" I typically respond, "how would *you* write it"? Beginners who can answer this question can learn to read and write—they can, in the sense of the word I am arguing here, *translate*.

15. It is a commonplace of Dante criticism that in *Inferno*, the punishment fits the crime. It is equally true that the problematic fits the locale: in the canto of the thieves, Dante explores the problematic of the property of the text: who owns it?; in the canto of the lustful, that of desire in discourse; in the canto of the counterfeiters, that of fiction and the true, etc.

16. For a preliminary overview of the crisis of convention in the *Commedia*, see my article in *Allegoresis* (note 2 above), which studies the evidence in *Inferno*, cantos 30-34. The following segment of my larger argument on convention was completed and accepted for publication before the appearance of Margherita Frankel's "Dante's Anti-Virgilian *Villanello* (*Inf.* XXIV, 1-21)" in *Dante Studies* 102 (1984): 81-109. Although I agree with many of Frankel's positions, I rather sharply disagree with certain other, crucial arguments (pp. 91-92 esp.); obviously, this is not the place, however, to engage the issue, a task better left to the longer study I am preparing of the crisis of convention in the *Commedia*.

17. In what follows, note that I quote both Dante's text and Mandelbaum's translation; to do so clearly makes my text awkward to read—the page seems crowded. And yet to pursue a detailed analysis of Dante's text otherwise is impossible because the presumption of a general knowledge of Italian is also impossible. Since this dilemma is part of the motive of my text, I resist elision of it, I do not simplify it, in the form of my text—such "awkwardness" is part of what I am writing about.

18. According to Francesco Mazzoni, *assempra* "deriva da *exemplare* (così *assempro* da *exemplum*) e significa trascrivere, ritrarre, rendere imagine ecc"— *La Divina Commedia, "Purgatorio,"* con i commenti di T. Casini, S. A. Barbi e di A. Momigliano, ed. Francesco Mazzoni (Florence: Sansoni, 1977), p. 469.

19. Cf. Benjamin, "The Task of the Translator," pp. 71, 73, 78-79, 81. As part of a book on Chaucer entitled, tentatively, *"The Substaunce Is in Me": An Essay on Error in the "Canterbury Tales,"* now in progress, I am writing a chapter on "The Clerk's Tale" as one of Chaucer's major essays into the problematics of translation: the crux, I argue, is the moment "whan [Griselda] *translated* was in swich richesse" (IV E 385, emphasis added)—Chaucer sees in the relation between Walter and Griselda a figure of the relation between the translator (who is also a reader) and the original and explores in this figure the problem of the identity or, say, the continuity or "afterlife" (Benjamin) of the original.

20. See Paget Toynbee, *Specimens of Old French* (Oxford: Clarendon Press, 1892), p. 314, for Deschamps's tribute to Chaucer. A bibliography of recent studies on the practice and the theory of translation in the Middle Ages themselves would include Gianfranco Folena, " 'Volgarizzare' e 'tradurre': Idea

e terminologia della traduzione dal medio evo italiano e romanzo all'umanesimo europeo," in *La traduzione: saggi e studi* (Trieste: Lint, 1973), pp. 57-120; Caroline D. Eckhardt, "The Art of Translation in *The Romaunt of the Rose*," *Studies in the Age of Chaucer* 6 (1984): 41-63; Tim William Machan, *Techniques of Translation: Chaucer's "Boece"* (Norman, Okla.: Pilgrim Books, 1985); and Rita Copeland, "Rhetoric and Vernacular Translation in the Middle Ages," *Studies in the Age of Chaucer* 9 (1987): 41-75.

21. Gen. 10:8, 11:1-4 (Douay-Rheims Version).

22. *Beowulf*, lines 64a-65a, 67b-70b, 78b-79b; Howell D. Chickering, Jr., ed. and trans., *Beowulf: A Dual-Language Edition* (New York: Anchor, 1977), pp. 52-53.

23. Cf. my analysis with Hrothgar's description of the inception and development of pride in his famous sermon (lines 1724-84)—the similarities lend weight to the notion that the poet could have been imaging the parallels between Heorot and Babel.

24. Others have similarly observed parallels between Heorot and Babel, though their readings of the parallels and mine are very different; Chickering in his edition (p. 283) cites an unpublished paper by Martin Bickman, for example; W. F. Bolton also discusses the parallel in *Alcuin and Beowulf: An Eighth-Century View* (New Brunswick: Rutgers University Press, 1978), p. 106.

25. I do not mean that Grendel cannot translate; I mean that he does not. Nor do I mean that he cannot understand—he understands the scop's song of creation (lines 89-98); I mean that he understands and still chooses not to cross the site of loss demarcated and occupied by translation. This is what is monstrous about Grendel: he can only live on the other side of that site.

26. In what follows I am informed by the work of Mary Douglas, *Purity and Danger: An Analysis of Concepts of Pollution and Taboo* (London: Routledge and Kegan Paul, 1966) and *Implicit Meanings: Essays in Anthropology* (London: Routledge and Kegan Paul, 1975), esp. "Self-Evidence," pp. 276-318; George Lakoff, *Women, Fire, and Dangerous Things: What Categories Reveal about the Mind* (Chicago: University of Chicago Press, 1987); and Victor Turner, *From Ritual to Theatre: The Human Seriousness of Play* (New York: Performing Arts Journal Publications, 1982), esp. pp. 20-60. I am also indebted, though to a lesser extent, to Michel Serres, *The Parasite*, trans. L. R. Schehr (Baltimore: Johns Hopkins University Press, 1982).

27. Here my argument makes its nearest approach to the "revisionism" of Harold Bloom, especially in the sense that the context of contexts for literature is contest—every context and its adherents contest the relevance and priority of other contexts (I developed these positions and terms before the appearance of Laura Kendrick's *The Game of Love: Troubadour Wordplay* [Berkeley: University of California Press, 1988], esp. chap. 1, and I use them in some respects quite differently from the way she does—although I am in sympathy with many of her related comments on "indeterminacy"). However, I differ from Bloom finally in that I do not privilege the psychoanalytic model of "revisionism" (see, esp., *Poetry and Repression: Revisionism from Blake to Stevens*

[New Haven: Yale University Press, 1976]); translation rather is a verbal event, where language is understood to precede and found the psyche. In this, I acknowledge my debt to Heidegger; see, esp., "The Nature of Language," in *On the Way to Language*, trans. Peter D. Hertz (San Francisco: Harper and Row, 1982), pp. 57-108.

28. See, esp., lines 867b-871a: "hwilum cyninges þegn, / . . . word oþer fand / soðe gebunden" (At times the scop, / a thane of the king . . ./ found new words, bound them up truly), where "gebunden," I might observe, corroborates my claim that Heorot and the conversations that transpire within it are structures of exclusivity—the words of the song, being bound, bind out as well as in.

29. *King Lear* 5.3.324-25 (emphasis added).

30. In a sense here I continue, though in a different direction, J. R. R. Tolkien's argument about the importance of the monsters to *Beowulf* and to understanding *Beowulf*—"*Beowulf*: The Monsters and the Critics," *Proceedings of the British Academy* 22 (1936): 245-95; rpt. in *An Anthology of "Beowulf" Criticism*, ed. Lewis E. Nicholson (Notre Dame, Ind.: University of Notre Dame Press, 1963), pp. 51-103.

PART TWO

Rethinking Texts

Toward a
Curriculum in Textual Studies

The remarks I am about to make are addressed to my fellow English teachers but they are not meant to be private. They may touch, occasionally, upon technical matters; still they are intended to be public remarks on issues that are important to all of us concerned with education. In particular I hope that students will take some note of what I say and, above all, those who are students now but hope someday to teach others under the aegis of this troubled discipline called "English."

In calling this discipline "troubled," I draw not only upon my own experiences as a teacher and chair of an English department, but also upon what I have learned recently as a member of the MLA's Commission on Writing and Literature—which has conducted an extensive investigation into the situation of college and university English teachers—and as a representative of the MLA on the English Coalition, a group that includes officers and representatives of some nine organizations of English teachers—at all levels of schooling—in this country. These experiences have clarified my knowledge of the extent and nature of our troubles, and I am grateful to my colleagues in those organizations for educating me in many matters. The description of our situation that I am about to present, however, and the solution I am about to propose, are not authorized by any group or organization. They are intended, I should add, not as definitive statements but as points of departure for further discussion. Let us begin with a description.

English as an academic discipline is housed in departments. Within such departments we regularly find a deep division between those who primarily teach writing and those who primarily teach literature. This division is often written into the title of such departments as a distinction between "English Language and Literature." There are other divisions in many departments as well: between American and English literature people, for instance, or between history and theory people, or even between what were once called ancients and moderns. But none of these goes as deep as the literature and writing division that is felt at every level of our profession. It is acutely present in training for the Ph.D., where we prepare people primarily in literary history, even though they will, in many cases and for many years, end up teaching more composition classes than anything else. And when it comes to preparing those who will teach English in secondary schools, we seem totally incapable of deciding what to do.

As I see it, there are only two possible solutions to the division that troubles our discipline: we must either split up along the lines that presently divide us or we must radically reorient our practice so as to eliminate the division. At present most of our college and university English departments are dominated by people whose primary commitment is to literature. In the very maintenance of this commitment they have kept the language and composition part of our activities in a peripheral or marginal position. This means that change can only be effected if our view of literary study itself is changed.

Literary study is presently grounded in two principles, which we may call "coverage " and "exegesis." According to the principle of coverage, the student of English should "cover" as many of the major works and authors in English and American literature as possible. This is how most undergraduate English majors are organized. Graduate study is organized exactly the same way of course, so that the student who has covered English as an undergraduate gets to cover it again as a graduate student—more thoroughly, one presumes, but the principle of coverage is such that—in principle—there is always more to be covered. The canon is both finite and inexhaustible.

The principle of exegesis requires that the student of English be able to attend closely to any of the works in the canon, extracting from such texts the truths and beauties put there by the author for just such extraction. It is usually forbidden to discover truths and beauties not attributable to the author—or to find lies and ugliness in canonical works. Like the canon itself, exegesis is both finite and inexhaustible, since there is no limit to meanings of the right sort that can be generated out of any work accorded canonical status. Meanings of the wrong sort, like uncanonical texts, are simply ruled out.

This is a curriculum calculated to produce a certain kind of person—or subject, as theoreticians say—a subject that is verbally aware and sensitive, docile, a better reader than writer, whose very writing is a kind of reading: correct but unadventurous. The traditional English major in my experience does produce this kind of subjectivity; indeed, it attracts this kind of person to begin with. Conversely, it rarely attracts or produces the aware, critical, writerly subjectivity that seems to me more appropriate for our present cultural situation.

In secondary schools, of course, the idea of coverage is already a thing of shreds and tatters. English literature, except for a token Shakespeare play, is largely gone while American literature is either surveyed or represented by a few masterworks. But exegesis or literary interpretation is still an avowed curricular aim. More important, nothing very coherent has replaced coverage. Courses or units may be constructed around themes or topics, problems of language and written composition are certainly addressed and sometimes emphasized, but it is not easy to find any notion of a discipline called English in all this. Still, teachers are doing the best they can with the material they have and the situations they confront every day.

I am not making an indictment here and have no blame to assign. We do what we do because that is what we learned, what we were trained to do, and most of us do it as well as we can. It is extremely difficult, in fact, to do anything but, as they say, "Keep on keeping on." This will not solve our troubles, however, because they will mount up until they overwhelm us unless we do something about them. As I have been suggesting, this means doing something about the way we have conceived our task and in particular about three things: the division between writing and literature, the central position of literature with the consequent marginalization of writing, and the model of English as a discipline based on coverage and exegesis.

What I am suggesting will, I know, sound heretical to many English teachers, or, at best, unprincipled. But I am not arguing that we should abandon coverage and exegesis to embark on some irrational nihilistic quest. I am saying, rather, that we have forgotten principles that are deeper and more consequential than coverage and exegesis, principles that, if we remember them, will help us rethink our aims and restructure our activities.

In speaking of principles I am not about to spring upon you some Platonic absolute that I have up my metaphysical sleeve, but to ask those of you for whom English has become a central part of your lives what you remember about how this happened. In the choice between this academic subject and that one, between this field of study and that one, some important part of what we are emerges, and in our professional commitment to such a field we may find what Ruskin called in just such a connection "The Roots of Honour."[1] In this spirit, asking you to think back to your own first interest in English, I raise the question of what this profession and those of us who teach it actually stand for.

We do stand for something, do we not, we who love English, who have come to consciousness and culture through this language, who have found in it not merely a medium of expression but a vocation, a calling, the professional center and public justification of our lives? We stand, I believe, for something far deeper than our particular curricular or institutional settings. We stand for whatever dignity this language can afford the human beings who find expression in and through it. We stand, above all, for sharing the powers and pleasures of this language with one another and with all those who seek our guidance in attaining those powers and pleasures. That is what I believe we stand for and I am certain that, though you may well have much to add to what I have said, you share in that belief.

What we stand for then is a hope, a desire, that takes concrete form in a certain linguistic or textual practice. For each of us, learning this language has had, and continues to have, costs and benefits that range from the psychic to the financial. Our relationships to the English language are never finished. A writer's skill may grow rusty with disuse, age or injury may plunge us into aphasia—surely one of the worst fears that can haunt such beings as we are; but at the same time, through practice and devotion and, of course, play, a person we know and care about—a child, a student, a friend—may come into greater powers, find their proper discourse, and produce texts that renew and refresh our own sense of the possibilities of life and language. This is what English is all about—our precarious relationship with this intimate impersonal thing, the English language.

For those of us who teach English, this volatile entity, our relationship to the language, must be institutionalized, departmentalized, and curricularized. Our hopes for our students must also be translated into this same institutional medium—which is itself another code, another language. In such translation much may be lost. In particular, what is most precious, our feeling for the language, our linguistic touch, may be sacrificed to the institution's needs for safety and regularity. The fixed curriculum, an assembly line on which we have our set, chronological place, is calculated to turn us into alienated laborers, automata twitching to the rhythms of that line. That is exactly the situation in which many of us find ourselves. Others are aimlessly trying to cope with anomalies. Trained for a place on the coverage line, they find themselves in the jungles of composition, missionaries among the heathen hordes, preaching from a book they never studied and cannot quite believe in.

In short, the institutional setting in which English teachers find themselves is terribly distant from those exhilarating experiences with language through which the call to this profession was first heard. It is possible, however, for us to change all this. But to do so we shall have to give up the comforts of our familiar setting, put coverage and exegesis aside, so that we can reconsider our true aims and devise a set of practices more in accord with those aims and more attuned to the cultural setting in which we and our students must find our functions and live our lives.

Our true aims as English teachers can be summed up as a desire to increase the textual competence of our students: to help them gain the ability to read with interpretive and critical acumen and to write with clarity, power, and grace. In short, we would like our students to be able to function textually in a society that constantly bombards them with texts. The system based on coverage and exegesis, I have suggested, does only a fair job on the reading side of textuality and a poor job on the writing side. It does so because coverage functions more as an end in itself than as a means to the end of textual competence, because exegesis leads to a passively receptive rather than an actively critical mode of reading, and because the dominance of consumption in this system relegates the production of texts to a deprived and marginal position.

Obviously it is not enough to carp and criticize, it is not enough to deconstruct our curriculum, we must reconstruct it as well. Assuming that our function as English teachers is to give our students fuller access to the powers and pleasures of textuality, how can we best accomplish this? The answer, in general terms, is by enabling them to understand how texts work and by giving them practice in the generation of texts themselves: by practice, then, and by theory also, for theory is nothing more than the understanding of how texts work. Let us try to envision a new curriculum based upon the theory and practice of textuality.

By the practice of textuality I mean the actual production or composition of texts. To base a curriculum on this practice we shall have to give a central emphasis in designing courses to the kinds of texts the students in those courses are going to produce. If we begin with the end product—the texts that will be composed in any given course— we can then consider such other matters as what theoretical information will help them in their productive work, what models or examples they will need, and what other textual material they should have for information or stimulation. The assumption operating here is that the student's work is the measure of what he or she has gained from any particular course of study. What a course accomplishes is not to be found in what it has supposedly "covered," but in what its students have done and can do as a result of having taken that course.

The relation of theory to this practice is crucial in two respects. First, it is only by theorizing over our discipline that we can move from our desire to enhance the textual powers and pleasures of our students to some concrete curriculum. Only by analyzing what textual power and pleasure mean for us in this society at this time can we begin to specify what kinds of production our students should undertake. Second, we must not think of theory as something that belongs only to the designers of curricula. We must think of theory as the form taken by knowledge about textual production.

We teach two kinds of knowledge: one is a tacit knowledge that comes from practice and can be called "skill"; the other is an articulate knowledge that situates skill and makes it intelligible. By articulate knowledge I do not mean knowing how to do something, but knowing how something works and, even more, knowing how any skill or activity is related to other things. Ultimately, we are talking here about what lies beyond what to do and how to do it; we are talking about why one thing should be done rather than another. This knowledge that goes beyond skill and helps to situate it may be called "consciousness." Theory is not consciousness, but it is the path to consciousness. And since the skill we are talking about here is a linguistic or textual skill, it is more thoroughly saturated with consciousness than most other skills. For this reason—because linguistic skill is such an intricate mixture of conscious and unconscious processes—our courses and methods must offer a balance between theory and practice.

At a very simple level this means that students should never be asked to do something without knowing why. At a more complex level it means that every kind of discourse they are presented with should be situated theoretically: that is, the rules and codes operative in its production should be made as explicit as possible. One of the lessons to be learned is that no text comes from nowhere. All uses of language are governed by rules and codes. What we are calling theory is, in its most accessible mode, the making explicit of rules and codes that normally function implicitly. To the extent that we have taught grammar and rhetoric we have been teaching theory all along, but we have often given the wrong impression about how the rules work and what aspects of them are really important. And we have seldom found the right relationship between theory and practice.

All too often we have presented theory (grammatical theory, for instance) as rules for correctness, with the admonition that trespassers will be punished. Such rules are indeed a part of theory and they can be used—and are used—for social and economic rewards and punishments. We should not ignore this. But we must always (in teaching grammar, for instance) go beyond these brute realities in two directions: we must teach not only the rules of the game, but the principles that lead to victory as well. We must theorize the positive as well as the negative. A basketball coach must not only teach players that on offense they must not stay in the paint for more than a few seconds or risk being called for a violation that will cost their team possession of the ball, he or she must also teach those players how to station themselves near the paint and when to make their moves through it. We must teach grammar and everything else in just that manner: how to avoid penalties, yes, but also how to reach the goal.

We must also theorize in another direction. We must show how textual practice is always situated in social structures. The speech, writing, and other signs that we produce inevitably tell more about us than we mean to reveal. Conversely, to produce certain kinds of texts we shall have to acquire textual habits that modify what we actually are. The boy from the barrio who learns to speak and write in ways that enable him to succeed as a banker is no longer the boy from the barrio; he has gained and lost something by entering this new textual process. To sum up, theory means the rules or boundaries of a given textual practice; it means the principles that lead to mastery of that practice; and it means the social situation and implications of learning that practice: who gets to produce texts in this way, how they get to do so, and what they become by doing so.

A curriculum based on theory and practice always linking these two aspects of study must, like any other curriculum, be divided into segments, that is, courses or units. Such segmentation may easily lead to coverage once again. To avoid this, and to address the problem in a manner that may be helpful to a broad spectrum of teachers and curriculum designers from secondary school to graduate study, I propose to offer here not a rigid set of courses, but a set of topics and principles that would be essential to a curriculum in textual studies—without claiming that these elements are either inevitable or complete.

Such a curriculum could be founded upon the study of four topics, each of which brings a different dimension of textuality into the foreground. There is no magic in this number four. It does not correlate with the seasons, or the evangelists, or the horsemen of the apocalypse. Think of these four, rather, as the first in an incomplete sequence. The four topics I propose as curricular necessities are *persuasion, narration, subjectivity,* and *figures.* The first two are discursive structures that we encounter daily and need to understand. They are traditional topics of rhetoric, about which we have learned more in recent years. The third topic involves the relationship of human subjects to language and discourse. This is a topic that has only been made available to us by recent theory. The fourth involves the fundamental processes by which language shapes our thought. It has long been a central topic in rhetoric and poetics. Recent theory has, if anything, enhanced its centrality. Let us begin with persuasion, which I would situate at the gateway to the formal study of English.

The theory of persuasion has sometimes been at the center of English studies. We know it as rhetoric and think of it as having special affinities with the oral discourse of the legislative chamber, the courthouse, and the pulpit. In this era, however, we encounter it largely in the form of advertising, in which verbal and visual signs are mixed, the verbal being spoken on television but written in magazines, billboards, and other displays. Our students know this discourse quite well when they come to us; hence, it can be used as the basis for an elaboration of the principles of persuasion, which is to say, rhetorical theory. Beginning with advertising, with students producing ads that are collages of cutout words and images, we can move to incorporate political advertising, letters to the editor, and finally current editorials and political speeches—articulating the principles of persuasion all the way. This century has been quite rightly called the age of propaganda. It is time we acknowledged this and put advertising and propaganda squarely into our curriculum in English textuality.

The theory taught in relation to advertising and propaganda can be drawn from traditional rhetoric to some extent. The practice should be both the production of texts in this mode and the critical analysis of such texts. To produce such analyses, students must read and discuss analytical texts, such as Roland Barthes's famous critique of the printed image of a black soldier saluting the French tri-color.[2] In effect, modern semiotic and ideological analysis will have to be added to traditional rhetorical theory in any contemporary course in persuasive discourse. The sophistication of this material should vary depending on the level of students in such a course, but the great advantage of beginning with advertising and propaganda is that students already have tacit knowledge of the formal qualities of these texts: knowledge that theory can make explicit and articulate.

Students can also draw upon considerable tacit knowledge of the other major discursive formation that we need in our curriculum: narration. In this case we have not only film and video experience to draw upon, but also the oral form that William Labov and Mary Louise Pratt have called "natural narrative," that is, oral narratives of personal experience. Pratt summarizes Labov's research in her excellent book, *Toward a Speech Act Theory of Literary Discourse.* I would recommend integrating the Labov/Pratt theory of the six-part structure of natural narrative with written practice based on both oral delivery of such narratives and study of written (printed) anecdotes. Once again, tacit knowledge that the student already possesses can be developed and articulated by theoretical discussion.

Narrative, of course, is an exceptionally rich and important field of study, which has been theorized enough in the last few decades to have generated its own name: narratology. Having worked in this field myself, I have some idea of the bewildering complexity of theoretical materials available. Certainly, no one is going to "cover" all this stuff adequately in a single course—and coverage, as I have been saying all along, is not the idea. The idea governing this approach is that theory will be presented as a way of enabling and enhancing the student's practice in textual production. The principles governing the selection of textual materials in all cases may be exemplified here with respect to the study of narrative. We must begin with what is basic and formal or structural: in this case Labov's six-part structure of a fully developed personal narrative. Then move to more complex principles, always working with the smallest and clearest examples and always integrating writing in narrative form with discussion of theory and oral or written work in analysis of sample texts—either texts produced by the class or examples from appropriate literary sources. I believe, for instance, that Gérard Genette's theory of the temporal order of narrative can be presented (in slightly simplified form) in classes at a quite elementary level, as can Propp's theory of how folktales are constructed. And certainly (as Nancy R. Comley has demonstrated) Umberto Eco's notion of "ghost chapters" can be put to excellent practical use.[3]

Ghost chapters are the parts of a story that must happen (by the narrative logic of what has been told) but are not actually narrated in the text. As Eco explains it, the reader writes these ghost chapters mentally as part of his or her role in the productive act that constitutes the reading of a written text. John Berger is also aware of the gaps to be found in all narratives. He has expressed this awareness with his customary eloquence:

> *The dog came out of the forest* is a simple statement. When that sentence is followed by *The man left the door open,* the possibility of a narrative

has begun. If the tense of the second sentence is changed into *The man had left the door open,* the possibility becomes almost a promise. Every narrative proposes an agreement about the unstated but assumed connections existing between events. . . .

No story is like a wheeled vehicle whose contact with the road is continuous. Stories walk, like animals or men. And their steps are not only between narrated events but between each sentence, sometimes each word. Every step is a stride over something not said.[4]

The gaps in narrative texts that the reader fills tacitly are perfect places for students to enter the play of narrative. One has only to ask students to begin writing these ghost chapters for the fun to start. They can produce written versions of events that have been skipped, or things assumed to have influenced the characters' lives before the story began, or they can continue the narration after the end of a printed text. Some stories, like Hawthorne's "Wakefield," positively require a concluding ghost chapter. We have only to ask students to write it and we are on the way to some enjoyable and fruitful activity. Of course, understanding the structure of narrative will enhance this kind of performance considerably. A theoretical framework such as that developed by Genette will enable us to locate the most fruitful points for ghost chapters and give us some clues about their dimensions as well.

Writing ghost chapters is just one of a number of activities that recent theoretical studies have taught us to think of as *intertextual* behavior. The principle of *intertextuality* is absolutely crucial to the development of a curriculum based on textual theory and practice.[5] Recent theory has demonstrated to an unprecedented extent how new texts are in fact made out of old ones. The poet does not, as Sir Philip Sidney urged him to, look in his heart and write: he does as Sidney actually did: look into Petrarch, Wyatt, and Surrey—or the appropriate equivalents—before he can generate a word. Whoever writes enters a discourse that was in progress before the production of his or her own text. This can be an intimidating situation, and all our well-meant strictures against plagiarism make it even more so. When we order students to produce "research" papers which are free from "plagiarism"—that is, work that is "original" but fully "documented"—we are setting them a virtually impossible task. Pastiches of others' thoughts, others' styles—in a word, of others' texts—are all we can manage until we are mature in scholarship, and even then it is terribly difficult to move so much as an inch out of the shade cast by our predecessors.

That we have set too much store by originality is one of the great lessons taught by textual theoreticians, as it is by historians of science.

Inventions and discoveries belong to their moment more than to the individuals who have the luck and the preparation to seize that moment for textualizing something new. Even those who seem to epitomize unique achievement—a Shakespeare in drama or a Coleridge in criticism—will be found to have helped themselves most liberally to the work of others, to have retextualized the texts of others. One way to empower our students textually is to encourage them to play irreverently with the texts of others. The ghost chapter, for instance, may be done in a faithful manner—and no doubt should be done in this way at least some of the time. It is important that a student have the experience of trying to write a chapter that fits the gap it fills as neatly and seamlessly as possible. Once a student can do this, however, the way is open to a disruptive intertextuality, to ghost chapters that clash deliberately with their contexts, that cause impossibilities to arise, thus generating new texts and new debates about what the original or "pre" text was about in the first place.

Other forms of intertextual intrusion are also possible and fruitful. A story can be rewritten from a different viewpoint than that of its original. In this way another side of a situation may be revealed, another style of narration be deployed. Obviously, such work will be performed best by those who understand the principles involved. The theory of fictional point of view as developed by Wayne Booth, for instance, will be of great service to the student asked to rewrite a section of a story from a different viewpoint.[6] When students turn to theory as an aid in their own practice, theory is most thoroughly understood. Using this approach we make writers and theoreticians at the same time.

Intertextuality is not always interpersonal. We make new texts out of our own pretexts as well as those of others. In some recent field tests of a new textbook, my associates and I have had considerable success using excerpts from the English translation of a delightful little book by the French writer Raymond Queneau called *Excercises in Style*. In this book Queneau begins with a brief notation describing two extremely casual encounters with an unknown man. Queneau then takes his original brief text (just 125 words) and proceeds to rewrite it in dozens of ways, including all sorts of grammatical, semantic, and discursive variations, ranging from a version totally in the passive voice, to one full of animal imagery, to a technically perfect haiku. Using a selection of Queneau's stylistic excercises for models, we have encouraged students to generate their own brief texts and then transform them exactly as Queneau had done. This has proved to be both easy and very pleasurable for first-year college students at Queens College, New York, and the University of Florida. It can certainly be undertaken at more elementary levels with every prospect of success, it being that truly rare phenomenon: an intellectual activity in which one size fits all.

In addition to ease and pleasure, these exercises offer opportunities to discuss styles and discursive codes in terms that are both concrete and oriented to the student's own future production. If you are going to write a haiku or a dozen sentences in the passive voice, you need to know the rules and procedures for doing so. The exercises offer opportunities for wit and creative skill to be displayed as well. As most English teachers know, one of the hardest jobs we have is getting students to see writing as writing. They find it more natural to look through writing toward the meanings it conveys or the objects to which it refers. One of our major functions is to obstruct this "natural" process and help them to see writing itself as the object of their interest. To see writing as writing—an always unfinished process of perpetual revision—is absolutely crucial to the development of writers and readers. There are few things that accomplish this as well as intertextual exercises in the manner of Queneau.

Once we are free from the idea that there is a body of literary texts that must be covered by our curricula, we are also free to address with much greater thoroughness our responsibility to the English language and its textualizing powers. So far we have considered the two macrostructures of persuasion and narration with their accompanying theories of rhetoric and narratology, and we have contemplated briefly the uses of intertextuality. In an ideal curriculum there would be substantial work in both persuasive and narrative discourse—perhaps a year in each at the secondary school level and substantial work in college, though this might vary depending on what knowledge and ability students bring to college from previous work. Intertextuality, on the other hand, seems to me not so much a subject for study as a ubiquitous aspect of writing itself, to be considered in all English courses. There are, however, some other substantial topics that deserve positions in the textual curriculum that we have been considering. Two of them are fundamental to the workings of human language. Let us call them *figures* and *subjectivity*.

By *subjectivity* I mean to indicate a range of topics that have been articulated by recent semiotic theory.[7] Drawing upon linguistics and psychoanalysis, this theory can be epitomized as the problematic of the pronoun *I*. What does it mean to say "I"? And, conversely, what does it mean to produce discourse in which the word *I* does not appear? The problems of subjectivity are inevitably connected to those of objectivity. We English teachers have sometimes seen our task as helping our students develop an objectivity of address. We have seen intellectual maturity as measurable by the attainment of objective ways of thinking deployed in an objective style of writing. Obsessed, perhaps, by a vision of ideal objectivity, we have sometimes forbidden the use of *I* in our students' discourse. In the study of subjectivity, these and other dimensions of language will occupy the foreground.

Such a study can quite properly begin with the grammar of those shifty characters: the pronouns. Drawing on the work of Bertrand Russell and Emile Benveniste, we can direct attention to the function of the pronouns *I* and *you*, which, according to Benveniste, are the distinguishing features of human language:

> Consciousness of self is only possible if it is experienced by contrast. I use *I* only when I am speaking to someone who will be a *you* in my address. It is this condition of dialogue that is constitutive of *person*, for it implies that reciprocally *I* becomes *you* in the address of the one who in his turn designates himself as *I*. Here we see a principle whose consequences are to spread out in all directions. Language is possible only because each speaker sets himself up as a *subject* by referring to himself as *I* in his discourse. Because of this, *I* posits another person, the one who, being, as he is, completely exterior to "*me*," becomes my echo to whom I say *you* and who says *you* to me. This polarity of persons is the fundamental condition in language, of which the process of communication, in which we share, is only a mere pragmatic consequence. It is a polarity, moreover, very peculiar in itself, as it offers a type of opposition whose equivalent is encountered nowhere else outside of language. This polarity does not mean either equality or symmetry: "ego" always has a position of transcendence with regard to *you*. Nevertheless, neither of the terms can be conceived of without the other; they are complementary, although according to an "interior/exterior" opposition, and, at the same time, they are reversible. If we seek a parallel to this, we will not find it. The condition of man in language is unique.[8]

I have quoted Benveniste at some length, but even so have omitted much that is of interest in his discussion of the pronouns. These matters should be given serious attention in English courses at the secondary school level and beyond, because they are the foundation of human communication. I would recommend studying Benveniste's theory in some fashion, however rudimentary, along with discussion of texts in which the use of *I* and *you* is crucial. One such text is part three, section four of Samuel Delany's science fiction novel, *Babel-17*, in which a character who is subhuman because he speaks without pronouns begins to learn what it means to say "I" and "you." Delany, who is entirely aware of the theoretical implications of his fiction, shows us this brutal creature (known as "The Butcher") struggling with the pronouns, first using them as proper nouns, as if *I* and *you* were the names of himself and his interlocutor, and finally grasping both the grammatical principle and his own human subjectivity at the same moment.

The study of subjectivity can be extended in various ways: for instance, through writing practice in which scenes are rewritten so that someone referred to in the third person by the narrating voice of a text becomes the subject of a new text, expressing this subjectivity in his or her own discourse and seeing things from that point of view. It is even possible to ask for writing from the viewpoint of subhuman organisms or objects, as W. S. Merwin writes in his poem "Things," which ends like this:

> Be a gentleman: you acquired us when you needed us
> We do what we can to please, we have some beauty, we
>   are helpless.
> Depend on us.

To give things a voice is to give them subjectivity, to give them life, but to speak to us they must learn our language, speak like us.

In more advanced classes, in college or graduate school, I would strongly urge extending the study of subjectivity in the directions opened up by Freud and Lacan. With suitable texts, what Freud called the psychopathology of everyday life can be presented for study, along with jokes, dreams, and other revealing forms of textual behavior.

The situation of the subject in discourse extends from Benveniste and the pronouns all the way to Michel Foucault and the study of discursive formations.[9] Foucault has sharpened our sense of the way in which every different kind of text that is produced for public scrutiny stems from some institution or social structure that governs many dimensions of the discourse to which any particular text belongs. A simple instance of this is an act like the writing of a prescription for drugs. Any of us can try to write one but the drugstore will not recognize all of our utterances as texts in the proper medical discourse. Even if we use the right words, if we are not recognized as physicians by pharmacologists our prescriptions will be treated not as texts but as noise—meaningless gibberish or, at best, criminal forgeries. Other discursive formations are not so explicitly controlled, but it is one thing to say one has written a poem and another to have our text accepted as a poem by potential publishers, critics, and already established poets, all of whom share in the institution of poetry.

Obviously, the full study of such works as Foucault's *Archaeology of Knowledge* is a matter for advanced courses in college or for graduate school, but high school teachers who have mastered that book and the theory of discourse it presents will be able to introduce their students to the notion of discursive formations in an engaging and useful fashion. Such a notion is crucial to the project I am sketching out here, because it offers the best theory available to account for the way in which our individual human subjectivity is socialized by institutions.

This concept of a discursively socialized subjectivity is crucial to our enterprise because it is the concept that describes this enterprise itself. What we have to offer our students is an entry into discursive formations that will give them a certain power: a power that can be exercised only at the price of being subjected to the rules and limits established by that discourse. Try to think of this in terms of a parable. Suppose a young woman is visited by a god who shows her in his own language everything that is wrong with her village—everything that her tribe does that displeases the gods. In learning the god's language, however, she has forgotten her own. She must tell the village elders what she has learned, and they are eager to hear it, for they can see the mark of the god upon her. Painstakingly, she relearns her own language, but as she puts the god's words into this tongue, they seem enfeebled and distorted. Finally, she can remember the originals no longer and has lost all faith in her own translation. When she is ready to speak, the mark of the god is no longer visible, and she has aged. In fact, she has become one of the village elders herself, and does as the other do, says what the others say.

Discourse creates subjectivity. We want our students to have power in their own society. We want to help them learn to express themselves in the ways to which power is attentive and responsive. And we have no magic that will spare them the price, that will preserve their initial apprehension of themselves from fading as they acquire their new subjectivities. We can, if we do our jobs very well, make them aware of the price they pay. That is, we can show them how discourses work, even as we help them to master those discursive structures that they need to know.

To function in academic situations, to survive schooling, our students need to learn the antisubjective discourse of the academic paper, and we must teach it to them. Such writing turns on the suppression of *I* and *you*, as well as on other formulas of exposition and objectivity. This suppression of subjectivity can be seen as the ultimate subjection, or the acquisition of an objective mode of subjectivity. This is the discourse of science, of knowledge, as it prevails in our culture, and it would be a serious betrayal of responsibility to ignore or trivialize it. In such writing our greatest power over objects is obtained at the cost of objectifying ourselves. We must read, study, and teach the theory and practice of objective discourse, along with other modes of textuality. By situating it in relation to subjectivity, however, we can avoid the great error of ignoring what such discourse does to us. By seeing it as one discourse among others, we can also avoid the error of thinking that such objectivity escapes from the problematic of language. It, too, has its irreducible formal structures. It is a way of mediating between us and the world. It is simply the mediation that tries to conceal itself, to present its ration of reality directly. Its modes of concealment are its form, and this can be studied. One dimension is grammatical objectivity. Another has to do with certain figures of speech.

Figuration is the fourth element of the scholastic plan I have been sketching here. To recapitulate, we have two master forms or macrostructures: *persuasion* and *narration,* and we have two features of discourse: *subjectivity* and *figuration.* By figuration I mean those processes by which language extends its semantic domain. Our linguistic base of operations is a domesticated territory of relatively stable associations between signs and meanings. Within this pale we perform our basic verbal functions as best we can, but language is imperialistic, always pressing outward, extending the pale. This, at least, is the way language works for those peoples who have entered history. It would be a brave scholar who claimed to sort out causes and effects in this area.

The metaphor of the extended pale is of course an example of a figure—a common one, to be sure—used to give an abstract notion sufficient concreteness to be communicated. The management of such ordinary figures is an important part of what every student of composition has to learn. The understanding of how figures work is even more important than that. The distinction between what is literal and what is figurative may be thought of as the first figure, the one that enables all the others. Some distinction between truth and falsehood is basic to all human language. To know how to speak is to know how to lie. It is a step beyond this to understand an utterance as literally false but figuratively true. Once we think of language as having layers or levels of meaning, the way is open to such basic forms as riddles and parables—and to all the subtleties of poetry and allegory.

The study of figures and their workings can be undertaken in many ways, including the traditional taxonomies of tropes. I, personally, would privilege parables, poems, and essays in which irony, metaphor, and other figures flourish as materials for study and models of production. But I would resist all impulses to confine the study of figuration to texts assumed to be literary. The study of figures is the place to show how all the strategic moves of exposition and argument are in themselves figures also: comparison, contrast, connection by cause and effect, association. Explanation and exposition, the most objective forms of textuality, rely on such figures for the very fabric of their discourse. We extend knowledge by thinking of the unknown in terms of the known. The study of figures will take us deep into the workings of textual power and pleasure. This is one of the directions emphasized by the best of deconstructive critics—such as the late Paul de Man— from whom we have much to learn that will strengthen us as teachers of the fundamental matters that concern us here.[10]

In studying figures, then, we are not considering some superficial or ornamental aspect of textuality. We are looking into the deepest processes of language itself. Metaphor, for instance, as George Lakoff and Mark Johnson have shown in their exemplary book, *Metaphors We Live By*, affects thinking about many crucial matters. Metaphors are both illuminating and blinding (and both those terms are of course themselves metaphorical). To raise the consciousness of students about the presence and power of metaphor and other figures in all kinds of texts would be a major function of the curriculum I am proposing. This can be done by a mixture of theory, analysis of all kinds of texts, and production of new texts in which various kinds of figuration are emphasized.

Where the study of subjectivity (and objectivity) takes us into the heart of communication—the text as an exchange of meaning between persons—the study of figures takes us to the central processes of language itself. If we combine these two topics with the study of those potent discursive structures, persuasion and narration, we would succeed in assisting our students toward their proper grasp of textual pleasure and power. These topics might well fill a whole secondary school program in English, or the general education requirements in English at a college or university. They would probably not, in themselves, constitute a curriculum for an entire major in English or in textual studies, but they could easily constitute the core for such majors, around which could be located courses devoted to particular problems, discourses, historical studies, or even major texts. All such studies, I believe, would be enhanced if students had the grasp of textuality that could be attained through the curriculum I have described. It is also my belief that through such a curriculum the lives of our individual students and our collective life as human beings in a shrinking world would also be enhanced, extended, and enriched.

NOTES

1. See *Unto This Last*, essay 1.

2. In the essay "Myth Today," included in *Mythologies* (New York: Hill and Wang, 1975), pp. 116-17 in particular.

3. For further information see Gérard Genette, *Narrative Discourse* (Ithaca, N.Y.: Cornell University Press, 1980); Vladimir Propp, *Morphology of the Folktale* (Austin: University of Texas Press, 1968); and Umberto Eco, *The Role of the Reader* (Bloomington: Indiana University Press, 1979). Comley's discussion appeared in G. Douglas Atkins and Michael L. Johnson, eds., *Writing and Reading Differently* (Lawrence: University Press of Kansas, 1985), p. 131, entitled "A Release from Weak Specifications: Liberating the Student Reader."

4. John Berger and Jean Mohr, *Another Way of Telling* (New York: Pantheon, 1982), pp. 284-85.

5. For the best single discussion of intertextuality, combined with a useful list of references on the topic, see Thaïs E. Morgan's "Is There an Intertext in This Text?" *American Journal of Semiotics* 3, no. 4 (1985).

6. For Booth the classic reference is *The Rhetoric of Fiction*, recently issued in a revised edition by the University of Chicago Press.

7. The best single discussion of this complex topic is that by Kaja Silverman in *The Subject of Semiotics* (London: Oxford University Press, 1983).

8. *Problems in General Linguistics* (Coral Gables, Fla.: University of Miami Press, 1971), pp. 224-25.

9. The fullest statement of Foucault's theory of discourse is in *The Archaeology of Knowledge* (New York: Pantheon, 1972), now available in a Harper Torchbook. A useful further treatment of the subject of discourse in Foucault, Althusser, and others may be found in Diane Macdonell's *Theories of Discourse: An Introduction* (London: Basil Blackwell, 1986).

10. See especially de Man's *Allegories of Reading* (New Haven, Conn.: Yale University Press, 1979).

GREGORY L. ULMER

Textshop for an
Experimental Humanities

The Humanities Laboratory

A book devoted to critical theory and pedagogy is an appropriate place
to continue my discussion of the function of a "laboratory" in the
humanities classroom (Ulmer 1985). Annoying neologisms such as
"textshop"—derived from Roland Barthes's essay "From Work to Text"—
are necessary due to the misunderstandings that so easily occur when
talking about a pedagogy based on contemporary theory, a body of
texts that some people insist has no practical value. My own view is
somewhat different in that I am convinced that modern experimental
arts and theory have finally shown us how to make the language and
literature disciplines equal partners with the other divisions of knowledge in the university.

The need for a textshop emerges out of the difficulty students have
understanding our object of study (language, literature, the arts) exclusively by means of analytical modes of thinking and writing borrowed from the social sciences (which borrowed them from the sciences). Having worked with a textshop for a few years now, and having
even helped design a "Text Book" for composition courses (with Nancy
Comley and Robert Scholes for St. Martin's Press) using the laboratory
method, I have concluded that it is impossible to comprehend an
aesthetic phenomenon anesthetically, despite the tremendous efforts of
most of us (myself included until recently) to do so. Barthes, as might
be expected, provides the rationale and the statement of value (even
in the ethical sense) for the textshop.

> Why is the writerly our value? Because the goal of literary work (of
> literature as work) is to make the reader no longer a consumer, but a
> producer of the text. Our literature is characterized by the pitiless divorce

which the literary institution maintains between the producer of the text and its user, between its owner and its customer, between its author and its reader. This reader is thereby plunged into a kind of idleness—he is intransitive; he is, in short, *serious*: instead of functioning himself, instead of gaining access to the magic of the signifier, to the pleasure of writing, he is left with no more than the poor freedom either to accept or reject the text: reading is nothing more than a *referendum*. (Barthes 4)

The textshop, then, is designed to supplement (not replace entirely) the readerly classroom, where reading and writing are taught as a specialized knowledge, with a writerly laboratory, where our materials are approached with the pleasure of *amateurs* (a term whose respectability Barthes attempts to revive).

Let me delay satisfying any curiosity about how the textshop works by offering another source for my rationale. While attempting to distinguish the essay from the treatise as a writing that introduces art into the treatment of concepts, T. W. Adorno invoked the example of Proust as "dilettante":

No one would have thought to dismiss as unimportant, accidental or irrational the observations of an experienced man because they are only his own and as such do not lend themselves readily to scientific generalization. Those of his discoveries which slip through the meshes of science certainly elude science itself. Science, as cultural science, negates what it promises to culture: to open up its artifacts from within. The young writer who wants to learn at college what an art-work is, what linguistic form, aesthetic quality, even aesthetic technique are, will only haphazardly learn anything at all about the matter; at best he will pick up information ready culled from whatever modish philosophy and more or less arbitrarily slapped on to the content of works currently under discussion. (Adorno 156-57)

Here we have one key to the textshop, in which is practiced an immanent critique—an object of study serves as a model for making another text. Thus the hierarchy of explanation is reordered, such that the means of our own materials—figurative language, dramatic narrative, imagery and the like—are put to work cognitively. The literary arts shift from being an object to being a subject of knowledge: irreducible in themselves, they become a source for representing knowledge in other disciplines and for organizing the solutions of problems confronted in everyday life.

From this perspective we may better appreciate the actual function of the avant-garde art movements of our century. Until recently it had been supposed that our period was distinct from any other period of history in having a major component of cultural workers—artists and intellectuals—alienated from and in rebellion against the dominant values of the age. But now we begin to realize that this illusion had to do with our misunderstanding of what our cultural values are. In fact, the experimental operation of the avant-garde is a good expression of the scientific episteme, and indicates that the conventional arts have produced a dimension of pure and applied research, in the same way that traditional reason (philosophy) produced pure and applied science. It is disappointing that the humanities disciplines working at the centers of learning have failed to appropriate for our own practical work the inventions and discoveries of arts—the by now extensive accumulation of experiments generated by the avant-garde in every area of the arts. One of the best examples to work with as an illustration of how a textshop might appropriate an experimental art is surrealism. The value of this example has to do with the explicit relationship of the art experiment to an extant theory—psychoanalysis.

Psychoanalysis and Surrealism

In a textshop the relation of psychoanalysis to teaching is approached through André Breton's invention of surrealism. If our concern is with the lesson of Freud for reading and writing, then one obvious place to start is with the avant-garde movement that devised its program as an application of Freud's theories to the arts. Educators have already mined this vein with some success, including, for example, Peter Elbow, whose *Writing without Teachers* features a method of "freewriting" derived from surrealist automatic writing.

Considering that the National Council of Teachers of English recommends Elbow's book, I am surprised that other educators have not followed his lead, have not produced similar applications to language instruction of the many other avant-garde experiments, most of which demonstrate procedures equally useful for us as those developed by the surrealists. Indeed, part of my purpose is to point out this neglect and to suggest ways to remedy the situation, opening what I believe could be a new dimension of applied scholarship in the humanities.

We have been slow to recognize the avant-garde as the humanities equivalent of pure research for several reasons. The primary reason is that, despite the aesthetic or artistic character of our object of study, ours is a profession trained exclusively in the rationalist, analytical, calculative paradigm of reason. Consequently we are ready to import into our curriculum any theoretical position so long as it is represented to us in the familiar expository form of literary criticism. Thus the formalism derived from Husserl, the various hermeneutics derived from

Marx, Nietzsche, and Freud, the deconstruction derived from Derrida, all have found a place in our courses in literary criticism. The first thing that might come to mind in the context of psychoanalysis and the teaching of reading probably will involve utilizing the various psychologies of reader response to improve the writing of interpretive essays. But there is another resource available.

My only objection to literary criticism as it is now taught, generally speaking, is that it tends to sustain an ideological bias against the cognitive value of the arts themselves as systems of representation. The language and literature disciplines have benefited enormously from the infusion of theory into our thinking. The textshop approach simply offers an alternative way to bring together theory and practice, drawing on the example of the vanguard movements. The vanguard artists, like their counterparts among academic critics, based their thinking on the best theoretical texts of the day. The difference between the critics and the artists has to do with their respective modes of representation, with the latter preferring to demonstrate the consequences of the theories for the arts by practicing the arts themselves, generating models or prototypes that function critically as well as aesthetically. When I say that they function critically I am thinking, for example, of the manifestoes that such movements produce, operating in the best tradition of the polemical essay to set forth a fully self-conscious program for the generation of certain kinds of texts. I will talk about Breton in a moment, with surrealism serving as an example for the phenomenon in general, but I want to stress again the still-untapped pedagogical potential of such artist-theorist pairs as Gertrude Stein/William James, Bertolt Brecht/Karl Marx, John Cage/R. Buckminster Fuller, The Art and Language Group/Ludwig Wittgenstein (to name only a few).[1]

I hasten to add that far from being a rival of literary criticism, the textshop is an extension of the logical development of critical theory in our curriculum. Courses in criticism won approval originally in the role of practical aid to the historical syllabus, providing students some of the basic techniques of specialized commentary that could be applied to the canon. Soon, however, as more of the apparatus of interpretation was exposed, these courses became increasingly theoretical, moving away from practical criticism to focus on the sources in philosophy and the human sciences from which the practical critics derived their hypotheses and concepts. More recently the tendency is to further extend the frame to include not just the content of critics and sources, but the processes of thinking, of concept formation, of explanation, and of learning how to learn—these conceived now directly and as things teachable in themselves. This most recent step might seem to be a move toward still greater abstraction, but because of the textshop it turns out to be, on the contrary, a return to "concreteness," to an immanent critique, unifying theory and practice.

This critical function distinguishes the way surrealism is taught in the textshop from its use in, say, Peter Elbow's method. Specifically, the textshop is designed to teach undergraduates how ideas such as surrealism are invented. The lesson counters the Platonism that most of our students have absorbed indirectly from their schooling—not that the students know anything about Plato's dialectic. The problem is precisely that they know very little about thinking or concept formation, however much some of them are able to perform thought. They have mostly acquired certain habits of mind that, for Plato, would not count as knowledge at all, but only as belief. The assumptions most students hold with respect to the nature of ideas bear a striking resemblance to Plato's theory of the idea as *eidos*, as absolute, universal form. For these students a concept is not a set in the mathematical sense of a collection of similar qualities (as modern epistemology maintains), but is set, fixed, given, finished, permanent, true (as Plato believed). No wonder they are dismayed when they are asked to write an essay giving their own point of view on some idea of the day, as if it were possible to renegotiate the configurations of reality. In the textshop, the student has an opportunity to discover the epistemological assumptions at work in culture and in one's own thinking. Textshop is "epic" in that it shares with Brecht's epic theater the desire to show people that culture (or society) is not natural, given, but is made, invented, and hence changeable.

The textshop is a laboratory in which the students attempt to reproduce the experiments of the humanities. Think of something like Rom Harré's *Great Scientific Experiments: Twenty Experiments that Changed Our View of the World*. In learning science, students not only read about a given idea (anything from Aristotle's "Embryology of the Chick" to Otto Stern's "The Wave Aspect of Matter and the Third Quantum Number"), they are expected to be able to reproduce the experiments themselves, finally reaching a point when they face a problem without solution (yet). Similarly, textshop teaches surrealism as one of the ideas that changed our view of culture and that cannot be fully understood until it is practiced. The point in both divisions of knowledge is to produce a person capable not only of reciting the history of invention, but of inventing something. The lesson should be that imagination is an integral part of thinking. We will be a truly theoretical discipline when our students find that their imaginations are as heavily taxed in their work as are such qualities as taxonomy and description.

Textshop, then, complements traditional approaches to literary criticism, which tend to neglect the fact that theorists have influenced the practice of the arts as much as they have the interpretation of art. The issue is sometimes raised in criticism courses in a paradoxical form with the suggestion that, for example, a psychoanalytic reading of a text authored by someone explicitly influenced by Freud has questionable hermeneutic value. Since psychoanalysis functions as a hermeneutics of suspicion, there may seem little point in using it to identify an author's conscious intention. Freud, in fact, encountered a similar problem in treating patients who had read his books.

In a textshop, however, the two principal ways in which theory is assimilated into the humanities—by critical interpretation and by artistic practice—are considered to be of equal cognitive and pedagogical value. My remarks, in this context, focus on just one side of the assimilation or appropriation of Freud by the humanities—the side of production rather than of interpretation—featuring André Breton's invention of surrealism. Breton's approach may itself be considered as a critical methodology operating at a macro level, capable of testing Freud's theory itself, for such is the function of the experimental arts. The relevant question for productive cognition is not "if Freud is right what might be the meaning of a conventional work," but "if Freud is right how might literature be composed?"

> We are still living under the reign of logic. . . . In the guise of civilization, under the pretext of progress, we have succeeded in dismissing from our minds anything that, rightly or wrongly, could be regarded as superstition or myth; and we have proscribed every way of seeking the truth which does not conform to convention. It would appear that it is by sheer chance that an aspect of intellectual life—and by far the most important in my opinion—about which no one was supposed to be concerned any longer has, recently, been brought back to light. Credit for this must go to Freud. (Breton 66)

The goal of textshop is, in part, to show that Breton's lesson is as useful for critics and students as it is for poets and artists. He demonstrated the arbitrariness of the rigid division between analytical and imaginative practices. "If the depths of our minds conceal strange forces capable of augmenting or conquering those on the surface, it is our greatest interest to capture them; first to capture them and later to submit them, should the occasion arise, to the control of reason. The analysts themselves can only gain by this" (66). The experimental setting of textshop is designed to promote the practice of the arts themselves as methodologies productive of knowledge and understanding.

Assignments: Ideology and Resistance

In a textshop a work is read as a set of instructions for making a text. This approach, while applicable to any genre or mode, makes immediate sense with avant-garde manifestoes such as Breton's that function as programs for the generation of art. The pedagogical strategy is to begin the lab with a writing assignment. (I will be discussing a typical project, different versions of which have been used in freshman courses— Writing about Literature and Honors: Creativity—and with upper division majors—Modern Criticism and The Age of the Avant-Garde.) At the same time that the students are asked to read Patrick Waldberg's *Surrealism* (including an introductory essay and selections by Breton, Dali, and Max Ernst), they receive a handout describing the lab project: to produce a fragment of a "false novel" using the technique of automatic writing. Selections from Breton's automatic text, "Soluble Fish," are assigned as well, to provide a model. The "novel" (minimum length 10-12 typed pages—the length is needed to allow the writer to shift fully into the automatic mode) is illustrated with at least one example each of a collage, frottage, decalcomania, and exquisite corpse.

In a related experiment each student is to present a modified ready-made sculpture in an exhibition to be held during class. No exam is given on the readings. Rather, the motivation for reading carefully and for asking questions during the lab meetings is to establish for oneself as clearly as possible what exactly all these terms mean, and where in the readings the instructions for making them are located. Discussion focuses, for example, on the section in Breton's manifesto entitled "Secrets of the Art of Surrealist Magic," in which several passages provide explicit directions.

> Supply yourself with writing materials, after having settled yourself in a place as favourable as possible to the mind's concentration on itself. Attain the most passive or receptive state of mind possible. . . . Write quickly with no preconceived subject, so quickly that you retain nothing and are not tempted to re-read. The first sentence will come by itself, since it is true that each second there exists a sentence foreign to our conscious thoughts which asks only to be brought out into the open. . . . Trust in the inexhaustible spirit of the whisper. If silence threatens in the least to establish itself you have made a mistake—a mistake shall we say of inattention. Make a break at the too-intelligible line immediately. After the word whose origin seems suspect place any letter, the letter *l* for example, always the letter *l*, and restore the arbitrary by making this letter the initial of the next word. (74)

These instructions may be supplemented with the directions for "How to Write False Novels."

Here are some rather dissimilar characters; their names in your hand-writing are a question of capital letters and they will behave with the same ease towards active verbs as the impersonal pronoun *it* towards words like *rains, is, must be,* etc. They will control them, as it were, and where observation, reflection, and the ability to generalize have been no help to you, rest assured that these characters will lend you a thousand intentions you never had. Thus provided with a small number of physical and moral characteristics, these beings who in truth owe you so little will no longer swerve from a certain line of conduct to which you need only apply yourself. (75)

The merger of the automatic text with the false novel helps the writers avoid the less interesting possibilities of the experiment that sometimes develop, such as remaining stuck at an initial level of itemizing one's worries and hopes, or passing beyond the level of discourse into gibberish. That the experiment is to tell a "story" also exploits a property of avant-garde aesthetics, which tend to be defined as much in negative terms as in positive ones. Breton's opposition to the traditional conventions of realist or naturalist fiction, then, serve in the lab discussions as a negative model—the elements of a conventional story—as well as in the features of the positive model, "Soluble Fish."

The real value of the readymade sculpture lab emerges at this point in that while most students are able eventually to explain the automatic method in principle along with its rationale (a derivation of Freud's talking-cure intended to avoid the censorship of repression), and even able to identify the main features of surrealist style and its intended effect (to produce bewilderment or wit by means of unexpected juxtapositions), they do not yet believe any of it. To take up again Plato's distinction between knowledge and opinion (*episteme* and *doxa*), their knowledge has changed but their opinions are still intact, the problem being that at their stage of education they still think with their opinions rather than with their knowledge. Most students have so completely accepted the culture's presuppositions about art (the very values challenged by surrealism and the other vanguard movements—for example, that only a genius possessed of specialized craft training is capable of producing a real work of art), that even at this late date in the twentieth century and despite the easily recognized influence of surrealist style on the entertainment and advertising industries, they still resist the claims of the original surrealists.

Now this resistance is a considerable advantage for pedagogy, first because in the discussion of their objections to surrealism (not to the style, which they like, but to the political, aesthetic, and metaphysical elements of the surrealist program) the students reveal explicitly and often for the first time to themselves and to each other the articulation of their cultural ideology. Such discussions have a powerful critical effect. The second pedagogical advantage has to do with the phenomenon of resistance itself. In psychoanalysis there is no cure without transference (which includes the problematic of resistance). The patient agrees to be in the care of the analyst, but then may resist all attempts of the analyst to cure him or her. Similarly, our students sign up for our classes with the intention of being educated, but then not infrequently they refuse to cooperate with the process, in part, as I indicated, and as the sophists first noted, because people tend to accept only that which corresponds to the opinions they already hold. One of the chief tasks of pedagogy is to help the students in the learning situation to shift their stances from the domain of opinion that governs daily life to an attitude of learning that organizes knowledge. Avant-garde texts provide an excellent resource to force this shift because, to the extent that they still retain any of their original power to shock and provoke (the effect aimed at by most experimental programs of our century) they stimulate resistance, and once the resistance has manifested itself it is possible to recognize it for what it is—ideology—and to deal with it in a constructively critical way.

Surrealism retains at least some of its critical, defamiliarizing power. No amount of the usual arguments used to impose *Paradise Lost* and the like on undergraduates will convince the class that "Soluble Fish" or a collage by Max Ernst are important works of art or even that they are "art" at all. The texts in question are too easy to produce and could be made by anyone, even themselves. Of what value could such items possibly be? But the avant-garde revolution, with surrealism in the forefront, is located precisely within this issue—the invention of a democratized art practice accessible to everyone, against the capture of art by concepts of genius (during Romanticism) and specialization and professionalization (during Modernism). The value of a vanguard experiment is not so much in the product (the lab discussed at length the ironies of the commodity value of a Duchamp readymade) but in the process of creation. The value and power of surrealist automatic practices cannot be comprehended externally but only by means of experience. They exist precisely for the user as actions, and are writerly through and through.

The proof of this assertion comes after the experiments have been completed in the lab, when the students find themselves amazed by their own work and by the works of their peers. The exhibition of readymades is especially revealing in this regard in that it allows everyone to experience each other's work. Having been quite (properly) skeptical that the mere juxtaposition of unrelated items (including an unrelated title)—the formula for a modified readymade—could produce the effect of wit, the students are surprised to find themselves laughing throughout the entire exhibit as each artist presents each work in turn, framed in a brief narrative describing the process of composition. One object—a vise with a letter addressed to the artist's mother clamped firmly in the grip, swathed in a pair of men's briefs with the screw lever protruding through the flap, entitled "The Whore Moans"— quite stunned the group with its provocative implications. The mere fact that each sculpture was different, perhaps in contrast with the traditional assignment in which the products (exams or essays) tend to be as similar as possible, took the group by surprise. Some people declared that they had never in their entire lives actually made a metaphor and had assumed only trained poets could do so.

Evaluation: Conceiving Culture

Which raises the question of how to evaluate the lab projects. The criteria for evaluation are the same ones that might be used to determine the success of work in a scientific laboratory. Did the procedure produce the predicted results? When the chemicals were mixed did the solution explode or turn solid? Does the writing or sculpture possess the qualities of the genre or not? Remember, the goal is not to invent a new, unheard of text (despite the assumption by many students that surrealism, perhaps because of their misunderstanding of the concept of the "unconscious," deals with the unthinkable), rather, it is to replicate a major experiment whose results are now a known quantity. Just as Freud demonstrated, or at least argued, that dreams and madness manifest a specific form and pattern and so cannot be just anything at all, so too did the surrealists develop a specific style based on the representational and linguistic properties described in psychoanalytic theory. The undergraduate participant in a textshop is not expected to invent a new form or to be "original" in her creations any more than is her counterpart in the sciences expected to find a cure for cancer.

In short, creative or imaginative projects function with the same features of identifiable criteria as do analytical assignments. The student's work must have the qualities established during the lab discussions, and to the extent that it falls short of manifesting these properties it is a less successful experiment and may be graded accordingly. Thus it turns out to be a relatively easy matter to grade the projects if one wants to, especially since in my experience most college students are capable of following instructions and using models and hence do quite well on these exercises. Occasionally, of course, someone, unable to overcome his preconceptions about the unconscious, fails to direct the automatic process toward the production of a false novel, so the result lacks any elements of a story line. In the case of the readymades, someone may fail to follow the method of randomness, trying instead to think up a title first for which some object must be found as an illustration, resulting in a piece without unrelated juxtapositions. The evaluation, in other words, is done in formal terms, based on a set of criteria established in lab discussion, and does not entail a judgment of the "contents of my unconscious," as some students early on fear it will.

Part of the evaluation process is carried out by the students themselves in the readerly or analytical part of the course. They are asked to write a separate paper, of the more conventional sort, assessing the value of the lab experiments in the context of a study on creativity written from a psychoanalytic point of view. Actually the assessment is aimed as much at the claims of the study as it is at the value of the experiment. I have sometimes used Freud's own writings on the arts for this readerly study, but more recently I have preferred to use Silvano Arieti's *Creativity: The Magic Synthesis*. The class reads (at least) the section on "The Psychological Components of Creativity," with chapters on "Imagery," "Amorphous Cognition: The Endocept," "Primitive Cognition," and "Conceptual Cognition," and a chapter from the next section, "Creativity in Wit."

This study works well with surrealism because a collection such as Waldberg's reads almost as a demonstration of the cognitive processes Arieti describes. Arieti discusses ideation as a dialectical interplay oscillating between concepts and endocepts—between socially accepted, collective, and public sets on one hand and on the other hand private, inchoate drives—with the interchange mediated by a paleological dimension of primitive cognition that is organized by a non-Aristotelian system of dream logic. This paleological cognition will be recognized as a kind of synthesis of the various attempts in our century to describe an alternative mode of reasoning, beginning with Freud himself and including the Russian psychologists of inner speech (Vygotsky and Luria), Lévi-Strauss on "the savage mind," and right-brain thinking. In this context, as indicated, the apparent irregularities of the surrealist style are recovered as systematic attempts to develop a means of representation adequate to articulating this alternative cognition.

The practical value of associating the writerly experiments with a readerly comprehension of the theories of mind and knowledge explored by the experiments is that most students for the first time thus become self-conscious about thinking not only as a biological given, but as a cultural skill. Student Platonists suppose that concepts and ideals spring from the heads of thinkers the way Athena is said to have been born full-grown out of the head of Zeus. They know next to nothing about the invention process (an aspect of rhetoric that fell out of the curriculum, but which textshop proposes to revive): Freud somehow one day must have thought of "psychoanalysis." A reading of Arieti helps set them straight. They learn that ideas begin as the slightest sort of glimmer, a flash of emotion associated with some item one happens to encounter—the endocept. To think, one must learn how to watch out for these glimpses and to have the confidence to grab them and to hold them tightly to develop them (as the German term for *concept* suggests we must do—*begreifen, Begriff*). That Breton's account of how he got the idea for surrealism fits Arieti's generalization of the process is not only convenient, but exemplary.

> One night, before falling asleep, I became aware of a most bizarre sentence, clearly articulated to the point where it was impossible to change a word of it. . . . It was something like: "A man is cut in half by the window"; but it can only suffer from ambiguity, accompanied as it was by the feeble visual representation of a walking man cut in half by a window perpendicular to the axis of his body. It was probably a simple matter of a man leaning on the window and then straightening up. . . . Immediately I had the idea of incorporating it into my poetic material, but no sooner had I invested it with poetic form than it went on to give way to a scarcely intermittent succession of sentences which surprised me no less than the first. . . . Totally involved as I was at the time with Freud, and familiar with his methods of examination which I had some occasion to practice on the sick during the war, I resolved to obtain from myself what one seeks to obtain from a patient—a spoken monologue uttered as rapidly as possible, over which the critical faculty of the subject has no control. (Breton 70-71)

Arieti generalizes the power of images to assist with discovery: "Imagery thus emerges not only as the first or most primitive process of reproducing or substituting for *the real*, but also as the first or most primitive process of creating the *unreal*. . . . To the extent that the image, not by faithfully reproducing reality, is an innovation, a state of becoming, and a force of transcendence, we shall be very much concerned with it" (49).

The lessons of textshop, then, do not stop with the exercise of making a text. They include as well an examination through conventional analysis of the relation of the art experiment to cognition and problem solving in general, the purpose being not to produce surrealists or psychoanalysts, but educated men and women who understand how their cultural equipment actually works.

Epic Treatise

I have mentioned Brecht's epic theater as one of the sources for text-shop. It may be useful to consider a laboratory assignment based on Brecht, repeating the procedure applied to Breton, to emphasize that the lab approach is not confined to one movement, but draws on the entire repertoire of the avant-garde.

In preparation for the lab the class read some of the pieces in *Brecht on Theatre*, including "A Short Organum for the Theatre" (for freshmen, "The Street Scene: A Basic Model for an Epic Theatre" suffices), and several of the learning plays. In normal class discussion, using conventional analysis, the class identified the contrasting features of epic and tragic theater. With these features in mind, the students in the lab were asked to generate a similar set of oppositions for the treatise or research paper. They set up a proportional analogy to generate with respect to the conventional academic research paper an equivalent of what Brecht provided for conventional psychological drama: an epic treatise. Aristotelian tragedy : epic theater :: research paper : ———?

The problem posed in the lab was the invention of an epic version of the treatise. Part of the project is an exercise in the logic of discovery, in which analysis and imagination are not held apart (as they rarely are in practice, regardless of what logical positivists say). The exercise requires recourse to problem-solving strategies, which, working as a group, the class has to devise for itself (although it is also possible to list the steps in recipe fashion). To identify the properties of the treatise the class suggested using a college composition textbook with a how-to approach to writing the research paper. They could then generate, by a kind of triangulation from the lists of epic properties and the textbook treatise properties, a list of features that an epic treatise might be likely to possess. We identified this strategy as a kind of extrapolation, noting that it could be used as an invention procedure with any sort of materials. Part of the interest of this experiment is that the lists thus generated tend to differ as well from the properties of the "essay" itemized by Adorno in his attack on the treatise (personal vs. public; reflective vs. scholarly; subjective vs. objective; opinion vs. knowledge). It would be feasible to include Adorno's essay on the essay as part of the lab materials if the emphasis of the exercise were shifted somewhat. In any case, the project involves two parts—the discovery of the features of an epic treatise and the writing of an epic treatise. For the latter experiment the students are asked to select a conventional topic but to treat it in an epic fashion.

A related project relevant to this material is the generation of a model for a vanguard manifesto. The exercise arises out of the previous one in that some students produce a formula for the epic treatise that reflects, as it turns out, the qualities of a manifesto. A formula for the manifesto was again generated analytically by comparing the features of the manifestoes by Breton and Brecht. The juxtaposition revealed the following common elements:

1. Contrast: both poetics developed their aesthetics in contrast to a traditional form—Breton versus the realist/naturalist novel; Brecht versus Aristotle's (realist) drama. Both oppose the mimetic tradition.

2. Analogy: both poetics propose an analogy between their mode and a neighboring discourse—Breton and the discourse of dreams or schizophrenia (offered nonetheless as a discourse of knowledge, as in Dali's paranoiac-critical activity); Brecht with "critical science." The poetics intervene in epistemology, although in this instance they take up positions opposed to one another with respect to logic.

3. Theory: both poetics base their epistemology on the work of a theorist, proposing a genre to embody the aesthetic implications of the theory in question (Freud for Breton, Marx for Brecht). Again, the features of each poetics may be recognized as extrapolations from the premises of the theory.

4. Target: both schools identify a specific domain of application or function to which the new poetics is to be applied. In both cases the target domain is politics—specifically, bourgeois ideology. The strategies for political action varied in either case according to the same distinction noted at the level of logic: the surrealist jest or the epic gest.

The four categories are assigned a generic status and are assumed to be generalizable within the logic of discovery, the development of which is part of the purpose of textshop (Nickles).

In principle, although this possibility has not been tested, the formula developed to describe the extant poetics of Breton and Brecht could be extended beyond its present status as a genre of learning to function also as a genre of invention in the modern rather than in the rhetorical sense of the term. It could, in the manner of the vanguard manifesto, predict the production of certain kinds of texts, based on which materials were introduced into the places of the categories, prior to the actual existence of such works. In short, the manifesto does not compete with the critical article, but complements it, being positioned differently in relation to the artistic work (generative rather than interpretive). It remains to be seen whether or not learning and discovery really are related in the way suggested here—whether learning to replicate experiments in the lab may also lead to genuinely original work (Brannigan). One way to find out is to use the formula to generate a new description of a poetics, and then to extrapolate a text out of that poetics. I have given that assignment to myself, but without a deadline. I hope other textualists will take up the experiment. The acronym for the categories (contrast, analogy, theory, target) is CATT, which as a name serves as a mnemonic image for the genre (the class suggested a halloween cutout of a black cat, arched back and hissing, as an appropriate representation for the magic quality by which it appeared to operate).

Meanwhile, the class did not attempt to invent a new poetics (although I plan to assign that project to my next graduate seminar in theory). They did, however, compose manifestoes for a new pedagogy, using Brecht and Breton as the theorists, in contrast with the conventions of the traditional "course," by analogy with vanguard art, targeting television as the institution for application. The integration of imagination and analysis in such experiments leads to unusual and exciting work, to such an extent that the next step is to put the lab in contact with the school's literary magazine, since much of what comes out of the lab is creative and smart at once. The paradoxical result of the lab, whose pedagogy is the replication of models, is the extent to which it produces thinking in student work.

Mystory (The Subject of Knowledge)

To actually produce a surrealist work oneself teaches at least one lesson that could not be learned any other way—that however difficult many experimental texts might be to understand, they are easy to make. This insight might serve as an axiom for the avant-garde, and the key to the pedagogy of textshop—easy to make, hard to understand. By applying analytical thinking to one's own experiment as if it had been made by another, the student becomes familiar with the difference between making aesthetic effects and explanatory effects. But the understanding of surrealism itself, or even of the productive act from both sides, is only part of the goal of the lab.

Its further goal is to discover or invent a way for the humanities disciplines to contribute more directly to an epic education. Textshop explores the possibility that the creative imagination is as educable as reflective judgment, which is to say that the discovery/invention stage of thought, as much as the verification/testing phase, might be included in our education. As Paul Feyerabend pointed out in *Against Method* in a way that applies to all divisions of knowledge, pedagogy in the academy is based strictly on the way science is verified, not the way it is invented. Invention, rather, is left to chance or luck. I see this condition to be at least partly the fault of the humanities, which has been imitating the wrong aspects of science—the experiment as verification rather than as invention. The humanities, with its arts materials and methods, should intervene in education on the side of invention.

Gerald Holton provides an idea of the level at which such an intervention might occur. In his study of the creative genius of Einstein, Holton proposes two generalizations to account for the elements of an act of invention: (1) "There is a mutual mapping of the mind and lifestyle of the scientist and of the laws of nature"; (2) "There is a mutual mapping of the style of thinking and acting of the genial scientist on the one hand, and the chief unresolved problems of contemporary science on the other" (366, 374). The two points might be collapsed if we keep in mind that "the laws of nature" refer to the descriptions honored by the scientific disciplines. Attempting to articulate the "themata" of Einstein's cognitive style that enabled him to solve the problems of electromagnetism confronting the physics of his time, Holton traces Einstein's interest in such matters back to what Arieti would describe as an endocept captured in an image—to Einstein's persistent memory of the compass given to him by his father when he was four years old.

Einstein's compass turns out to be a good emblem of his themata, identified by Holton as balanced between the relative and the fixed, and could be generalized into an emblem of what the humanities should teach everyone to look for—the "text" of one's personal story—what I have discussed elsewhere as the *mystory*—that constitutes the guidance for invention. This notion strikes some people as deterministic because they interpret the mystory as if it were an essence rather than a construction selected and elaborated by the teller from his or her personal and public experience. To the extent that the story acquires a specific style it serves its teller not as a declaration of fate, but as a compass needle. Once we know which direction is north, it is possible to go in any direction at all. The systematic or formal knowledge of style that constitutes the humanities as a discipline is applied in textshop to help each student articulate the coherence of his/her mystory, in which is manifested the student's cognitive style or personal themata.

The images and themes of the life story may prove useful (judging by the history of invention) in the creation of models and metaphors needed for problem solving or theory formation in the student's field of study.

Arieti helps us understand what such a project involves in practice. At one level the artistic or aesthetic aspects of reasoning as a style have to do with the association of certain emotions with our concepts. The semiotic notion of the "interpretant" (the semiotic version of the "concept") suggests that our personal experiences of things serve as generalizations about the world — when one thinks of the concept of "dog," one does so by means of the image of one's own pet. In short, the concept carries an emotional overtone that contributes inevitably to one's thinking practice. It would be safe to assume in this context that Einstein's feelings about his father were an integral part of his cogitations on electromagnetism, mediated paleologically by the image of the compass.

Paleology is the crucial dimension — not a lesser form of thought, as implied during the era of the "two-cultures" debate, but a full and distinct partner in the reasoning process. Paleological thinking supplements the analytical mode of thought (functional in the dimension of verification) with a reasoning that draws on the full range of rhetorical and aesthetic procedures. Arieti simplifies the matter by summarizing the two modes as *logical* and *analogical*. Analogy, he explains, is essential to the productive powers of *synectics*, "the joining together of different and apparently irrelevant elements" — the formula, significantly, of surrealism. Arieti's discussion of Arthur Gordon's synectics includes a point important to the goals of textshop. "Gordon distinguishes four types of analogy: personal, direct, and symbolic analogy, and fantasy. In personal analogy the individual imagines himself to be the material with which he works. For example, Kekulé identified himself in a dream with a snake swallowing its tail, and saw an analogy to the benzene molecule as a ring rather than a chain of carbon atoms" (376).

The exploration of personal analogy is precisely the method for discovering the themata of one's cognitive style, the very element until now excluded from schooling in a curriculum dominated by an incomplete understanding of the scientific process of knowing. In fact, the Kekulé case is even more suggestive in this regard than Arieti implies, and provides an interesting example of the mystorical dimension of reason. Meredith Skura, in her discussion of the implications of Kekulé's example for creativity in general, notes that the universal symbol of the snake with its tail in its mouth was invested in Kekulé's life with some powerful emotions. "There was a fire that destroyed the house next to Kekulé's when he was eighteen, killing the countess who lived there. The local investigators, deciding that the episode constituted a deliberate murder, connected it with the simultaneous theft of the countess's jewelry—which included a ring in the shape of snakes biting their own tails. Eventually a trial was held, and Kekulé was called as an eyewitness" (132). At the time of the trial Kekulé was living through a disturbing conflict concerning his career choice, abandoning his father's influence for that of a mentor in chemistry. Skura speculates that since this particular conflict was an ongoing problem for Kekulé, it is possible that at the time he had the dream he was again experiencing personal difficulties that merged with his efforts to solve (as Holton would say) a major problem of his discipline. As he stared into the fire, Skura says, alluding to the circumstances of this famous anecdote in the history of science, the countess's murder stirred in his memory. Skura's conclusion supports Arieti's notion of paleology—Kekulé's discovery was "the result of very personal, preconditioned, and eccentric ideas working illogically below the level of consciousness to reshape conscious thinking" (133).

The murdered countess and her snake ring, associated with the discovery of the benzene molecule, constitutes a mystory—the contribution of personal anecdotes to problem solving in field of specialized knowledge. In this context we may see that the invention of psychoanalysis offers a fundamental lesson for educators. The lesson is so basic it does not depend at all on whether or not Freud was right in his account of human behavior and thought. What counts is the example he sets for the process of invention itself. Kekulé and Einstein and everyone else, if Holton is right, could not have solved a single scientific problem without mixing their mystories with the histories of their disciplines. But Freud is the first innovator in the history of science to propose a system of knowledge and a practical institution whose "subject" (object of knowledge) is precisely this mystory—Freud's own story.

Let us think about Freud's invention for a moment. It consists of the generalization of his peculiar personal, familial circumstances, mediated through a major work of world literature (*Oedipus Rex*), into the discourse of medical science. There may be a formula available in this example, joining a strong personal, emotional experience, a work of art, and an unsolved problem in a field of knowledge. For now, I want to try to summarize what I take to be the specific approach of the humanities laboratory. What textshop learns from Freud is not so much concerned with the theory and practice of psychoanalysis, but with the act of invention: the way Freud carried the styles and languages of humanities materials (folklore, popular culture, dreams, the fine arts, literature) into the dimension of science. His most important lesson for us is not the secondary possibility of interpreting literature by means of psychology, but the use of literary and other cultural artifacts as primary and irreducible sources of knowledge and explanation. What is psychoanalysis but the frame through which our aesthetic culture has intervened in a society committed to science?

To learn from Freud, then, we should repeat not psychoanalysis, but his discovery procedure itself, drawing upon our private experience and popular culture in the context of a given disciplinary problem. Our problems, both personally and disciplinarily, will be different from Freud's. The stories we grew up with will be different too: Greek tragedy does not have for contemporary America the importance it had for nineteenth-century German culture. In textshop we use psychoanalysis to learn about invention, but not only psychoanalysis. The productive relationship between psychoanalysis and surrealism suggests in our contexts the possibility of other theories providing similarly generative or inventive guidelines for the production of new styles of representation. Instead of waiting for another Breton to happen along, textshop proposes to test systematically any and all theories for their poetic potential, as well as to interrogate existing avant-garde movements for their theoretical implications. The genres and modes of representation generated in this manner will be made available to the students in textshop as vehicles for mystoriographical research.

NOTE

1. The practical applications of these pairings for textshop will be developed in a future study. A related approach to the texts of Roland Barthes and Jacques Derrida is developed in *Text Book*, by Robert Scholes, Nancy Comley, and Ulmer—designed for introductory composition courses in "writing about literature." I explore the concept of "mystory" in two articles: "Teletheory: A Mystory," and "Mystory: The Law of Idiom in Applied Grammatology."

WORKS CITED

Adorno, T. W. "The Essay as Form," *New German Critique* 11 (1986): 151-71.
Arieti, Silvano. *Creativity: The Magic Synthesis*. New York: Basic Books, 1976.
Barthes, Roland. *S/Z*, trans. Richard Miller. New York: Hill and Wang, 1974.
Brannigan, Augustine. *The Social Basis of Scientific Discoveries*. Cambridge: Cambridge University Press, 1981.
Brecht, Bertolt. *Brecht on Theatre*, trans. John Willet. New York: Hill and Wang, 1964.

Breton, André. "Surrealist Manifesto." In Patrick Waldberg, *Surrealism*. New York: McGraw-Hill, n.d. 66-76.

Holton, Gerald. *Thematic Origins of Scientific Thought: Kepler to Einstein*. Cambridge, Mass.: Harvard University Press, 1973.

Nickles, Thomas. *Scientific Discovery, Logic, and Rationality*. Boston: D. Reidel, 1980.

Scholes, Robert, Nancy Comley, and Gregory L. Ulmer. *Text Book*. New York: St. Martin's Press, 1980.

Skura, Meredith. "Creativity: Transgressing the Limits of Consciousness," *Daedalus* 109 (1980): 127-46.

Ulmer, Gregory L. "Mystory: The Law of Idiom in Applied Grammatology." In *The Future of Theory*. Ed. Ralph Cohen. New York: Metheun, 1988.

———. "Textshop for Post(e)pedagogy." In *Writing and Reading Differently: Deconstruction and the Teaching of Composition*. Ed. G. Douglas Atkins and Michael Johnson. Lawrence: University Press of Kansas, 1985. 38-64.

———. "Teletheory: A Mystory." In *The Current in Criticism*. Ed. Clayton Koelb and Virgil Lokke. West Lafayette, Ind.: Purdue University Press, 1987.

GEORGE P. LANDOW

Changing Texts, Changing Readers: Hypertext in Literary Education, Criticism, and Scholarship

What Is Hypertext *and Why Should Those Who Read Books Care?*

It is eight P.M., and after having helped put the children to bed, Professor Jones settles into her favorite chair and reaches for her copy of Milton's *Paradise Lost* to prepare for tomorrow's class. A scholar who specializes in the poetry of Milton's time, she returns to the poem as one returns to meet an old friend. Reading the poem's opening pages, she once again encounters allusions to the Old Testament, and because she knows how seventeenth-century Christians commonly read these passages, she perceives connections both to a passage in Genesis and to its radical Christian transformations. Furthermore, her previous acquaintance with Milton allows her to recall other passages later in *Paradise Lost* that refer to this and related parts of the Bible. At the same time, she recognizes that the poem's opening lines pay homage to Homer, Virgil, Dante, and Spenser and simultaneously issue them a challenge.

Meanwhile, John H. Smith, one of the most conscientious students in Professor Jones's survey of English literature, begins to prepare for class. What kind of poem, what kind of text, does he encounter? Whereas Professor Jones experiences the great seventeenth-century epic situated within a field of relations and connections, her student encounters a far barer, less connected, reduced poem, most of whose allusions go unrecognized and almost all of whose challenges pass by unperceived. An unusually mature student, he pauses in his reading to check the footnotes for the meaning of unfamiliar words and allusions, a few of which he finds explained. Suppose one could find a way to allow Smith to experience some of the connections obvious to

Professor Jones. Suppose he could touch the opening lines of *Paradise Lost*, for instance, and the relevant passages from Homer, Virgil, and the Bible would appear, or that he could touch another line and immediately receive a choice of other mentions of the same idea or image later in the poem or elsewhere in Milton's other writings— or, for that matter, interpretations and critical judgments made since the poem's first publication.

Hypertext, or electronically linked text, enables students to do all these things. Unlike books, which contain physically isolated texts, hypertext emphasizes connections and relations, and in doing so changes the ways texts exist and the ways we read them. It also changes the roles of author and reader, teacher and student.

Because hypertext has the power to change the way we understand and experience texts, it offers radical promises and challenges to students, teachers, and theorists of literature. *Hypertext*, a term coined by Theodor H. Nelson in the 1960s, refers to nonsequentially read (and written) texts: "Both an author's tool and a reader's medium, a hypertext document system allows authors or groups of authors to *link* information together, create *paths* through a corpus of related material, *annotate* existing texts, and create notes that point readers to either bibliographic data or the body of the referenced text. . . . Readers can browse through linked, cross-referenced, annotated texts in an orderly but nonsequential manner" (Yankelovich et al.). Writers on hypertext trace the notion to a 1945 article by Vannevar Bush in *Atlantic Monthly* that called for mechanically linked information retrieval machines in the midst of what was already becoming an explosion of information. In the 1960s Douglas C. Englebart and Nelson began to design computer systems that could implement some of these notions of linked texts, and today *hypertext* refers almost exclusively to electronic hypertext systems that rely on computing equipment and software.

Originally the idea of hypertext did not depend upon computers. In fact, the standard scholarly article in the humanities or physical sciences perfectly embodies the underlying notions of hypertext as nonsequentially read text. For example, in reading a critical article on James Joyce's *Ulysses*, one reads through the main text, encounters a number or symbol that indicates the presence of a foot- or endnote, and leaves the main text to read it. The note might contain a citation of passages in *Ulysses* that support the argument in question as well as information about the author's indebtedness to other scholars, disagreement with them, and so on. The note might also summon up information about sources, influences, and parallels in other literary texts. In each case, the reader can follow the link to another text indicated by the note, thus moving entirely outside the text of the article itself. Having completed reading the note or having decided that it does not warrant a careful reading at the moment, one returns to the main text and continues reading until one encounters another note, at which point one again leaves the main text. This combination of excursionary reading outside the main text and returning to it constitutes the basic experience of hypertext.

Suppose now that one could simply touch the page where the symbol of a note or reference appeared and instantly bring into view the material contained in a note or even the entire other text—here all of *Ulysses*—to which that note refers. Scholarly articles situate themselves within a field of such relations, but the print medium keeps most of these intertexts out of sight and relatively difficult to follow because the referenced (or linked) materials lie spatially distant from the corresponding note. In contrast, electronic hypertext makes individual references easy to follow and the entire field of textual interconnections easy to navigate. Changing the rapidity and ease with which one can orient oneself within such a context of information radically changes both the experience of reading and ultimately the nature of what is read. For example, if we had a hypertext system in which our putative Joyce article existed linked to all the materials it cited, it would appear to the reader as part of a much larger system whose totality might count more than the individual document. The article would now be woven much more tightly into its context than would its traditional print technology counterpart. The ease with which readers traverse such a system has additional consequences for as they move through this web of texts, they continually shift its center—and hence the focus or organizing principle of their investigation and experience. Hypertext, in other words, provides an infinitely recenterable system whose provisional point of focus depends upon the reader, who becomes truly a user of knowledge.

Hypertext offers enormous possibilities to the student and teacher of literature, all of which derive from its fundamental connectivity, a quality that greatly speeds up certain processes involved in skilled reading and critical thinking, while also making them far easier to carry out. The greater speed of making connections in hypertext permits and encourages sophisticated forms of analysis. Since hypertext facilitates the making of connections among literary texts and arrays of concepts, images, and maps, it seems an obvious tool to use in basic college courses that aim to enable students to assimilate large bodies of information while developing the habits of analysis necessary to think critically about this information. Unfortunately, until very recently neither computing equipment nor programming that could make use of these educational and research possibilities existed.[1] Relatively powerful and inexpensive minicomputers that could join together to share information were needed before even prototypes of systems both convenient and economical enough for educational and scholarly use could develop.

Brown University's Scholars Workstation Project, which is supported by a grant from IBM, offered the promise of adequate computing machinery, and the Institute for Research in Information and Scholarship (IRIS) of Brown University set out to develop a hypertext system for use in university education and scholarship. In 1985 IRIS received a three-year grant from the Annenberg/Corporation for Public Broadcasting Project to develop the educational materials that would employ it.[2] English 32, English Literature from 1700 to the Present, and Biology 106, Plant Cell Biology, were the two courses chosen for the pilot project.

After describing the application of hypertext to English 32, I shall discuss the materials on *Context32*, or that part of the system devoted to this English course, and then narrate how a student uses the system during a typical session in an electronic laboratory. Next, I shall present evidence of the effect of such a hypertext system on student performance, after which I shall examine the relation of hypertext to contemporary critical theory—in particular, to the ideas of decentering, intertextuality, and anti-hierarchical texts.

Critical Thinking: The Uses of Intermedia and Context32

In spring semester, 1987, the forty-five students in my section of English 32, English Literature from 1700 to the Present, used *Context32*, a corpus of linked documents created using Intermedia software designed at IRIS. (See Meyrowitz "Requirements," Yankelovich "INTERMEDIA," and Yankelovich et al. "Creating Hypermedia Materials.") At first glance this course resembles the traditional, rather old-fashioned survey found in many English departments, for it is intended to allow beginning students to sample a wide range of authors (e.g., Pope, Dickens) and literary movements (e.g., Neoclassicism, Victorianism) and to get some sense of the historical continuities of major forms and genres (e.g., epic and mock-epic, the realistic novel). However, English 32 has other goals not found in many traditional literary surveys, among which the most important is to enable students to describe the interrelations of authors, movements, and various extraliterary cultural contexts, including those provided by social, religious, political, intellectual, artistic, and technological history.

In addition, I also intended the course to foster critical thinking, my conception of which centers on the notion that an educated intelligence perceives any particular phenomenon as potentially multidetermined and subject to multicausation. *Context32*'s graphic presentation of data and its capacity to allow multiple links to individual documents encourages the habit of approaching any literary (or other) fact from multiple directions. This aspect of Intermedia markedly differentiates it from many other computer-assisted education projects that encourage students to sit passively before a screen while information is fed to them, as if they had found a McDonald's of education whose products they can engorge in passivity.[3] In contrast, Intermedia encourages the student to map out pathways of information for him- or herself. Intermedia is designed, in other words, to free students rather than confine them. Indeed, by allowing the student to create his or her own route through knowledge, it permits—or rather demands—choices. Intermedia thus provides support for Roland Barthes's demand that the "goal of literary work (of literature as work) is to make the reader no longer a consumer, but a producer of the text" (4).

Much of the sheeplike behavior that one observes in students, particularly when they first arrive at a college or university, comes from their having both so little information and so little idea of what to do with that information they do have. One cannot discover or create connections between fact A and six other facts if one knows only fact A, and this lack of factual knowledge tends to make one think in a reductive manner. Just offering additional factual information, however, will not help a student think critically unless she has techniques for relating facts to each other and to everything else already known. College liberates us because it both provides us with facts and offers examples of the way we can make connections for ourselves. Intellectual freedom derives from an ability to make choices. Anything that can thus help us make information available to those who want it and also provide them with techniques to relate it to what they already know provides a model for education. The critical habits of mind thus encouraged apply to all kinds of activities inside the classroom and out; education and thinking are both active procedures. Intermedia has the capacity to speak to all these educational issues. Above all, it encourages the student to ask questions and to make choices.

Intermedia extends hypertext to include other media, and it is therefore most accurately described as a hypermedia system. As Nicole Yankelovich, IRIS project coordinator, explains: "*Hypermedia* is simply an extension of hypertext that incorporates other media in addition to text. With a hypermedia system, authors can create a linked corpus of material that includes text, static graphics, animated graphics, video, sound, music, and so forth."[4] *Context32*, the body of materials created specifically for English 32, though now used by other courses as well, draws upon these hypermedia capacities of the system. The redesigned, computer-assisted version of English 32 has essentially the same reading list used in past versions. With the addition of Intermedia, the course now has five components: assigned readings; student-directed class discussions; a weekly lecture; out-of-class writing assignments, other exercises, and examinations; and hypermedia materials of *Context32* that were created specifically for the course by four graduate and postdoctoral assistants and myself. These materials, which are intended to help students read with greater skill and pleasure, supplement the main reading but do not replace it.

Students make use of *Context32* and Intermedia in the electronic classroom—really a learning laboratory. This laboratory, which is in the same building as the room in which English 32 meets, is open from 9 A.M. to midnight weekdays and from noon to midnight weekends. After doing the assigned readings and while attending lecture and class discussions, students use Intermedia materials on fourteen IBM RT/PCs that join together to form a network. *Context32*, which comprised approximately 1,000 text and graphic files joined by some 1,300 links by the end of the course, employs various parts of the IRIS Intermedia system including its text, timeline, graphic functions, as well as its link-creating process, which "is modeled after the 'copy/paste' techniques found in standard Macintosh programs."[5]

InterVal documents are timelines for individual authors as well as more general subjects, such as political history, science, literature, and the women's movement. Since Intermedia permits opening many documents at the same time, one can juxtapose timelines, placing, for example, Tennyson's next to the history timeline. *InterWord* documents include biographies of individual authors; brief essays on literary technique, both general and specific, e.g., "Narration and Point of View" and "Imagery in D. H. Lawrence's 'Prussian Officer'"; and discussions of nonliterary topics related to more than one author, e.g., "Social Darwinism," "Ages of Technology," "Biblical Typology," and "Freud and Freudianism." Most essays contain questions that refer students back to the reading, ask them to apply their newly acquired information to an included portion of text, or encourage them to follow links to other files.

In addition to these, two other kinds of materials have been added to the original *Context32*: lyric poems that either exemplify particular difficulties (Hopkins's "The Windhover") or function as a crux in the course and are frequently referred to ("Ode on a Grecian Urn") and annotated bibliographies. Although we considered including bibliographies on the original system, my assistants and I did not do so for several reasons. English 32 had a particularly heavy list of readings, so we did not wish to suggest that students should read secondary materials as a requirement for the course. If members of the course had the time to do additional work, we all preferred that they either read additional authors or read more widely in the authors assigned. Second, since studies at Brown had revealed that only the smallest percentage (3 percent) of students do recommended readings, I did not want to create the impression that students should try to read materials when we did not expect them to do so. Now that various advanced courses use *Context32*, I wish to make such bibliographies available for those working on independent projects or research papers, and placing such materials on the system no longer creates a false impression of the teacher's expectations for student reading.

In contrast to InterWord documents, which contain only formatted text, those in InterDraw contain both graphic images and text. InterDraw documents take various forms, the most important of which is the index diagram, one of the most educationally important parts of *Context32*. These diagrams serve as directories or overviews, thus informing the user about various information available in relation to individual authors, works, and topics, and also including links to that information. By surrounding an individual phenomenon, say, Tennyson (Figure 1), Tennyson's *In Memoriam*, or Victorianism (Figure 2), with a series of relatable phenomena including biographical information, contemporary science, and so on, these overview diagrams immediately reinforce one of the main educational points of the course—that any literary or other phenomenon exists surrounded by relatable contributing texts and events. This graphic presentation simultaneously shows the student existing links and cultivates the habit of making such connections.

By abandoning the table of contents or list mode that characterizes page-bound, printed text, one liberates hypertext from the restrictions of print and enables it to do what it does best—present networks of relationships while also enabling the user to traverse those relationships easily, establishing connections between paired sets of data and among larger groupings of material. I emphasize this crucial aspect of our implementation of educational hypertext since it lies at the heart of our particular project and its educational purposes, but also at the heart

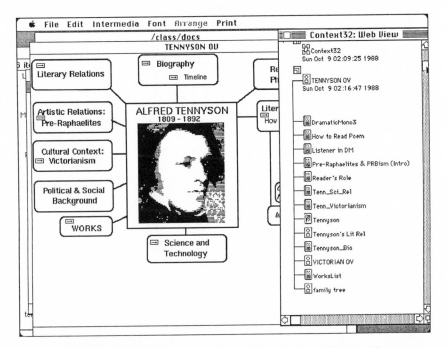

FIGURE 1. "Tennyson OV," a graphic overview (OV) or directory document that provides a convenient starting place for readers interested in the topic to which it refers. In *Context32*, multiple overviews provide the reader with alternative ways of organizing given bodies of material. In addition to the "Tennyson OV," the folder for that author contains overviews for *In Memoriam* and other poems as well as for the images and motifs in *In Memoriam* and for that poem's intertextual relations. In this illustration of the most recent (or Macintosh II) version of Intermedia, the web view, which the system generates automatically, overlays the right side of "Tennyson OV." The web view contains icons representing documents linked to the document the reader is currently examining, and the reader can use these icons to travel to the linked documents.

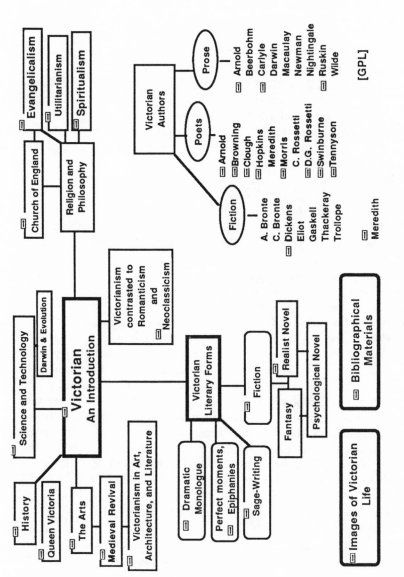

FIGURE 2. "Victorianism OV."

of hypertext systems themselves. If hypertext is characterized by connectivity, to realize its potential one must employ directories that focus on that quality. Lists, tables of contents, or indexes do not work in this manner.

One cannot overemphasize the centrality of these directories, or overview files, to teaching students critical thinking. These graphic presentations of information have several purposes, the first and most obvious of which is to organize a body of complex ideas so that users can better comprehend them. At the same time, the overview file suggests that all these various other ideas link to or impinge upon the central point, which may take the form of an author, chronological or period term, idea or movement, literary genre, or other concept. The implied and often reinforced message of such arrangements is simply that any idea that the user makes the center of his or her investigations exists situated within a field of other phenomena, which may or may not relate to it causally. Such graphic presentation of materials depicts the informing idea or hidden agenda of *Context32*, namely, that the student or scholar proceeds in understanding any particular literary or other phenomenon by relating it to other contexts. In addition to such overviews, *Context32* also contains representations of literary influences and interrelations as vector forces (Figure 3). Unlike overview files, literary relation files and similar analyses of complex historical and cultural phenomena emphasize a unidirectional flow of forces.

Digitized images, such as works of art, cartoons, and maps, are included with appended texts to make the images more educationally effective. The texts provide some factual information, encourage the students to relate that information to a problem, and contain links that allow students to pursue various investigations. For example, Figure 4, which has been scanned from a reproduction of the catalog for the first world's fair, the Great Exhibition of 1851, has much to tell the student engaged in formulating a working definition of *Victorian* or *Victorianism*. The appended text reads: "This curiosity from the Crystal Palace exhibition of 1851 is not a suit of armor but a stove built in the shape of one. What do such bizarre glances back at the past tell us about the Victorian age, which invented the idea of Progress as we know it? Can you find any examples of thus presenting contemporary purposes (or issues) in ancient forms in the poems you have read?" Students who highlight the link marker and issue a command to follow it receive a menu of various Victorian literary works, including Tennyson's "Morte d'Arthur," a poem set in medieval England, and "Tithonus," one set in the Greece of ancient myth. The visual information also supports the principle that relevance is in the mind of the beholder

Relations of In Memoriam 60 to Other Sections
by Kristen Langdon '88

In 60 concern is more for passing of the friend and the earthly loss;
Compare: 95:33-36 "So word by word, and line by line/The dead man though'd me from the past."
116:15-16 "Less yearning for the friendship fled
Than some strong band which is to be."
129:9 "Strange friend, past, present, and to be"

BUT with spiritual awakening in 95, he can see friendship in both present and future terms
(Cp 116, 129)

60

He past, a soul of nobler tone;
My spirit loved and loves him yet,
Like some poor girl whose heart is set
On one whose rank exceeds her own.

He mixing with his proper sphere,
She finds the baseness of her lot,
Half jealous of she knows not what,
And envying all that meet him there.

The little village looks forlorn;
She sighs amid her narrow ways,
Moving about the household ways,
In that dark house where she was born.

The foolish neighbours come and go,
And tease her till the day draws by;
At night she weeps, "How vain am I!
How should he love a thing so low?"

9:18 "Till all my WIDOW'D race be won"
85:113 "My heart, tho' WIDOW'D, may not rest"
52:13 "So fret not, like an idle GIRL"
97:7 "And of my spirit as a WIFE"
(In 48 and 49, sorrow is identified as "she" when the speaker is overwhelmed by sorrow. Likewise, knowledge and wisdom are females in 114)

Imagery of circles and spheres:
61:3 "With all the CIRCLE of the wise"
63:11-12 "The CIRCUITS of thine ORBIT ROUND"

97:31 "She knows but matters of the house"

environmental description reflects speaker's mood:
7:1-2. "Dark house, by which once more I stand/Here in the long unlovely street
No. 119 shows same setting with happier mood, thus reflecting a change of attitude. [follow for discussion by R. Fletcher]

Others around the girl of 60 and women of 97 question her position in love:
97:13-16 "Their love has never past away. . .
Whate'er the faithless people say."

FIGURE 3. A student contribution—a text document within a graphic document: Kristen Langdon's "Relations of In Memoriam 60 to Other Sections."

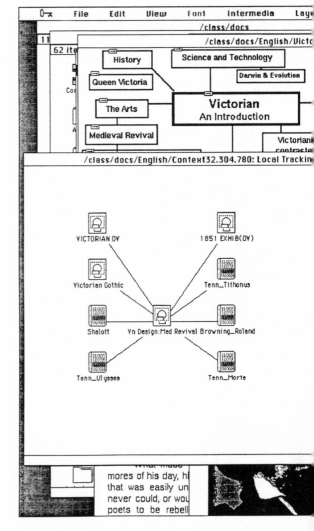

FIGURE 4. In this illustration of the earlier version of Interm
which operated on IBM RT/PCs, "Victorian Design: Med
Revival" appears at the right while at the left appears the
tracking map. This feature, which the web view has rep
in the newer versions of Intermedia (see Figure 1), shows li
documents but does not itself provide a means of opening t
Beneath both the local tracking map and "Victorian De
appear portions of three other documents — "Tenn

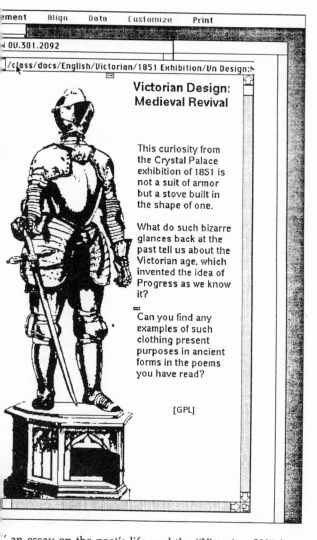

Victorian Design: Medieval Revival

This curiosity from the Crystal Palace exhibition of 1851 is not a suit of armor but a stove built in the shape of one.

What do such bizarre glances back at the past tell us about the Victorian age, which invented the idea of Progress as we know it?

Can you find any examples of such clothing present purposes in ancient forms in the poems you have read?

[GPL]

' an essay on the poet's life, and the "Victorian OV" from ch the reader reached "Victorian Design." Beneath these uments one can see the edges of the main English folder the desktop containing folders for each discipline. Clicking the computer mouse upon any portion of a visible doc- nt or folder immediately brings that document or folder to top of the pile, activates it, and shows its linked documents he local tracking map or web view.

and that the investigator's function in any field is to inquire what connections might exist among various kinds of data and how their relative importance might be evaluated.

A student uses *Context32* in the following way. After logging onto a PC, the student types the command "Intermedia" once a prompt appears. After several minutes half a dozen icons in the shape of folders appear, at which point the student uses a mouse to activate and then open the folder labeled "English." When that has been opened the student double-clicks "*Context32*" and waits 25 seconds for this action to generate the over two thousand links that bind the system together. A student who wishes to use the system to prepare for written exercises concerning Tennyson and the Victorians can begin by opening either the Tennyson or Victorian folder.

When opening poet folders, students generally open the overview file first (Figure 1) since this provides an idea of what kind of information relates to an individual author and also permits them to use the links to gain access to such data. Students can follow links to bring up a biography of the poet, essays on individual works, or relations to contemporary history and politics, religion and philosophy, other authors, and the general cultural milieu, in this case Victorianism. The student might first look at "Tennyson's Literary Relations" and follow it to other authors, such as contemporaries like Browning or Arnold, or to influential predecessors, such as Keats and Wordsworth. Conversely, a student concerned to discover an adequate working definition of *Victorian* could explore the link to the poet's cultural context and bring up the overview file on Victorianism (Figure 2), which presents a wide range of information about the period in visual and verbal form. Following the link to "Medieval Revival" (Figure 4), for example, the student encounters the stove in the shape of a suit of armor, and following the links in that file finds five files on the poetry of Tennyson and Browning. The student might choose "Morte d'Arthur," and from there might examine several poems or either return to overview and go from there, examining the file "Biblical Typology" or "Darwinism," since both relate to Tennyson's major poetry, or search files about literary technique. Links to discussions of literary technique offer the student a choice of a general introduction to techniques common to all relevant authors and a file containing brief passages from the assigned work together with discussion and additional queries. After students used a sample set of documents I had appended to a single author, they told me that they found this kind of information particularly helpful, so I created them for all major authors and placed links in the overview (OV) files.

Hypertextual Pedagogy: Results

English 32 employed Intermedia as a means of providing information that students rarely obtain in surveys and most other courses while also helping them to develop critical thinking. The role of the Office of Program Analysis (OPA), the social science part of IRIS, was to evaluate how successfully Intermedia fulfilled our plans as well as to study the process of developing Intermedia and the course materials themselves. To have a standard of comparison once English 32 began to use Intermedia, several ethnographers from OPA examined how students study and learn in courses without computer enhancement.[6]

The OPA analysts proceeded by attending, taping, and transcribing all meetings of software and courseware developers and by interviewing faculty and graduate student authors of the materials frequently—at times, weekly. One analyst attended all classes before, during, and after the development of the Intermedia component of English 32. The analysts conducted surveys, had students keep diaries, and repeatedly interviewed them. Charts and statistics summarizing student use, attitudes, and time spent appear in the project report, as do copious quotations from the student interviews.

As we had hoped, students in the *Context32* section demonstrated a markedly better grasp of the materials than had members of previous classes. They also introduced more biographical and historical information of all kinds into class discussions and examinations than had members of previous classes, and they also cited many more specific passages and related many more works to each other. For example, during class discussion both the number of student comments and of individual students participating increased by 300 percent. Perhaps even more impressively, the nature of comments changed from vague expressions of interest ("I was interested in the way Swift said this.") and need for help ("I wonder if anybody could tell me why . . .") to factual statements and critical judgments. We had early indications that *Context32* was doing some of the things we hoped it might accomplish, for immediately after the students worked with the system for the first time, they began to introduce factual material about the author's life and times into class discussions—something the teaching staff and social scientists evaluating the course had not observed previously. For example, during discussions of Jonathan Swift's "A Modest Proposal" and *Gulliver's Travels*, students introduced relevant materials about Swift's life, British colonialism and England's relation to Ireland, and satiric devices and their relation to the Roman satirists. As the course progressed, student exercises, such as diagrams of literary relations and imitations of Pope's neoclassical heroic couplets, proved markedly superior to those in previous years.

Furthermore, Intermedia helped many students learn how to use books more effectively. Studies of novice readers and our own OPA researchers both confirm what many teachers have long suspected—that inexperienced or unskillful students fail to make use of introductions, footnotes, glossaries, and other apparatus created specifically for them. Lacking developed reading skills and the knowledge to recognize the relevance of the information offered, many novice readers do not find it of interest because they do not know what to do with it. Our ethnographic researchers report that, after using Intermedia, students make much greater use of these materials in books. Thus, one might say, having used electronic hypertext they better understand how to use its print version. In any case, Intermedia both taught students crucial reading skills and demonstrated that computer-assisted instruction can reinforce reading books rather than replace them or drive students away from reading.

My grader for the course, an experienced graduate student teacher who judged the take-home midterm and in-class final examinations the most rigorous she had ever seen, found that answers to both identification and essay questions were in general far more detailed and intellectually sophisticated than any other work by students at this level she had encountered previously. Although after first looking at the examination she warned me that she might have to fail a considerable number of my students, she did not—and in fact discovered that more than 10 percent of the class scored over 100 percent.

In addition to such results, some of which we had hoped would occur, several others took us somewhat by surprise. The course's emphasis upon connectivity and interrelatedness convinced many students that since everything in the course related importantly to everything else, they could not omit any of the reading since all appeared crucial to them. Teachers have been trying for centuries to convince students to do all their assigned readings: here we have a case in which the linking capacity of Intermedia had achieved this result without our expecting it to do so!

A second pleasant set of surprises concerns the willingness of students in the section to consider *Context32* as a body of knowledge to which they can contribute and whose shape they can determine. This new student attitude apparently begins with the first week's assignment, which instructs them to explore files relating to Graham Swift's *Waterland* (1983) and then suggests additional links among files that they would like to see and texts that they would append to graphics, such as maps depicting the growth of British railways and canals. Having been asked their opinion once, they proceeded to give it freely ever afterward. Throughout the semester students thus offered proofreading and criticisms of the nature and placement of links as well as requests for documents on subjects like labor history or critical theory that they thought would be useful. Certain students' belief that they played a role in developing materials for use by the entire class continued beyond the end of the course. Several students, unasked, mailed in a fifteen-page, single-spaced evaluation that contained corrections, suggestions, and requests for improving Intermedia materials.

This student activity and interest beyond the course itself appears significant, particularly since any computing or other enhancement seems likely to work only if it develops grass roots appeal. This appeal seems to exist at both extremes of the educational scale: freshman not in my section of English 32 expressed serious interest in using Intermedia, and at least one student used it intensively throughout the semester. At the same time two graduate students have continued to use Intermedia in preparing for their preliminary oral examinations for the doctorate. And students enrolled in English 32 reported to me that they used *Context32* to study for other courses, including those not in the English department.

Hypertext and Critical Theory

Hypertext has the capacity to emphasize intertextuality in a way that page-bound text in books cannot. Scholarly articles, as we have seen, offer an obvious example of explicit hypertextuality in nonelectronic form. Conversely, any work of literature—which for the sake of argument and economy I shall here confine in a most arbitrary way to mean canonical literature of the sort we read and teach in universities— offers an instance of implicit hypertext in nonelectronic form. Take Joyce's *Ulysses*, for example. If one looks, say, at the "Nausicaa" section in which Bloom watches Gerty McDowell on the beach, one notes that Joyce's text here "alludes" or "refers" (the terms we usually employ) to many other texts or phenomena that one can treat as texts, including the Nausicaa section of *The Odyssey*, the advertisements and articles in the women's magazines that suffuse and inform Gerty's thoughts, facts about contemporary Dublin and the Catholic Church, and other passages within the novel. Again, one can envisage a hypertext presentation of the novel that would link this section not only to the kinds of materials mentioned, but also to other works in Joyce's career, critical commentary, and textual variants. Hypertext here permits one to make explicit, though not necessarily intrusive, the linked materials that an educated reader perceives surrounding the novel.

Thaïs Morgan suggests that intertextuality, "as a structural analysis of texts in relation to the larger system of signifying practices or uses of signs in culture," shifts attention from the triad constituted by author/work/tradition to another constituted by text/discourse/culture. In so doing, "intertextuality replaces the evolutionary model of literary history with a structural or synchronic model of literature as a sign system. The most salient effect of this strategic change is to free the literary text from psychological, sociological, and historical determinisms, opening it up to an apparently infinite play of relationships"(1-2). Morgan describes well a major implication of hypertext (and hypermedia) intertextuality: one gains an opening up, a freedom to create and perceive interconnections occurs. Nonetheless, although hypertext intertextuality would seem to devalue any historic or other reductionism, it in no way prevents those interested in reading by means of author and tradition from doing so. Our experiments thus far suggest that hypertext does not necessarily turn one's attention away from such traditional critical approaches. What is perhaps most interesting about hypertext, though, lies not in whether it fulfills certain claims of structuralist and poststructuralist criticism, but that it provides a rich means of testing them.

Intermedia does not work in the manner of most first-generation computer-assisted instruction. Most such programs and materials, which follow the model of printed workbooks, take the user through a pre-arranged sequence of exercises and experiences. Such systems constrain the users by forcing them to follow a single sequence or relatively few possible sequences. Intermedia, in contrast, reflects the fundamental characteristic of hypertext and hypermedia systems: they are bodies of linked texts that have no primary axis of organization. In other words, Intermedia has no center. Although this absence of a center can create problems for the teacher and researcher, it also means that anyone who uses Intermedia makes his or her own interests the de facto organizing principle (or center) for the investigation at the moment. One experiences Intermedia as an infinitely decenterable and recenterable system.

Hypertext then is related to the ideas of Jacques Derrida and Louis Althusser, both of whom emphasize the need to shift vantage points by decentering discussion. As Derrida points out in "Structure, Sign, and Play in the Discourse of the Human Sciences," the process or procedure he calls decentering has played an essential role in intellectual change. For example, "Ethnology could have been born as a science only at the moment when a de-centering had come about: at the moment when European culture—and, in consequence, the history of metaphysics and of its concepts—had been *dislocated*, driven from its locus, and forced to stop considering itself as the culture of reference" (251). Derrida makes no claim that an intellectual or ideological center is in any way "bad," for as he explains in response to a query from Serge Doubrovsky, " I didn't say that there was no center, that we could get along without a center. I believe that the center is a function, not a being—a reality, but a function. And this function is absolutely indispensable" (271).

Intermedia, like all hypertext systems, permits the individual user to choose his or her own center of investigation and experience. What this principle means in practice is that *Context32* does not lock the student into any kind of organization or hierarchy. For the person who chooses to organize a session on the system by making use of author overview files, moving from Keats OV to Tennyson OV, the system would represent an old-fashioned, traditional, and author-centered survey course. On the other hand, nothing constrains the student to work in this manner, and any students who wish to investigate the validity of period generalizations could organize their sessions in terms of such periods by using the Victorian and Romantic OV files as starting or midpoints, while others could begin with ideological or critical notions, such as overviews of Feminism or the Victorian Novel. In practice, however, students employ *Context32* as a text-centered system, since they tend to focus upon individual works with the result that even if they begin sessions by entering the system at an individual author overview file, they tend to spend most time with files devoted to individual works, moving between poem and poem (Swinburne's "Laus Veneris" and Keats's "La Belle Dame sans Merci") and between poem and informational texts ("Laus Veneris" and files on chivalry, medieval revival, courtly love, Wagner, and so on).

As the capacity of hypertext systems to be infinitely recenterable suggests, they have the corollary characteristics of being antihierarchical and democratic in several different ways. First, as the authors of "Reading and Writing the Electronic Book" point out, in such systems "Ideally, authors and readers should have the same set of integrated tools that allow them to browse through other material during the document preparation process and to add annotations and original links as they progress through an information web. In effect, the boundary between author and reader should largely disappear" (Yankelovich et al. 21). One sign of the disappearance of boundaries between author and reader is the fact that the reader, not the author, largely determines how the reader moves through the system, for the reader can determine the order and principle of investigation. Intermedia has the potential, thus far only partially realized, to be a democratic or multicentered system in yet another way: as students who use the system contribute their comments and individual documents, the sharp division between author and reader that characterizes page-bound text begins to blur with several interesting implications: first, by contributing to the system, student users accept some responsibility for materials anyone can read; second, students thus establish a community of learning, demonstrating to themselves that a large part of any investigation rests on the work of others.

Although students, particularly beginning students, do not have sufficient knowledge of either primary materials or their contexts to create adequate treatments of more complex issues, they often produce excellent brief discussions of relatively limited, specific topics, such as aspects of technique in specific texts or ways in which one text relates to others. Although students in the survey contributed relatively little original material to *Context32*, those in English 61, the Victorian poetry seminar, contributed much more. Members of this and subsequent classes have created a wide range of materials including brief comparative essays, annotated bibliographies, analyses of particular passages, annotations to maps or other graphical materials illuminating individual works, and their own versions of concept maps and literary relation files. I offer as examples two pieces of student work that now have become part of the Intermedia materials: Kristen Langdon's "Relations of *In Memoriam* 60 to Other Sections" (Figure 3) and Jacqui Olkin's "Lady of Shalott" (Figure 5), another InterDraw file that takes the form of an overview or directory. I draw the reader's attention to the quality and amount of information in the materials created by these students and also to the fact that Olkin's contribution, which fulfilled an assignment during the opening weeks of the course, connects a Victorian poem to works she had read in other courses. Intermedia's emphasis upon connections and relations encourages students to integrate materials from a single course with everything else they know.

There is another form of democratization or absence of hierarchy: in hypertext systems, links inside and outside a text—intertextual and intratextual connections between points of text (including images)—become equivalent, thus bringing texts closer together and blurring the boundaries among them. Consider what happens to the distinction between intra- and intertextual links in Milton in a hypertext system like Intermedia. Examples of hypertext intratextual links could be created by Milton's various descriptions of himself as prophet or inspired

LITERARY RELATIONS

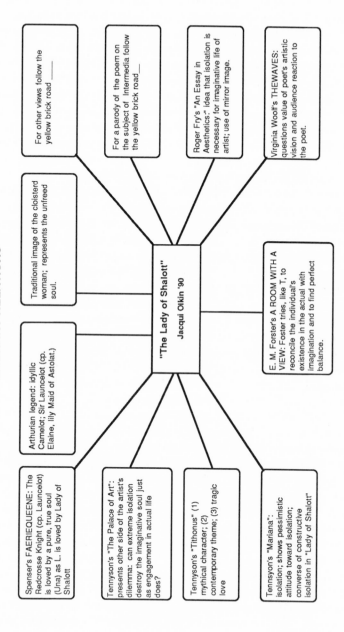

For other views follow the yellow brick road ____

For a parody of the poem on the subject of Intermedia follow the yellow brick road ____

Roger Fry's "An Essay in Aesthetics:" idea that isolation is necessary for imaginative life of artist; use of mirror image.

Virginia Woolf's THE WAVES: questions value of poet's artistic vision and audience reaction to the poet.

Traditional image of the cloisterd woman; represents the unfreed soul.

"The Lady of Shalott"
Jacqui Olkin '90

Arthurian legend: idyllic Camelot; Sir Launcelot (cp. Elaine, lily Maid of Astolat.)

Spenser's FAERIEQUEENE: The Redcrosse Knight (cp. Launcelot) is loved by a pure, true soul (Una) as L. is loved by Lady of Shalott

Tennyson's "The Palace of Art": presents other side of the artist's dilemma: can extreme isolation destroy the imaginative soul just as engagement in actual life does?

Tennyson's "Tithonus" (1) mythical character; (2) contemporary theme; (3) tragic love

Tennsyon's "Mariana": isolation; shows pessimistic attitude toward isolation; converse of constructive isolation in "Lady of Shalott"

E. M. Forster's A ROOM WITH A VIEW: Foster tries, like T, to reconcile the individual's existence in the actual with imagination and to find perfect balance.

FIGURE 5. A student contribution—a graphic document presenting a concept map of a single work: Jacqueline Olkin's "Lady of Shalott."

poet in *Paradise Lost* or by linking his citations to Gen. 3:15 within the poem. Intertextual links, in contrast, are exemplified by links between a particular passage in *Paradise Lost* that mentions prophecy and his other writings in prose or poetry that make similar points as well as those between this passage in the poem and biblical texts, scriptural commentaries throughout the ages, comparable or contrasting poetic statements by others, and scholarly comment by students of literature. Similarly, Miltonic citations of the biblical text about the heel of man crushing the serpent's head and being in turn bruised by the serpent link to the biblical passage and its traditional interpretations as well as to other literary allusions and scholarly comment upon all these subjects. Hypertext linking simply allows one to speed up the usual process of making connections while providing a means of graphing such transactions—if one can apply the word *simply* to such a radically transformative procedure. The speed with which one can move between passages and points in sets of texts promises to change the way we read and write, just as high-speed number-crunching computing changed various scientific fields by making possible investigations that before had required too much time or risk. We do not know all the ways hypertext will affect reading (and production) of texts, but one effect is already clear: the distinction between intratextuality and intertextuality will become harder to maintain than it is with book technology, and this crucial change comes from the fact that electronic linking permits the reader to move with equal facility between points inside a text and those outside of it. Once one can move with equal facility between the opening section of *Paradise Lost* and a passage in book 12 thousands of lines "away," or between that opening section and a particular anterior French text or modern scholarly comment, then, in an important sense, the discreteness of texts, which print culture creates, has radically changed and possibly disappeared.

These observations about hypertext suggest that computers bring us much closer to a culture whose qualities have more in common with those of preliterate humans than even Walter J. Ong has been willing to admit. In *Orality and Literacy* he argues that computers have brought us into what he terms an age of "secondary orality" that "has striking resemblances to the old [oral, preliterate culture] in its participatory mystique, its fostering of a communal sense, its concentration on the present moment, and even its use of formulas" (136). Nonetheless, although Ong finds interesting parallels between a computer culture and a purely oral one, he still insists, "The sequential processing and spatializing of the word, initiated by writing and raised to a new order of intensity by print, is further intensified by the computer, which maximizes commitment of the word to space and to (electronic) local motion and optimizes analytic sequentiality by making it virtually instantaneous" (136). In fact, hypertext systems, which insert every text into a web of relations, produce a very different effect, for they allow nonsequential reading and thinking.

Such nonsequential reading weakens the boundaries of the text, either correcting the artificial isolation of the text from its contexts or violating one of the chief qualities of the book, depending on one's point of view. Another possible result of hypertext may also be disconcerting. As Ong points out, books, unlike their authors, cannot really be challenged: "The author might be challenged if only he or she could be reached, but the author cannot be reached in any book. There is no way to refute a text. After absolutely total and devastating refutation, it says exactly the same thing as before. This is one reason why 'the book says' is popularly tantamount to 'it is true.' It is also one reason why books have been burnt. A text stating what the whole world knows is false will state falsehood forever, so long as the text exists" (79). The question arises, however, if hypertext situates texts in a field of other texts, can any individual work that has been addressed by another still speak so forcefully? One can imagine hypertext presentations of books (or the equivalent) in which the reader can call up all the reviews and comments on that book, which would then inevitably exist as part of a complex dialogue rather than as the embodiment of one voice or thought that speaks unceasingly and authoritatively.

As one might expect at this relatively early stage in the history of hypertext systems, those involved in developing them have devoted most attention to the simple fact of linking and to the effects upon discourse of such electronically linked text. Now we need to develop a rhetoric and stylistics of hypertext. To begin with, we must recognize that although hypertext redefines some of the basic characteristics of page-bound, printed discourse, such as the rigidly hierarchical distinction in scholarly works between a main text and its annotation, it still depends upon many of the same organizing principles that make page-bound discourse coherent and even pleasurable to read.

Designers of hypertext and hypermedia materials confront two related problems, the first of which is how to indicate the destination of links, and the second, how to welcome the user on arrival at that destination. Drawing upon the analogy of travel, one can say that the first problem concerns *exit* or *departure* information and the second *arrival* or *entrance* information. In both cases the designer must decide what users need to know at each end of a hypertext link to make use of what they find there. The general issue here is one of interpretation—

namely, how much interpretation in the form of encoding or markup must the designer-author attach to the points at which one both leaves and enters a text?[8]

Thoughts about Teaching with Intermedia

Developing the hypermedia materials for the survey and other courses has demanded greater self-awareness of my goals and methods as a teacher. In particular, my work on this project has made me think much more both about my role as teacher and about the kinds of information that students could use. Normally in a survey like this instructors have the chance to provide some background, maybe a few interesting facts about the author's life, and some broadly sketched aspects of the political, religious, philosophical, and scientific changes taking place at the time the work was written, but most of their time and energy must be devoted to close readings of the text and teaching the students how to read. Intermedia offers more opportunities and hence more choices. When providing the materials for a hypermedia system that can give the student far more detailed information than possible by other means, the teacher must think carefully about the nature of the materials. One keeps encountering questions not encountered in teaching a course like this before, because in most cases there had been no possibility of presenting that information. This system creates an opportunity to do things not possible before, both in terms of quantity and quality, so one must continually rethink what one wants. This rethinking, like the actual preparation of materials, has turned out to be both extremely exhilarating and extremely demanding.

The semester before I joined the Intermedia project I had already decided to move away from my usual mixture of lectures and discussions to a different format. Convinced that students, particularly at the beginning undergraduate level, benefit most from discussions they initiate themselves, I experimented with ways of promoting such discussion. Finally, announcing that students had to take larger responsibility for their education, I warned my section of English 32 that at the next class meeting I would not speak for the first twenty-five minutes of class, and I gave them reading and discussion questions related to that week's assigned reading. At the next class meeting I took a seat among the students and waited. For the first three or four minutes no one spoke, but finding the silence more painful than the embarrassment of speaking in the presence of their fellow students, several asked questions, offered interpretations, and argued with others. At times the discussion lagged, and as one whose many years of teaching had trained him to leap into these pauses in discussion and "help" the students, I found sitting quietly extraordinarily difficult. To my surprise, I discovered that the quality of discussions was far better than I had been able to achieve using the usual Socratic method, and the improvement derived in part from students' willingness to argue with one another. When I entered class discussions about halfway through each session to summarize or suggest new directions, students immediately displayed their former passivity and hesitancy once again, but after a few weeks I found that I could interrupt briefly without markedly affecting the quality of discussion. My teaching assistant and I noted that frequently these beginning students would discuss issues with sophistication that one had previously only encountered in graduate seminars. Nonetheless, despite all this obvious improvement, the student-directed discussions could not solve certain fundamental problems. The most troublesome to me was that students had no way to obtain information they did not yet know they would need for discussion. Intermedia offered an obvious solution to this major problem.

Intermedia clearly does not require any one particular philosophy or technique of teaching, for the successful biology course that employed it had a more traditional lecture format as, on occasion, does my seminar on Victorian poetry. One aspect of my precomputer experiment with student-directed discussion does seem to mesh perfectly with Intermedia: in both cases, students take more responsibility for their education. As a result, in relation to student-directed discussion and to use of *Context32,* my role as instructor, the OPA evaluators observed, becomes more that of coach than teacher. And as students contribute increasingly to the corpus of documents in *Context32,* the distance continues to narrow between teacher and student, author and reader, designer and user.

Hypertext and the University

By the end of the first term in which English 32 used Intermedia materials, *Context32* consisted of approximately 1,000 documents and 1,300 links, and since then the number of both has continued to grow. Thus far, *Context32* has required the efforts of myself, three graduate students, and a postdoctoral student, and a great deal more effort will be needed to add new materials to make the system match our expectations. Obviously, such hypertext materials demand a great deal of effort to prepare, so designing and creating all these materials for a single course hardly represents a practical enterprise. Fortunately, there is no reason why such materials should be created solely for a single course, and there are a number of reasons why Intermedia should be available to all students and faculty.

For a hypertext system like *Context32* to achieve anything like its full potential it cannot remain course-specific. In fact, I have already used it for English 61, Victorian Poetry, and (to a lesser degree) for English 137, Anglo-American Nonfiction, a course covering writers from Swift and Johnson to Didion and Chatwin. In Spring 1988, when I again used *Context32* to support the survey course for which it was originally designed, I also used it for a graduate seminar in Victorian poetry. *Context32* now needs to extend beyond my courses and indeed beyond those taught by the English department to history, classics, art history, and other disciplines, all of whose materials could support one another.[9]

NOTES

1. Englebart demonstrated the general viability of electronic hypertext with AUGMENT, which dates from the late 1960s. Using FRESS, a word-processing language he had created with hypertext capabilities, Andries van Dam also carried out a seminal experiment in hypertext and cooperative learning as part of a poetry course at Brown University in the 1970s. For FRESS, see Carmody et al.; for a description of the poetry experiment, see Catano.

2. Intermedia is the culmination of two years of intense effort by a large team of developers at IRIS led by Norman Meyrowitz. I would especially like to thank him and Nicole Yankelovich, our project coordinator, for their continual resourcefulness, tireless effort, and unfailing good humor. I would also like to thank Helen DeAndrade, John Bowe, Mike Braca, Tim Catlin, Brian Chapin, Steve Drucker, Page Elmore, Charlie Evett, Matt Evett, Nan Garrett, Allan Gold, Ed Grossman, Bernard Haan, Marty Michael, Karen Smith, Tom Stambaugh, Dan Stone, and Ken Utting for their contributions to the Intermedia system and David Cody, Glenn Everett, Suzanne Keen Morley, Kathryn Stockton, and Robert Sullivan for their contributions to *Context32*.

The work described in this essay was sponsored in part by a grant from the Annenberg/CPB Project and a joint-study contract with IBM.

3. I do not wish to suggest either that *all* CAI projects encourage such passivity or that only hypertext presentations succeed with complex subjects. Three outstandingly successful projects come immediately to mind. For Lougee's Stanford University role-playing game for the Apple Macintosh, see Lougee; for Miller's Carnegie-Mellon University *Great American History Machine* see Miller; and see Jones and Smith's University of Illinois *Computer Assisted Video-Disc Instruction for Chemistry*.

4. Yankelovich, Landow, and Cody, 1. According to Yankelovich, Meyrowitz, and van Dam, "hyper*text* document system allows authors to link together only information blocks created with a single application, a text editor,

while a hyper*media* document system provides linking capabilities between heterogeneous blocks created with different applications such as a painting program, a chart package, or a music editor" (19).

5. Yankelovich, Landow, and Cody, 15; see this article for detailed descriptions of Intermedia software and the equipment required to run it.

6. During the half-semester after the grant was received and then during the next semester the course was offered, Kenneth T. Anderson, Gail Bader, and Patrick McQuillan carried out extensive surveys of the entire process. The results are described in *Intermedia: A Case Study of Innovation in Higher Education*, a 200-page report to the Annenberg/CPB Project, so here I will only provide a summary of methods and results.

7. For a similar view of intellectual decentering, see also Althusser. I would like to thank my colleague Neil Lazarus for suggesting this similarity.

8. For first attempts to formulate the rules for both departure and arrival rhetorics demanded by this new form of text, see Landow, "Relationally Encoded Links" and "The Rhetoric of Hypermedia," 39-64.

9. One way to extend this body of materials beyond its present narrow bounds lies in a consortium of educators from institutions of higher learning who would write materials and guide the system's growth. With a planning grant from the Annenberg/CPB Project, IRIS is currently working out the details of such a multi-institutional consortium that would create a hypermedia body of materials supporting the teaching of courses including English and other literatures, the history of science and technology, cultural, political, and social history, and the life and physical sciences.

WORKS CITED

Althusser, Louis. *For Marx.* Trans. Ben Brewster. London: Verso, 1979. 131-51.

Barthes, Roland. *S/Z.* Trans. Richard Miller. New York: Hill and Wang, 1974.

Beeman, William O., Kenneth T. Anderson, Gail Bader, James Larkin, Anne P. McClard, Patrick McQuillan, and Mark Shields. *Intermedia: A Case Study of Innovation in Higher Education.* Providence, R.I.: Office of Program Analysis, Institute for Research in Information and Scholarship, Brown University, 1987.

Beeman, William O., et al. "Assessment Plan for a Network of Scholar's Workstations in a University Environment: A New Medium for Research and Education." Providence, R.I.: Institute for Research in Information and Scholarship, Brown University, 1985.

Bush, Vannevar. "As We May Think." *Atlantic Monthly* 176 (July 1945): 101-8.

Carmody, Stephen, et al. "A Hypertext Editing System for the /360." In *Pertinent Concepts in Computer Graphics.* Ed. M. Faiman and J. Nievergelt. Urbana: University of Illinois Press, 1969. 63-88.

Catano, James. "Poetry and Computers: Experimenting with Communal Text." *Computers and the Humanities* 13 (1979): 269-75.

Conklin, Jeff. "Hypertext: An Introduction and Survey." *IEEE Computer* (Sept. 1987): 17-41.

————. "A Survey of Hypertext." MCC technical report no. STP-356-86, Oct. 23, 1986.

Derrida, Jacques. "Structure, Sign, and Play in the Discourse of the Human Sciences." In *The Structuralist Controversy: The Languages of Criticism and the Sciences of Man*. Ed. Richard Macksey and Eugenio Donato. Baltimore: Johns Hopkins University Press, 1972. 247-72.

Garrett, Nan, and Karen Smith. "Building a Timeline Editor from Prefab Parts: The Architecture of an Object-Oriented Application." In *OOPSLA '86 Proceedings*. Portland, Ore., 1986.

Kahn, Paul. "Objective and Subjective Links: An Application of Hypertext to the Comparative Analysis of Chinese Literature." Providence, R.I.: Institute for Research in Information and Scholarship, Brown University, 1987.

Landow, George P. "*Context32:* Using Hypermedia to Teach Literature." In *Proceedings of the 1987 IBM Academic Information Systems University AEP Conference*. Milford, Conn.: IBM Academic Information Systems, 1987. 30-39.

————. "Course Assignments Using Hypertext: The Example of Intermedia." Providence, R.I.: Institute for Research in Information and Scholarship, Brown University, 1988.

————. "Relationally Encoded Links and the Rhetoric of Hypertext." *Hypertext '87*. Chapel Hill, N.C., 1987. 331-44.

————. "The Rhetoric of Hypermedia: Some Rules for Authors." NERCOMP 1 (1989).

Landow, George P., David Cody, Glenn Everett, Kathyrn Stockton, and Robert Sullivan. *Context32: A Web of English Literature*. Providence, R.I.: Institute for Research in Information and Scholarship, Brown University, 1986.

Larson, J. "A Visual Approach to Browsing in a Database Environment." *IEEE Computer* (June 1986).

Lougee, Carolyn C. "The Would-Be Gentleman: A Historical Simulation of the France of Louis XIV." *SICGUE Outlook* 18 (1986): 15-19.

McLuhan, Marshall. *The Gutenberg Galaxy: The Making of Typographic Man*. Toronto: University of Toronto Press, 1962.

————. *Understanding Media: The Extensions of Man*. New York: McGraw-Hill, 1964.

Meyrowitz, Norman. "Intermedia: The Architecture and Construction of an Object-Oriented Hypermedia System and Applications Framework." In *OOPSLA '86 Proceedings*. Portland, Ore., 1986.

————. "The Intermedia System: Requirements." Providence, R.I.: Institute for Research in Information and Scholarship, Brown University, 1985.

Miller, David W. "The Great American History Machine." In *Proceedings of the 1986 IBM Academic Information Systems University AEP Conference "Tools for Learning."* 5 vols. Milford, Conn.: IBM Academic Information Systems, 1986. I, 97-107.

Morgan, Thaïs E. "Is There an Intertext in This Text?: Literary and Interdisciplinary Approaches to Intertextuality." *American Journal of Semiotics* 3 (1985): 1-40.

Ong, Walter J. *Orality and Literacy: The Technologizing of the Word.* London: Methuen, 1982.

Scholes, Robert. *Textual Power: Literary Theory and the Teaching of English.* New Haven: Yale University Press, 1985.

Yankelovich, Nicole. "Hypermedia Bibliography." Providence, R.I.: Institute for Research in Information and Scholarship, Brown University, 1987.

———. "INTERMEDIA: A System for Linking Multimedia Documents." IRIS technical report no. 86-2. Providence, R.I.: Institute for Research in Information and Scholarship, Brown University, 1986.

Yankelovich, Nicole, Bernard Haan, and Stephen Drucker. "Connections in Context: The Intermedia System." Providence, R.I.: Institute for Research in Information and Scholarship, Brown University, 1987.

Yankelovich, Nicole, George P. Landow, and David Cody. "Creating Hypermedia Materials for English Literature Students." *SIGCUE Outlook* 19 (1987): 12-25.

Yankelovich, Nicole, Norman Meyrowitz, and Andries van Dam. "Reading and Writing the Electronic Book." *IEEE Computer* 18 (1985): 15-30.

PART THREE

Reading and Writing Otherwise

LORI H. LEFKOVITZ

The Subject of
Writing within the Margins

Theory

This essay is about the teaching of reading in writing courses, and it is at least implicitly about questions of gender, race, and class as they impinge upon the teaching of writing.[1] I will suggest that semiotic theory be used in writing courses, and that theory—with its elevated connotations in the academy—and so-called remedial writing—which connotes an underclass—may be brought together to correct some of our prejudices and help us confront social questions that show up in the writing classroom. Playing with several senses of the terms *subject* and *marginality,* I will explore ambiguities related to questions of remedial writing instruction. For example: is it more empowering to teach students a recognized canon or an anticanon? If academic institutions marginalize writing classes and writing students, should this marginalization be celebrated or should the marginal work instead to center themselves? I will answer "both" to these questions by suggesting a sample syllabus that raises questions about language deprivation.

The "subject" or topic of my title refers to the topic of this essay: writing or composition courses. The "subject" of my title refers as well to the person who is created by composition courses in the sense that writing courses can be deemed successful if the students are finally able to find selves on paper who are articulate, eloquent, and "self"-possessed. My assumption is that there is no core "self," but rather that one's subjectivity is constituted variously in language. Writing of his proposed analyses in *The Archaeology of Knowledge,* Foucault states that

> instead of referring back to *the* synthesis or *the* unifying function of *a* subject, the various enunciative modalities manifest his dispersion. To

the various statuses, the various sites, the various positions that he can occupy or be given when making a discourse. To the discontinuity of the planes from which he speaks. And if these planes are linked by a system of relations, this system is not established by the synthetic activity of a consciousness identical with itself, dumb and anterior to all speech, but by the specificity of a discursive practice. . . . Thus conceived, discourse is not the majestically unfolding manifestation of a thinking, knowing, speaking subject, but, on the contrary, a totality, in which the dispersion of the subject and his discontinuity with himself may be determined.[2]

Foucault's assumptions of the subject's multiplicity and self-discontinuity in discourse suggest that students who are helped to see the possibility for manifold selves in language will be able to compose these selves more effectively. In this sense, my "subject" is the subject of a sentence, the subject of the verb that, as such, asserts its subjectivity.[3]

But the "subject" in another sense, one subject to another kind of sentence—the sentences delivered by kings or courts—is subjected or subjugated. Again Foucault: "At the heart of the procedures of discipline, it [the examination] manifests the subjection of those who are perceived as objects and the objectification of those who are subjected. The superimposition of power relations and knowledge relations assumes in the examination all its visible brilliance."[4] Because I mean this sense of subject too, to be a subject is to be powerful (the subject who wields power rather than is its object, the subject rather than the object of the verb), and it is also to be powerless (to be subjected, subjugated, subject to king, law, rule of the other who holds the power to subject you).

The metaphor of "marginality" that analogizes socialization to textualization is available in the work of Jacques Derrida.[5] It has since been developed and adapted by feminist critics and theorists and by other readers who recognize a division between the language and discourses of power and the language of those who are "marginalized," presumed to be "outsider," by the dominant discourse. Josette Féral, for example, writes in the "Powers of Difference" that

To put discourse into question is to reject the existing order. It is to renounce, in effect, the identity principle, the principles of unity and resemblance which allow for the constitution of phallocentric society. It means choosing marginality (with an emphasis on *margins*) in order to designate one's difference, a difference no longer conceived of as an inverted image or as a double, but as alterity, multiplicity, heterogeneity.

It means laying claim to an absolute difference, posited not within the norms but against and *outside* the norms.[6]

In another article in *The Future of Difference,* "For the Etruscans: Sexual Difference and Artistic Production—The Debate over a Female Aesthetic," Rachel Blau DuPlessis and "Members of Workshop 9" compare women's writing to modernism and postmodernism on the basis of a shared "marginality": "*What I'd like to try to understand and explain to other people* (you yourselves are the riddle) *is how the* form *of women's writing is, if ambiguously,* (of double [sometime duplicitous] needs) *nonetheless profoundly revolutionary (as are, in their confusing ways, modernism and post-modernism, also written from positions of marginality to the dominant culture).*" Barbara Herrnstein Smith uses the metaphor differently in the title of her book *On the Margins of Discourse: The Relation of Literature to Language,* suggesting there that literature in general functions on the margins of ordinary language.[7]

Clearly the connection between marginal social groups and what Féral calls marginal writing is relevant to a consideration of writing curricula. This connection raises questions for the writing teacher as he or she designs a reading program and evaluates student essays: does one identify and proudly celebrate marginal writing, as Féral does, perhaps name it "revolutionary," or does one teach as the "margins of discourse," the niceties, the philosophical complexities that Smith might claim distinguish and elevate literary writing?

Writing as an academic discipline, students who are disciplined to write, and wild children may alike be construed as marginalized, rhetorically impoverished subjects. On the basis of such a construction, I want to build a case for teaching writing courses that have a unified subject matter grounded in a textual tradition. Any number of themes would serve my pedagogic ends and the needs of my constituency. The example that I will use, because I have used it in the classroon, is a thematic treatment of the figure of the wild child. Although I will have something to say about the syllabus, assignments, and lessons of the course, my larger purpose here is to press the urgency of this teaching strategy. To do so, I appeal to the authority of some basic assumptions of semiotic theory. But making my case necessitates a move from theory to practice, a move that we make whenever we enter the space of the classroom.

Despite the fact of teaching as practice, teachers are stereotypically defensive about not engaging in political practice. Setting up a related problematic for his book *Criticism and Social Change,* Frank Lentricchia writes that "those of us in the university who conceive of our political work . . . not as activity intrinisic, specific to our intellectuality . . . are being crushed by feelings of guilt and occupational alienation. We have let our beliefs and our discourse be invaded by the eviscerating notion that politics is something that somehow goes on somewhere else." He continues to insist that this notion is more than a little damaging: "To believe as university humanists that our political work can only be in the streets, or in the factories, or at best in writing essays and books about Reagan, Vietnam, or the Middle East is to leave traditional cultural power to those forces that wish to engender in us the feeling that we are ineffectual angels. The inside/outside distinction is killing us."[8] Given the assumption that we wish we engaged in practice more than we do, it is ironic that in this age of theory, generally to talk about practice at academic meetings or in volumes on literary theory can be embarrassing. If we are to challenge effectively such oppositions as theory and practice, scholar and teacher, literature and writing, world and academy, then it is important to confront this embarrassment, not as a psychological condition, but as the energy that keeps these categories divided, a product of textualization that inevitably locates some subjects embarrassingly close to the margins.

In most colleges the state of things is as follows: Writing courses have no recognized subject matter. Writing courses are part of English departments, though their marginality is evidenced by the numbers and titles that codify them. Writing may be English 1, 2, or 6 beside Romantic Poetry (English 200) or Semiotic Theory (English 2000). English 1, 2, and 6 are taught by "staff," while English 200 and 2000 are taught by professors with identifiably human, and sometimes even famous, names. "Staff" is not eligible for tenure or promotion or health insurance. Writing, a subject with no subject matter, is marginally English (the courses do not count toward a major in the subject of English); its teachers are marginally faculty, and often the students— the writing subjects—are on the margins too. English 2 or 6 may be populated by freshmen who are taking a course required of all entrants into the system, but English 1 is often named remedial, a required course for those who failed a writing assessment test. When I taught this course during my first year as a graduate student at Brown University, I was teaching numbers of men on the football team, and a disproportionate number of my students were on financial aid. When I later taught part-time at Queens College, CUNY, the remedial course was populated largely by immigrants. These people being subjected to the discipline of writing enter a discipline that enforces their own marginality in American culture. Small wonder that both staff and students desire to be closer to the center of the system.

Certainly the system is just a construct, and center and margins are just metaphors, but the material situation that these metaphors describe is real. I have already elaborated on some of the implications of these metaphors, but for my purposes here the center is where the power is. To be on the margins is to be in a social class and a classroom that embarrasses oneself. In such a class, all students want to learn is how to get out.

We are all implicated in the systems in which we teach. The problem is that to teach students to get out of their class (in its limited and sometimes larger sense) is to teach them to respect the boundaries that put us all there in the first place. And when we teach the so-called canon, we find these boundaries encoded in the very texts we teach. Given this situation, what materials do we use and what stance do we assume with respect to the literature? In *Criticism and Social Change*, Frank Lentricchia discusses the teaching of reading in a way that raises further questions about the teaching of writing:

> The activist intellectual needs a theory of reading that will instigate a culturally suspicious, trouble-making readership. Whether or not one calls oneself a Marxist, one could, I'd say one should, always check one's effectivity as a teacher of the literary classics by asking oneself the following questions: Does one's approach to the text enable or dis-enable—encourage or discourage—oneself and one's students and readers to spot, confront, and work against the political horrors of one's time?[9]

Beginning from the premise that literature should no longer be treated as a vehicle for sacred truths but rather as a vehicle for historical values, Robert Scholes writes in *Textual Power* that we must stop "teaching literature" and start "studying text." And because text must be studied from some perspective, students need to be provided with "the skill and knowledge" that will enable them to "determine their own interests, both individual and collective."[10] The distinction between skill and knowledge has been problematic for the subject of writing. Writing has had no proper subject because it is knowledge of a skill that we are presumably after. It is less clear, however, in what the skill of writing lies: grammar? the manufacture of subjectivities? Moveover, the distinction between individuals and collectivites begs the question of how one establishes the boundary between them.

The confusions underlie some of the theoretical debates on writing instruction. For example, Mina Shaughnessy offers a program for basic writers in *Errors and Expectations* that focuses on the acquisition of skills.[11] To teach people how to produce valued writing, writing that earns money, they must learn the rules that govern such writing, and they must learn them quickly, before they are graded as failures by teachers of more advanced classes.

John Rouse criticizes this emphasis on skills in an essay entitled "The Politics of Composition." In a developed analysis of Shaughnessy's approach to students, texts, and grammar, Rouse determines that this emphasis on skill ignores the socialization of the individuals who are likely to find themselves in Shaughnessy's remedial writing course. He concludes:

> The difficulties we have with these young people, then, lie not in their language itself, certainly not in any lack of grammar, but rather in their social experience, in the habits of feeling and thought they have learned. What should be the context of social experience in our classrooms? What should be the values implicit there? The answers we give will express not only our views of teaching but also of what society should be. Any decision about language teaching is a moral and political decision.[12]

Rouse asks whose expectations (whose values?) the title *Errors and Expectations* is addressing. Learning rules forces students into a position of passivity and submission. Rouse is disturbed that we study text only after we have created, and I am borrowing Foucault's term, "docile bodies." Foucault writes that "a body is docile that may be subjected, used, transformed and improved." The school, like the prison and the hospital or the asylum which emerge at close historical moments, creates docile bodies through discipline. Two kinds of discipline apply: corporal discipline, or punishment, and academic disciplines, or taxonomies. "Discipline produces subjected and practiced bodies, 'docile' bodies."[13]

From another political perspective we hear the opposite complaint. Ewa Thompson writes in *Chronicles of Culture* that we must save the humanities from the new intellectuals who teach students to question fundamental assumptions about reality before they teach the values of Western civilization themselves.[14] The more recent formulations of this debate come under the banner of "cultural literacy."[15] In the name of empowering students deprived of "crucial" cultural information, proponents of "cultural literacy" would impose a canon of great works in the classrooms of basic readers and writers. The nagging questions are, of course, who determines what is a great work and which values make it great. The project of "cultural literacy" as we have all heard it advocated by politicians and academicians threatens the teaching of critical thinking. Interestingly, those on both sides of this debate insist that their position serves to empower the less educated "class." One position prefers to teach the information in the Bible, for example, because the Bible is a "great book" and educated people know what it contains; the alternative view is to teach a method of analysis (what one analyzes is not so much the point initially) that will enable students to read critically and evaluate any text when they confront it.

These debates point to a problem that asserts itself in the composition classroom: in helping students position themselves with respect to texts, what relation should be established between teaching skills and knowledge? I faced this question when an Asian woman not long in America responded to the first writing assignment of the semester in beautifully poetic prose. Perhaps she was simply translating literally from her native Chinese into English. My own unfamiliarity with Chinese led me to perceive poetry. Her unfamiliarity with English led her to disrespect the margins of the page. Punctuation appeared at the beginning of lines, and lines began and ended with apparent arbitrariness. I worried that enforcing the rule of the margins would somehow interfere with the poetry of her discourse.

Similarly, the relation between valued writing and writing of value impressed me when I participated in a reading of college English papers being judged for Bedford writing prizes.[16] The submissions came from teachers all over America who sent what they regarded as the best of their students' essays. The serious silence of a room full of New York City college writing teachers engaged in reading was broken when someone muttered, "another grandmother bites the dust." We laughed our recognition because indeed the presence of a grandparent in the first paragraph of an essay was like a smoking gun: the beloved relative was sure to be dead by the essay's conclusion. There may be many ways to explain why this topic was so frequently chosen by students, but why was it so frequently selected by teachers? It occurred to me then that what American college teachers often value in writing is writing that expresses the right values. In this case the sentimental construction of the family and nostalgia for tradition are also the values of the right.

Designing curricula that are both intertextual and that focus topically on questions of marginalization (where and how texts fix a culture's boundaries) seems to me to handle these practical matters and theoretical disputes, because such oppositions as knowledge and skill and individuals and collectivities themselves provide the subject matter of our courses. In effect, I am suggesting that we foreground rather than mystify the extent to which the teaching of writing has always been a semiotic enterprise. Literature teachers may have sanctified what we know to be products of people and history, but with varying degrees of self-consciousness, what has been taught in composition classes are rules and modes of discourse (codifications), imitation of coded language, and the production of specifically cultural artifacts. Language as a signifying system, coding and textualization, and the relation of reading and writing are among the special topics of writing courses and semiotics courses, English 2 and 2000.

Practice

Producers of texts are necessarily critics of texts. The acquisition of writing skills is the acquisition of textual knowledge. Basic writing courses should, therefore, teach intertextuality so that the dialogic character of the writing enterprise is clear and so that cultural codes may be recognized as such by virtue of their repeated appearance in the space of a semester.

Michael Holquist, in his translation of Bakhtin's *The Dialogic Imagination: Four Essays,* offers this useful definition of "dialogism": "Everything means, is understood, as part of a greater whole—there is a constant interaction between meanings, all of which have the potential of conditioning others. Which will affect the other, how it will do so and in what degree is what is actually settled at the moment of utterance. This dialogic imperative, mandated by the pre-existence of the language world relative to any of its current inhabitants, insures that there can be no actual monologue."[17] Organizing materials that are intertextual, that is, choosing books that speak to one another and shed light on one another, is my first principle.

The second principle is that the course's subject address specifically the subject of marginality and language. We want to make students participants in the dialogic writing enterprise and self-conscious about the stakes. To teach students to write within the margins of the page and the culture, to obey the rules of the dominant discourse, and to be aware of the possibilities for challenging the placement of margins, we need to make the margins themselves visible. If this goal can be approached through syllabus design, then a first writing course will have a recognized and important subject, and the subject of writing itself will resist marginalization.

The "subject" of the wild child meets these criteria. The wild child is the course's subject because this figure has a history in representation that challenges our most fundamental assumptions about who we are and how we are supposed to live. Most important, speculations about children isolated in nature—whether these speculations are philosophical, scientific, or fantastic—share a concern for the role that language plays in empowering people. The history of representations of the wild child teaches that the better able we are to write and speak, the more highly we will be regarded; we discover that an abiding cultural prejudice favors the literate.

Among many suitable texts I chose Longus's third-century Greek romance, *Daphnis and Chloe,* Shakespeare's *The Tempest,* brief selections from Montaigne, Hobbes, and Rousseau, all concerning definitions of human nature and natural humans. I chose such "canonical" texts because we empower students by familiarizing them with works that are well known. But these are not the only kinds of texts deemed interesting by the syllabus. We read Itard's scientific reports on the wild boy of Aveyron, and we saw Truffaut's film adaptation. We read Brontë's *Wuthering Heights,* Brownings's "Caliban upon Setebos," the Mowgli stories from Kipling's *Jungle Books,* Burroughs's *Tarzan of the Apes,* Ted Hughes's poem "Wodwo," Adrienne Rich's "Meditations for a Savage Child," and Peter Handke's play *Kaspar.* We read from sensationalist newspapers, and we looked at comic strips. We found wild children in many environments.

Students wrote regularly in answer to two kinds of exercises: imitation and synthesis. Examples of the former, what has traditionally been called "creative writing," included writing a new ending to *Daphnis and Chloe* consistent with the style and assumptions of the original. Students learn to imitate voices that have been traditionally valued, and they learn that voice is a matter of imitation. After reading *The Tempest* and the philosophical essays but before reading Browning's "Caliban," students wrote an essay on nature, nurture, and God from the perspective of Caliban. In this way, they had been in the poet's position before they faced his difficult text. Students could see Browning as a student like themselves, one who also faced a writing task, one that they had already tried. They were encouraged to evaluate Browning's solution, and while most agreed that the professional poet had achieved a formal success, many of my students preferred the ideas expressed in their own responses. Browning, one student argued, did not appreciate the sympathy with which Shakespeare treated Caliban.

Students rewrote an entry from Itard's science reports from the perspective of the housekeeper. This exercise is meant to convey that because texts are not sacred, they may be shamelessly tampered with, and an author's perspective should be continually scrutinized. Before reading *Wuthering Heights,* which is then told from the perspective of the housekeeper, students described a childhood injustice from their own experience, indicating their response and what that response said about their own characters. Because this is a writing course, every text was seen as providing an opportunity for a written response, and these writing students thereby entered into a dialogue with a textual tradition.

Intermittently, students wrote analytic essays, but always treating two texts together, accounting for continuity and innovation in terms of changing historical assumptions. Such comparative analysis discourages students from treating the text under consideration as a timeless embodiment of truth. Just as their writing speaks to books, so books speak to other books. I suggested titles for papers that invited no single thesis. These included "The Nature of Nurture and the Nurture of Nature," "The Nature of Love and the Love of Nature," and "Servants of Freedom and the Freedom of Servitude." Such oppositions indicated to students that what had been contraries in one context became identities in another. We looked at apparent dichotomies to discover how changing assumptions about nature resulted in changing perceptions of children deprived of what was recognized, at a given moment, to be culture.

Responding to Itard's paternal efforts to teach Victor language, the Chinese woman whom I mentioned above wrote in a class diary entry: "I am a lazy student, and because I am lazy I am hurting my mother. If I were like other American teenagers, I would have written that I am hurting myself. I wish that I were home in China. Here, I am the wild child." This response exemplifies that students came to understand that culture governs much of what we take for granted in our lives and that cultural assumptions are expressed in our use of language. To recognize how one's own discourse would differ from a dominant discourse involves reading, writing, and acting from a position of seized authority. Students marginalized because of gender, race, or class discovered that because they are "wild," they may name themselves differently than books do.

It has been objected that this is too full a syllabus for what is usually regarded as a foundations course, with all that such a designation implies about limits. But because students consider a limited number of cultural codes, their attention is directed accordingly. The goal of such a class is not a full treatment of textual systems, because writing courses may still distinguish themselves from literature courses. I will illustrate with a small example from what is arguably the longest and most literarily complex text of the course, *Wuthering Heights*.

Early in the novel, Nelly Dean is grooming her young charge Heathcliff, apparently trying to refashion his soul as well as his body.[18] Heathcliff, feeling competitive with Edgar Linton, expresses a wish for Linton's fair hair and blue eyes; he envies Linton's aristocratic appearance because he envies the privileges that come with Linton's high birth, privileges that he fears will win Linton the coveted girl, Cathy. Nelly urges Heathcliff to switch codes: he must imagine himself the son of an Indian Princess and Chinese Emperor. His own darkness is not a sign of descent from poor English gypsies but the sign of exotic wealth. A passage such as this one may resonate for my students with passages from any of the works of the semester. They may remember that Daphnis and Dorcon competed in similar fashion for Chloe's kiss, and that Nelly's imagined scenario derives from pastoral romance where all foundlings are unusually articulate, and therefore lost nobility. And Nelly is not the first to recognize that beauty, with its attendant powers, is manufactured by rhetoric, because the beauty competition in *Daphnis and Chloe* is verbal rather than visual. Dorcon and Daphnis each assert their beauty and superiority by appeal to codes: when Dorcon says that Daphnis is as dark as a wolf, Daphnis too switches registers, saying that Dorcon is white as a lily town lady, while he himself is dark like the hyacinths. In the code of flowers to which Daphnis appeals, hyacinths are preferred.

Although both stories thus make the claim that rhetoric defines truth (knowledge is power), the stories define the natural so differently that students must discover as well that power is knowledge. With changing economies, truth (here the truth of what is wild and what is beautiful) changes. Students recognize that Heathcliff, relatively late in the tradition of wild men, gives Nelly a typically Victorian response when he says, in effect, that wishing will not make it so. In an emerging democracy, we are all foundlings who must make ourselves; no royal parents will materialize to prove that this peasant is noble.

While Nelly's advice thus seems outmoded, students can consult the limited cultural encyclopedia provided by the course to discover that this servant's ideas are, at the same time, more current than those of the narrow-minded families she serves.[19] Hobbes's brutish "man of nature" had been overthrown by Rousseau's "noble savage," a concept that made the wild boy of Aveyron particularly interesting when he stepped out of the woods in 1799. Itard's reports betray his assumption that a good grooming and language will transform his own savage into the equal of any noble. This simple scene from *Wuthering Heights* represents a Victorian voice within a long historical dialogue.

When young Linton arrives, he looks at Heathcliff's long hair and calls him a colt (as Dorcon, also in animal code, called Daphnis a wolf). But since linguistic ability is no longer inherited, Heathcliff, unlike Daphnis, lacks the vocabulary with which to phrase an appropriate response. Instead, he expresses himself in the violent manner of the wild boy of Aveyron. Heathcliff earns banishment, but ultimately acquires, perhaps through savage means, the money to buy out the lands of the Lintons. The aristocracy moves to the margins when the industrious foundling takes his revenge (not coincidentally, at the height of the industrial revolution).

The vocabulary of the course is thus continually reconsidered. Class, eloquence, and grace were once matters of birth, in the province of the divine, though by the twentieth century definitions had changed such that grace and class became skills learned in the classroom. How fragile is this myth? Literatures of colonialism—*The Jungle Books* and *Tarzan*—reveal themselves to be reactionary. Because of their low birth, Dorcon and Caliban (initially) lack linguistic power and are potential rapists; Tarzan, though raised by apes, is a linguist, and when he is tempted to take Jane by force, his high birth triumphs over his low breeding, and he shelters her instead.

As the boundaries that define knowledge shift with changing historical circumstances, students may see that woman is persistently encoded textually as a prize that may either be won through graceful rhetoric or seized by inarticulate savagery. Female writers, perhaps assuming the role of Jane, can produce their own texts that begin to challenge this construction of their sexuality. But they can do so only if they see these truths of the tradition as cultural constructs, if they learn to see themselves as subjects who have been subjugated in writing and who may assert their subjectivity by writing. Their own texts are treated on the same level as those which are printed and bound; they too are valuable and vehicles for value.

Some of the goals of the course are conservative: to provide an overview of a tradition and major genres by tracing the transfigurations of a subject who has long gripped the imagination, thereby familiarizing students with books known to an educated class; and to provide continuity in subject matter and variety in discursive models for writing. Other goals are differently liberating: to provide occasions for writing that is playful imitation on the assumption that successful reproductions both testify to viable readings of the original text and sharpen the skills of the novice artist; to provide occasions for writing about texts that function to integrate disparate material; to encourage an engaged and challenging relationship with the tradition; to demonstrate to students, in a way that is accessible to them, the workings of intertextuality, literary coding, and the relationship between literature and society; and finally, to engage students, through their own writing, in these vital processes of cultural and intellectual exchange.

In writing classes we must teach how the human subject is constructed in language (that is what writing is all about), and how the human subject can be marginalized by the discourse that we teach. Only if we teach our students not just how to write within the margins, but where the margins are, can they learn to use and subvert the discourse that enforces marginalization. We want to do more than theorize about textual operations; theory must be put in the service of teaching practice. Thus, we can use semiotics at the foundations of the curriculum. For each English 200 or 2000 there are dozens of English 1, 2, and 6: staff are more numerous than tenured professors. If we are to create a reasonable business for the two graduate students who take English 2000, then these two students have to be made ready to practice theory for the thousands who take English 1, 2, and 6.

NOTES

1. A briefer version of this essay was first delivered at the International Summer Institute for Semiotic and Structural Studies at Indiana University in 1985.

2. Michel Foucault, *The Archaeology of Knowledge and the Discourse on Language*, trans. A. M. Sheridan (New York: Harper and Row, 1972), pp. 54-55.

3. For Foucault's treatment of the relation between the subject and statements, ibid., pp. 95-96.

4. Michel Foucault, *Discipline and Punish: The Birth of the Prison*, trans. Alan Sheridan (New York: Random House, 1979), pp. 184-85.

5. Derrida's methods of reading suggest as well that the margin itself resists being fixed. In "Tympan," Derrida asks: "Under what conditions, then, could one *mark*, for a philosopheme in general, a *limit*, a margin that it could not infinitely reappropriate, *conceive* as its own, in advance engendering and interning the process of its expropriation (Hegel again, always), proceeding to its inversion by itself?" in *Margins of Philosophy*, trans. Alan Bass (Chicago: University of Chicago Press, 1982), p. xv. And later: "Can this text become the margin of a margin? Where has the body of the text gone when the margin is no longer a secondary virginity but an inexhaustible reserve, the stereographic activity of an entirely other ear?" (p. xxiii).

6. In *The Future of Difference*, ed. Hester Eisenstein and Alice Jardine (New Brunswick, N.J.: Rutgers University Press, 1985), p. 91.

7. DuPlessis quote ibid., p. 152; Barbara Herrnstein Smith, *On the Margins of Discourse* (Chicago: University of Chicago Press, 1978).

8. Frank Lentricchia, *Criticism and Social Change* (Chicago: University of Chicago Press, 1983), p. 7.

9. Ibid., pp. 11-12.

10. Robert Scholes, *Textual Power: Literary Theory and the Teaching of English* (New Haven: Yale University Press, 1985), pp. 12, 15.

11. Mina P. Shaughnessy, *Errors and Expectations: A Guide for the Teacher of Basic Writing* (New York: Oxford University Press, 1977).

12. John Rouse, "The Politics of Composition," *College English* 41, no. 1 (Sept. 1979): 1-12.

13. Cf. Michel Foucault, *Discipline and Punish: The Birth of the Prison*, pp. 136, 138; see also pp. 135-69. See also a related argument in Jacques Donzelot, *The Policing of Families*, trans. Robert Hurley (New York: Pantheon Books, 1979).

14. Ewa Thompson, "Saving the Humanities," *Chronicles of Culture: Letters and Arts, Morals and Manners* 9, no. 4 (April 1985): 4-5, 23.

15. Cf. *Salmagundi* 72 (Fall 1986), an issue partly devoted to "Cultural Literacy: Canon, Class, Curriculum," including contributions by Robert Scholes, E. D. Hirsch, J. Mitchell Morse, Marjorie Perloff, Elizabeth Fox-Genovese, and John P. Sisk.

16. The volume that resulted from this contest is Nancy Sommers and Donald McQuade, eds., *Student Writers at Work and in the Company of Other Writers: The Bedford Prizes* (New York: St. Martin's Press, 1986).

17. M. M. Bakhtin, *The Dialogic Imagination: Four Essays by M. M. Bakhtin,* trans. Michael Holquist (Austin: University of Texas Press, 1981), p. 426.

18. This analysis is more fully developed in my book, *The Character of Beauty in the Victorian Novel* (Ann Arbor, Mich.: UMI Research Press, 1987), pp. 115-56.

19. By cultural encyclopedia, I have in mind Umberto Eco's idea that reading always means consulting our culture for the information that we need to contextualize. See *Role of the Reader: Explorations in the Semiotics of Texts* (Bloomington: Indiana University Press, 1979).

NANCY R. COMLEY

Reading
and Writing Genders

In introductory literature and writing courses the use of reader-response
theory provides a natural start to the teaching of critical and analytical
reading and writing. Natural because starting with a consideration of
their initial responses to a text provides students with an entry to texts
previously denied them under New Critical strictures against subjectivity. However, reader-response theory and criticism, as Patrocinio
Schweikart has pointed out, has overlooked "the issues of race, class,
and sex, and [has given] no hint of conflicts, sufferings, and passions
that attend these realities" (35). As Schweikart so cogently puts it,
"reader-response criticism needs feminist criticism" (36). With its emphasis on re-vision, to use Adrienne Rich's term, feminist theory and
criticism has pointed the way to demystification of canonical texts, and
by taking reader-response theory another, and most important step,
has emphasized the politics of reading, pointing out the difficulty for
the woman reader contending with a canon that is male-oriented and
male-dominated. In *The Resisting Reader,* Judith Fetterley speaks of the
immasculation of the woman reader: "In such fictions, the female reader
is co-opted into participation in an experience from which she is explicitly excluded; she is asked to identify with a selfhood that defines
itself in opposition to her; she is required to identify against herself"
(xii). She calls upon the feminist critic to become "a resisting rather
than an assenting reader . . . to begin the process of exorcizing the male
mind that has been implanted in us" (xxii). To identify against oneself
is to devalue one's experience, and to place oneself—if one is a woman—
on the margins of (privileged) experience. "Male minds," or concepts
of masculinity, are partially shaped in our classrooms, for reading and
writing are certainly acts of gender construction. When students are
invited to see literature and writing as part of a cultural system that

helps to shape gender, they are likely to read and write more attentively, and they are likely to read and write in a new way.

Why is a new way necessary? Reading and writing in an academic setting adds further complications to the issue of gender construction. Because students are usually tested in some way on what they read, the form of the test determines the kind of reading that goes on. In an academic setting students almost always read for someone else, usually a teacher who stands above them perhaps literally, but certainly figuratively, in a power hierarchy in which the teacher is the holder of the "real meaning" of a literary text, as well as the dispenser of grades. This patriarchal condition prevails most often where New Critical reading and writing are still privileged. When students are asked to write, to produce critical texts about a literary work, they are encouraged to adopt an academic pseudogenderless discourse: "It would seem, when one considers the narrator of *The Great Gatsby*. . . ." The effect of this voice is to keep the reader outside the text, which is to say, to keep the reader's experience outside the text—especially if the reader is a woman. And especially if the canon in which she is immersed is predominantly, if not wholly, masculine.

Experience has recently proven to be a bone of critical contention, especially since Jonathan Culler, taking a deconstructionist stance, attempted to defer it in "Reading as a Woman." As Tania Modleski has pointed out, his motive "in calling this notion [women's experience] into question" is "to clear a space for male feminist interpretations of literary texts" (132). Culler latches onto Elaine Showalter's definition of feminist criticism concerned with "woman as reader—with woman as the consumer of male-produced literature, and with the way in which the hypothesis of a female reader changes our apprehension of a given text, awakening us to the significance of its sexual codes" ("Toward" 128). In her criticism of Culler's appropriation of Showalter's concept, Modleski finds the "notion of hypothetical woman reader" crucial in making "generalizations about the activity of reading. Yet it is equally important that we refer these generalizations to the experience of real women" (134). For Culler, however, "experience" is a "construct": "For a woman to read as a woman is not to repeat an identity or an experience that is given but to play a role she constructs with reference to her identity as a woman, which is also a construct, so that the series can continue: a woman reading as a woman reading as a woman. The noncoincidence reveals an interval, a division within woman or within any reading subject and the 'experience' of that subject" (64). For Robert Scholes, in rejecting Culler's definition of the woman reader, "Whatever experience is, it is not just a *construct* but something that *constructs*" (215). For the purposes of this paper, we shall use Teresa de Lauretis's definition of the term *experience*:

> the general sense of a *process* by which, for all social beings, subjectivity is constructed. . . . For each person . . . subjectivity is an ongoing construction, not a fixed point of departure or arrival from which one then interacts with the world. On the contrary, it is the effect of that interaction—which I call experience; and thus it is produced not by external ideas, values, or material causes, but by one's personal, subjective engagement in the practices, discourses, and institutions that lend significance (value, meaning, and affect) to the events of the world. (159)

The ways in which cultural constructs affect students' responses to a literary text can be seen in the written responses of a second-semester composition class to Ernest Hemingway's "Hills like White Elephants," a story structured by differences, sexual and otherwise. The students were asked to examine the roles of characters in the story by assuming one of the roles and rewriting the story from that character's point of view. Besides giving students experience in narrative production, such writing encourages a re-vision of the text that is frequently revelatory of submerged agendas, especially those of sexual politics. The students' readings of the text were strongly influenced by the roles the text asked them to play, and their rewritings of the text reflected their reactions to the inscription of gender in the text. Their comments consist of journal responses to "Hills" written both before and after class discussion of the text, their role-playing narratives and their commentaries on those texts, and their comments in class and in conferences.

Two very different reading styles appeared in the students' journal entries. The Hemingway fans, in awe of the Author and his "masterpiece," as two of them called it, responded with plot summaries of the story. This group read "Hills" as a Work, perfect and immutable; for them the story was, in Roland Barthes's terms, "the object of a consumption" (161). Having consumed it, they could only quote it, not question it. Those who disliked the story were more likely to examine their reactions to it, to try to find in the text the elements that triggered those reactions. Keith, one of the more tenacious readers in the class, claimed he had an "aversion to Hemingway" and considered "Hills" a "confusing and trivial" story: "She states she doesn't care about herself and for the rest of the story she holds an idealistic hopeful view of what they can share, and about their love. Then, she becomes angry and realistic. She switches back and forth like this, until the train comes for them to leave; however, at one point I was reminded of the book *Great Expectations*, and felt that he was leaving her behind. I can't really figure out their relationship."

In this journal entry, Keith does attempt to figure out how the story creates its effect. His use of the terms *idealistic* and *realistic* show that Keith has spotted the differences that divide the couple and that he is tuned in to the system of oppositions operative in the text. His reference to Dickens shows him trying to approach "Hills" intertextually, searching the "storage of his intertextual competence," as Umberto Eco would put it, for a frame through which to read a relationship he finds puzzling (21).

Michael, another student who found the story "unclear" because the characters were "too anonymous," best described the reader's work of interpreting the ambiguity of the modernist text: "I like this story for the interplay between the American and the girl. Every word has many levels of meaning, and every reading reveals a new facet to their personalities and views. On the other hand, I can't stand it when a story tells you nothing for certain, doesn't even give a decent conclusion. I want a second version, with translations for every line."

After reading my students' journal responses, I went back to the text to try to read it through my students' eyes, to see why so many of them termed the story "confusing." The class had provided me with a set of intertextual frames through which to read Hemingway, reminding me of what it felt like to be a freshman reader faced with a text like an alien field. This rereading made me aware of the unusually high incidence of the pronoun *it* in Hemingway's textual field. Hemingway's speakers frequently rely on this little word, but not to the degree found in "Hills," where there are fifty-six *its*—an unusually high number for so short a story. Tracking each one in search of its antecedent reveals that all too frequently the *it* either does not have a clearly defined referent or the referent is a generality, such as *everything*. The repetition of so many *its* produces a neutralizing effect because the same signifier (*it*) is used for both deliberately repressed and less important, obvious signifieds, as in the following exchange, where *abortion* is juxtaposed with *beer*: " 'The beer's nice and cool,' the man said. 'It's lovely,' the girl said. 'It's really an awfully simple operation, Jig,' the man said. 'It's not really an operation at all.' " The problem of assigning signifieds adds to this neutralizing effect: " 'You've got to realize,' he said, 'that I don't want you to do it if you don't want to. I'm perfectly willing to go through with it if it means anything to you.' " If signifieds are substituted for the *its* (and of course this can only be done if the reader has the cultural lexicon necessary to translate the man's description of the "operation"—" 'It's just to let the air in' " —into "abortion"), this passage would read: " 'You've got to re-alize,' he said, 'that I don't want you to have the abortion if you don't want to. I'm perfectly willing to go through with the pregnancy if the baby means anything to you.' "

However, these signifieds never appear in the text. The abortion is euphemistically (and callously) described by the man as a "simple operation. . . . It's just to let the air in." Otherwise, all references are to *it*, and there are no words other than *it* used to refer to *pregnancy* and *baby*. The reader must supply the signifieds for all those *its*, which, as signifiers of the neuter gender, work toward desexualizing, or "neu-tering," the discourse. *It* is the agent for the repression of the noun, as if to name were to own, to have, to make real. In this dialogue, the *its* act as a self-censoring private language, a way to speak as little as possible about an unspeakable situation: unspeakable for the man because his autonomy is threatened by the child, whom he clearly regards as other (" 'the only thing that bothers us' ") and hinders their return to a state where, as she drily notes, " 'you'll be happy and things will be like they were and you'll love me' "; unspeakable for the girl because all the signifieds connote death, and to name things is to deepen the pain of their loss. The dialogue moves inexorably toward the ul-timate loss, not only of a fetus but of their relationship, as the girl is only too aware. With surgical precision, she "neuters" the man's phal-locentric discourse by denying his hyperbolic assertions and reducing them to those neutral *its*:

> "What did you say?"
> "I said we could have everything."
> "We can have everything."
> "No, we can't."
> "We can have the whole world."
> "No, we can't."
> "We can go everywhere."
> "No, we can't. It isn't ours any more."
> "It's ours."
> "No, it isn't. And once they take it away, you never get it back."

Gender is inscribed in the text by means of binary oppositions, and the characters define themselves against each other by establishing their own set of differences, aligning them with the primary determining opposition, fertility-infertility. This opposition is reflected in the land-scape, the two sides of the valley, one with grain and trees, and the other, where the station is, hot and brown and dry. Fertility and crea-tivity, the latter a mental function and hence usually perceived as masculine, are linked to the girl. She looks at the hills and can see them as white elephants, but he can't, because, as he says, he's " 'never seen one.' " Her reply, " 'No, you wouldn't have,' " attests to his limited vision and alerts readers to their entry into an ongoing argument. Four times the girl looks off at the hills. The third time we read the landscape with her: "Across, on the other side, were fields of grain and trees along the bank of the Ebro. Far away, beyond the river, were mountains. The shadow of a cloud moved across the field of grain and she saw the river through the trees." It is then that she says " 'And we could have all this,' " as she gazes on the fertile landscape, a landscape of which she feels a part by virtue of her own fertility. Shortly afterward, her gaze shifts to "the hills on the dry side of the valley," while "the man looked at her and at the table." Then he looks at "the bags against the wall of the station. There were labels on them from all the hotels where they had spent nights." He looks "up the tracks but could not see the train." He looks at the people in the bar, "all waiting reasonably for the train." The man can't see very far; he reads his world denotatively, and it is left to the reader to see beyond the surface of all those labels. The man is primarily concerned with his own worries, the biggest one being the threat of the child now being carried by the (by implication) unreasonable girl. (Why else are all the others perceived as waiting "reasonably"? Of course, as Freud has shown us in *Moses and Monotheism*, the rational is traditionally considered to be a male trait.) That the girl will probably have the "simple operation" is signaled by the movement of her gaze from the fertile to the unfertile landscape. The other indication is the awful smile in which her face is fixed at the end—that (falsely) bright emblem of " 'I don't care about me.' "

Less experienced readers are given little help in orienting themselves in the story, but there is a reader's role prescribed in "Hills," one in keeping with Hemingway's other texts. As Walker Gibson has pointed out, the Hemingway narrator "behaves rather as if he had known us, the reader, a long time and therefore doesn't have to pay us very much attention" (31). Because this assumed reader is treated as a friend (a male friend, of course) who knows the places the narrator talks about, no explaining is necessary. This lack of explanation is strongly felt by readers of "Hills" because so much of the story is told in dialogue. The narrator is all but invisible after the opening passages; in subsequent brief passages the point of view shifts from that of the narrator to that of the girl or man. The narrator's sense of the presence of this friendly reader is signaled by definite articles and demonstratives, especially at the opening: "*The* hills across the valley of the Ebro were long and white. On *this* side there was no shade and no trees and *the* station was between two lines of rail in the sun. . . . It was very hot and *the* express from Barcelona would come in forty minutes. It stopped at *this* junction for two minutes and went on to Madrid." I would hazard a guess that some student readers were reacting against this role of "boon companion," as Walter J. Ong has described it, even though, as he says, "It is a flattering role. Hemingway readers are encouraged to develop high self-esteem" (63). Yet in their initial responses, male readers like Keith, Michael, and Jakob resisted rhetorical manipulation into a masculinist role they did not wish to play. They responded as resisting readers, in ways analogous to those described by Judith Fetterley for women readers. While these young men might not resist the initially chummy opening of "Hills," they might well resist taking the man's side in the ensuing dialogue, resisting the role of persuading a woman to have an abortion, because they did not want to imagine, or could not imagine, themselves in such a position. In their initial reading responses, most women readers claimed they could relate to the girl's situation—that is, to her being pregnant— and so they did not read against the text. However, as we shall see, some of them *wrote* against it. The injunction to write necessitated closer attention to the text, and some minds were changed.

Since the majority of the class considered "Hills" to be lacking as a story it seemed logical to ask the students to provide this missing narrative by rewriting "Hills" from the point of view of the American, the girl, or the woman who serves them in the station bar. In such an assignment, "Hills" loses its canonical status as Work, and functions instead as a pretext, a set of guidelines, a field of information to be transformed into the students' own texts.

Michael was one of three men who chose to write from the man's point of view. Though male students might relate sympathetically to the man's peripatetic lifestyle being threatened by family obligations, not many of them wanted to play the role of a man who was so obviously unsympathetic toward the girl's feelings. Michael decided to play the man's role as a shallow cad, and he proceeded with obvious enjoyment:

> Oswald G. Hargood hated riding on trains. He especially hated Spanish trains. But he might just enjoy this ride; just this one—if he could get her there on time; if the silly little thing didn't lose her head. But Oswald had doubts on that.
>
> When he had left the states with the girl, she had intrigued him. She seemed so insightful, so meaningful; not to mention her beauty. Sometimes, they seemed the same. The world was bright and exciting, and each new sensation seemed to flow from the next. Drink, see the sights, then back to the hotel room, and gone the next day, on to new drinks,

new sights, new rooms. Always, they had laughed. Only the train broke the steady trail of new sensations. It was always the same. The cars were dull and plain. There was nothing to do but talk. But a few hours later, the next place was there. New drinks, new sights, new rooms.

Then she had seen a doctor and he had told her of it. The answer was, of course, obvious. How else could they go on, see and feel more than before? There was no alternative. She agreed. But the next drink was too dry. The next sight held no hidden splendor. The next room, too, was suddenly lacking pleasure. She had changed.

Now, weeks later, he felt an urgency. Always she agreed to go through with it, but never *now*. He found himself trying to convince her of the need, to explain that it was right. But she had already agreed. One day he set the date himself, by phone to Madrid, while she took a rest in the room. When he told her, she nodded. "Of course," she had said quietly.

Now, at the station, he could sense something new, an added resistance. Once more he tried to explain to her its simplicity, its necessity. Finally, she voiced her unrest, giving him something to argue with. Damn her! Damn her insightfulness, and her meaning! She wanted to ruin everything. For what? It could all be the same, if only she would. But she wouldn't. He could sense her resolve growing, trapping him.

He must keep her going, keep up the momentum of the trip. Perhaps he could win the race. If he got her there fast enough, before she has time; maybe. Just maybe he could manage it.

The long ride was ahead. Oswald hated train rides. This one promised to be the worst ever. And maybe the longest.

As Michael put it, "The 'Hills' paper was made by putting myself in the man's place. I literally tried to think as he would, and that was what came out. I do not necessarily agree with his views, but I like the paper because I feel I imitated his thinking well." Michael's Oswald is a parodic interpretation of the American, and the name Michael has chosen—Oswald G. Hargood—has echoes of such fictional American businessmen's names as George T. Babbitt, Caspar Goodwood, or Frank Algernon Cowperwood. These are all solid, sensible American names that present a front of square-jawed, masculine rationality to the world. Michael has responded to the element of coercion in the story: the man's persistence in wearing down the girl's defenses. Michael's persona is the voice of male authority, expressing contempt for the girl ("the silly little thing") and an unwillingness to accept her change in attitude. Michael adopts the desperate, aggressive tone of a man who must dominate, for loss of this race means entrapment by the female. In this case, hypothesizing the masculine means virtually obliterating any trace of feminine discourse. The girl is permitted two words and later cursed for speaking: her "insightfulness" is dangerous, and thus her discourse must be written out of a text striving to maintain its masculinity. In playing this role, Michael has produced a reading similar to those of many of Hemingway's male critical readers who erase or write against feminine elements in Hemingway's texts. Michael's confidence in writing comes in part from his experience with masculine codes and his Oswald G. Hargood is a chilling parody of masculine codes as they are revealed in Hemingway's text.

A male student who also claimed ease in writing chose the role of the waitress (see Appendix A). Here is his comment on his paper:

> The assignment wasn't really difficult, for I wrote it through the eyes of the woman, and it was interesting trying to imagine the thoughts of a woman, who doesn't say a great deal. The most challenging part was trying to figure out the proper grammar, the word phrases with which to let the woman speak. I don't think I perfected that task, for I made purposeful mistakes (ex. me and the girl), while using words of someone with some degree of intelligence. I tried to give a unique impression to the reader of the woman's inner feelings instead of merely recounting the events of the story.

Like the others (both male and female) who assumed this persona, Keith made the waitress an older, more experienced woman, probably in response to the text's reference to her as "the woman," as opposed to Jig, "the girl." He sees the woman as a victim because she has been deserted by her man, because she has lost a child through abortion at the man's request, and because she is stuck in a boring job ("I needed the money"). If Keith is aware that men victimize women, he also believes that women form relationships more easily because they are sensitive to one another's feelings. Similarly, another waitress (also the work of a male student) who overhears the girl say, " 'I'll do it. Because I don't care about me,' " states, "When she said that, I could hear something in her voice (which only another woman can understand) indicating that she really didn't want the abortion." On the other hand, there is Keith's suggestion that women tend to romanticize relationships, for his woman seems to believe that love conquers all ("I just hoped they'd cling to their love tightly") even after she has read the American's "loving words" as meant to deceive. The other male student's waitress assumes that the couple is married, and finding them an unlikely match, can only say, "I guess it's true that opposites attract." This waitress also believes that the girl "wanted the baby so they would be forced to settle down and live a normal life . . . one that offered safety and security." However, women writers created waitresses that did not romanticize the situation. One in particular responded to the man's rhetorical tactics: "The man never shut his mouth. . . . I was proud of her when she asked him to stop talking." This waitress does not want the girl to be victimized: "I just hope she doesn't do anything that she doesn't want to do because of him, but I don't think she will—she's much smarter than he gives her credit for." And another found the man's actions "very typical of how men want the fun but can't accept the responsibility."

The issue of responsibility also loomed large with those who assumed the girl's persona. A male writer has her say, "I detected that he feared to take full responsibility for talking me into such a decision." Yet his girl, in acquiescing, shows her awareness of submitting to the role of victim: "I felt that I was letting myself fall into something where I was doing it more for him than for me." This young man, however, needed a reason other than her gender for the girl to submit, so he played up the drinking element: "I couldn't remember how many drinks we had. . . . Somehow they served their purpose. They helped me escape from the thought of my problems for a short while and I felt fine." Thus, this male writer tries to resist the role of victim even while he feels his feminine subject must play that role. Adopting the girl's role is more difficult than adopting the role of either the man or the waitress because of this position of victimization. The women writers who chose the girl's role said they could easily relate to her situation, but only one of them could accept abortion as the only choice, and the one who could had to revise the story to try to make abortion acceptable on an economic basis. However, her attempt to do so is overwhelmed by the posture of her girl as noble victim: "No matter what I do, I will always be somewhat polluted. . . . As I kissed him for the last time, I could tell he knew what I had to do."

The women who chose the girl's role responded not only to their own beliefs, but also to one of the most emotionally charged lines in the text, when the girl asks, " 'Doesn't it mean anything to you? We could get along.' " Here is the suggestion that a child brings a couple together, but that is not quite what the girl is willing to say, though the women who assumed her role wanted to believe that she does indeed subscribe to that (oft mistaken) credo. But at the same time, women writers had trouble relating to a girl who says, " 'Then I'll do it. Because I don't care about me.' " Women writers resisted this masochistic and life-denying statement by radically revising the story, while the three men who wrote from the girl's point of view stayed close to the original. Three of the women decided that the girl refused to have the abortion, and two of these revisions are especially revealing of contemporary mores, such as Lisa's:

> Didn't he know how much it meant to me? Couldn't he tell? Well, he made the decision. He finally said that he didn't want it and he didn't care anything about it. Imagine him not even being able to define "it". I felt relieved that he had finally come out and stated his decision; I thought if anything Sam would carry the guilt. Or would he? We both got on the train and got off at Madrid. Two weeks later I was back in America. I had made the return trip alone. My family was spared the disgrace by never knowing. I can't imagine the reaction my parents would have had, devout Catholics that they were. Their little girl, their pampered child who never had to make a decision. Well, I learned and on my own. I took charge of my own life. My husband Charlie and I have been married now for just about five years and we have a wonderful son and a beautiful baby girl. We love them both very much.

Gail's response is not as sanguine. Here are her opening and concluding paragraphs:

> What is wrong with me? Eighteen months ago. It seems more like a lifetime ago. I can't believe I did it. Why did I do it? What did I hope to gain? I know what, his eternal love. Great. Now what do I do with it?
>
> I was so young. He always made me feel so good. I never wanted to lose that feeling. I saw the way all the women looked at him. I knew if I didn't do something it would only be a matter of time before I lost him. So I slept with him. I gave him what he wanted. Now he would be mine forever, or so I thought.
>
> It didn't take long. This time he was looking back at them. I had to do something more permanent. . . . Could I do it? . . . Could I live without him? No. I had no choice.
>
> . . .
>
> I sit here now, in our little house, thinking and waiting. Thinking about my life—past, present, and future. Thinking about how life would be if I had decided not to. Thinking about how much I have grown and changed in such a short time. Thinking about how I told him I was pregnant the last time. Thinking about how he would react this time. Waiting. Waiting for him to come home from a long hard day's work. Waiting to tell him. Waiting to hear what he'll say. Waiting for the baby to wake up from her nap.

Because abortion is the issue, all students but one assumed the couple was unmarried. To be pregnant out of wedlock is still today seen as a disgrace, so Lisa invents Charlie, who makes an honest woman of her heroine. Lisa's narrative emphasizes the difference in age between the girl and the man—"Sam" in this case—to whom she has looked for guidance, as little girls look to their papas. While one can read Lisa's narrative as a conservative or stereotypically feminine desire for home and family, one should also take into account Lisa's emphasis on decision making; indeed, the title of her narrative is "The Only Decision." Her subtext shows a desire to break with male autonomy (the lover as father figure) through her own decision—yet she shows the girl still caught up in a patriarchal structure of church and Charlie.

Gail's long interior monologue is full of self-questioning. In her opening she explains why the girl got pregnant: "I knew if I didn't do something it would only be a matter of time before I lost him"; thus the girl assumes the active role and the man, a cad with a roving eye, becomes the victim. Gail's comment on the writing of her narrative suggests the extent to which she has taken over the text: "I loved this assignment because it gave me a chance to use my imagination to create whatever I wanted to. This somehow made me enjoy the story more. I had no problems because of the few restrictions there were. The story gave little information, so I was free to do anything to it." Her enjoyment came from taking over Hemingway's text to use as a pretext for her own story of pregnancy as entrapment of both the man and the girl. For many of the women, the writing could be considered therapeutic, a way to play out gender-based anxieties. For some, the issue of sexual politics was clearly on the line and they could express opinions through the voices and actions of their characters without worrying whether the teacher would agree with them. In their assessments of this particular writing assignment, the women described it as "fun" and said that they could "relate to" it, while the men tended to emphasize the technical choices they had to make in assuming a female persona (Keith's response is an example of this).

I read the women students' "I could relate to it" as the acknowledgment of the ability to play a particular role. Their pleasure in doing so lies, I think, in the fact that they were rarely, if ever, asked to write about or through feminine experience. Academic writing privileges objectivity, or obliteration of the writing subject, who is meant to stay outside the text. Yet the greatest pleasure in reading is the entrance into a text, into an engagement with it. Such an engagement, as we have seen here, may not always be on friendly terms, as the social, cultural, and literary contexts of readers confront those of the text. The writing assignment in this case highlighted this confrontation; the role-playing called for re-vision of the text and, for most of the men, provided a creative experience in cross-dressing which enabled them to investigate feminine experience. Such writing also forms the basis for a critical awareness of how we read—of the positions from which we read. Such an awareness includes an understanding of the experience we bring to a text, as well as how a text may work to add to or challenge one's experience—or, to use Teresa de Lauretis's terms, how reading is part of the construction of our subjectivity. It is here, I would suggest, that our teaching of reading and writing begins.

APPENDIX A

Keith's Narrative

The clock struck 4:00 P.M., signifying the start of my shift in the bar. Day after day, the monotony became more unbearable. The only thing keeping me going was the beauty of the landscape, and those hills that looked like white elephants in the sunlight beyond the trees. There was one other reason: I needed the money.

A lovely couple sat down outside the bar, he American, and she, well, I couldn't be sure. They looked so happy, and free, the way I remembered youth. As I placed their beers in front of them, I couldn't help staring at the two. "They look like white elephants," she said, as I stood astonished by her remark. Once again, I gazed into her eyes, before turning quickly, and receding into the bar. I remained by the beaded curtain, trying not to create suspicion while I listened to their conversation. That wasn't my style, eavesdropping I mean, but that remark made me feel something. No one else ever saw them like that, except me and the girl.

They appeared to be arguing, starting off with trivial matters, and continuing to ones of greater importance. The man started with a snappy reply as to possibly having seen a white elephant, and the girl later added her own sarcastic responses about everything tasting like licorice, and that trying new drinks and seeing things were the only things they did. I brought them two more drinks, this time Anis del Toro; the girl sat, again looking across at the hills. I reentered the bar, still trying to understand the feeling I had about the girl. Suddenly it all pieced together. The man stated, "It's really an awfully simple operation." He continued on this subject, as the girl, seemingly unnerved, questioned him about their future if she had the operation. They appeared to be in love, even stating it to each other; however, I couldn't help the bitterness that overcame me when he said they'd be fine afterward. I remembered myself in the same situation, hearing the same loving words, and naively believing every one. I went through with the operation, waking up to find that my man had left—not even a note! Time didn't relieve me of my bitterness, for I regretted not having the tenderness of the child that would have been mine. "Oh, stop," I told myself, as I went out to inform them that the train was scheduled to arrive in five minutes. Her piercing smile made its way straight to my heart, as I painfully refrained from offering assistance, and the knowledge of experience. The man proceeded to take their bags around the station to the other tracks. As he made his way back, I fumbled with some glasses so he wouldn't notice my continued listening to their conversation. He asked her if she felt any better, to which she replied, "I feel fine, there's nothing wrong with me. I feel fine." That was the last I heard, as I smiled at the two as they made their way to the train. Happiness still encompassed their faces, but it left my heart. I had seen myself and my man in the couple; I just hoped they'd cling to their love tightly, and live the future of which I had always dreamed.

WORKS CITED

Barthes, Roland. "From Work to Text." In *Image-Music-Text*. Trans. Stephen Heath. New York: Hill and Wang, 1977.

Culler, Jonathan. *On Deconstruction*. Ithaca: Cornell University Press, 1982.

de Lauretis, Teresa. *Alice Doesn't*. Bloomington: Indiana University Press, 1984.

Eco, Umberto. *The Role of the Reader*. Bloomington: Indiana University Press, 1979.

Fetterley, Judith. *The Resisting Reader*. Bloomington: Indiana University Press, 1978.

Gibson, Walker. *Tough, Sweet, and Stuffy*. Bloomington: Indiana University Press, 1966.

Gilligan, Carol. *In a Different Voice*. Cambridge: Harvard University Press, 1982.

Hemingway, Ernest. *Men without Women*. New York: Scribner's, 1928.

Jardine, Alice, and Paul Smith, eds. *Men in Feminism*. New York: Methuen, 1987.

Modleski, Tania. "Feminism and the Power of Interpretation: Some Critical Readings." In *Feminist Studies/Critical Studies*. Ed. Teresa de Lauretis. Bloomington: Indiana University Press, 1986.

Ong, Walter J. *Interfaces of the Word*. Ithaca: Cornell University Press, 1977.

Scholes, Robert. "Reading like a Man." In Jardine and Smith, eds., *Men in Feminism*.

Schweikart, Patrocinio. "Reading Ourselves: Toward a Feminist Theory of Reading." In *Gender and Reading*. Ed. Elizabeth A. Flynn and Patrocinio Schweikart. Baltimore: Johns Hopkins University Press, 1986.

Showalter, Elaine. "Critical Cross-dressing: Male Feminists and the Woman of the Year." In Jardine and Smith, eds., *Men in Feminism*.

———. "Toward a Feminist Poetics." In *The New Feminist Criticism*. Ed. Elaine Showalter. New York: Pantheon, 1985.

ELIZABETH A. FLYNN

The Classroom as Interpretive Community: Teaching Reader-Response Theory and Composition Theory to Preprofessional Undergraduates

> We neither capture nor create the world with our texts, but interact
> with it.
>
> Robert Scholes, *Textual Power*

The Summer 1986 *MLA Newsletter* reports the results of a survey indicating that courses in literary theory and criticism are offered by approximately 50 percent of the respondents with Ph.D. programs, but only 30 percent of other departments offer such courses ("ADE Study" 18). The theory courses that do exist are often marginalized, treated as peripheral. Too often the token theory course is one option among many and taught by a token specialist whose obligation it is to keep up with Derrida et al. so that everyone else can continue doing what they have always done in the way they have always done it. Faculty who do not teach theory may have read some, for it would be embarrassing if they had not, but their reading often has little effect on their teaching.

Paul de Man argues that a certain resistance to theory is inherent in the enterprise itself and that this resistance serves to rejuvenate the field—the more it is resisted the more it flourishes (20). This may be true in scholarly circles, but it is not necessarily true in pedagogical ones. Educational institutions are inherently conservative and resistant to change. Disciplinary developments do not find their way into the curriculum quickly or easily, and often large public institutions are the most resistant. The MLA survey indicates, for instance, that 63 percent of private institutions granting Ph.D.'s offer courses in literary theory whereas only 41 percent of public institutions do (18).

De Man also points out that New Criticism and the politically oriented alternatives that developed in the 1950s, though extremely diverse trends, shared a resistance to theory (6). If these critical positions continued on into the 1960s and '70s, and they no doubt did, several generations of college professors, many of whom are now in positions of authority within English departments, resist theory because they were trained to do so, because the critical positions they embraced repudiated the value of theory.

Theory is threatening because it is often difficult and because it demands so much time and attention. Keeping up with developments in literary theory is a full-time occupation, diverting time from literary texts themselves. But the threat is no doubt more deeply rooted than this. Theoretical developments force us to question our scholarly and pedagogical activities in fundamental ways. They force us to rethink and perhaps alter professional practices to which we have become accustomed. To become engaged in theoretical debate is to jeopardize our present beliefs and behaviors and almost certainly to repudiate much of our professional training.

Faculty resistant to theory may argue that literature itself is anti-theoretical in its refusal of classification or easy generalization. But much modernist and postmodernist literature—the works of Joyce, Beckett, and Woolf come immediately to mind—anticipates and illuminates contemporary literary theory by thematizing such subjects as the self-referentiality and playfulness of literary language, the elusiveness of linguistic meaning, and the inevitability of multiple and often contradictory perspectives. Such works often inscribe their own theoretical concerns within themselves (Prince 38). Theory and literature are not distinct entities; both should be the subject of literary studies.

I am hardly arguing that all teachers of literature should drop everything and become experts in literary theory. What we do need are specialists in theory, several per department perhaps, who are thoroughly conversant in the history of literary criticism and in contemporary theory. Such experts should offer courses on both undergraduate and graduate levels frequently, and these courses should be required. The nonspecialist, though, should also teach theory—by making clear her theoretical assumptions and by incorporating theoretical texts into her literature courses.

My primary concern here, though, is not with the training of English majors preparing for graduate programs in English or of graduate students in English programs but, rather, with preprofessional undergraduates who study literature and language but who do not plan to enter the English profession. These students will generally, upon graduation, find positions in business, industry, or the federal government or enter a professional school of one kind or another. How much literary theory do these students need? Why do they need it? I contend that the study of literary theory should be a part of all literature courses, those taken by majors and nonmajors alike, because an understanding of theory is indispensable in every conversation about literature.

Every speech act about a literary text, about the literary canon, about the process of interpretation, is grounded in assumptions that are not necessarily shared. Students who are asked to participate in a literary discussion, either in class or in informal or formal essays — and what students are not — need to learn how to identify their own critical assumptions and those of others with whom they are agreeing or contending. There is no such thing as a "pure" assertion or a universally acceptable claim. Positions about what literary texts mean or about how they mean differ from interpretive community to community, and differing positions will only be able to be negotiated if the assumptions that underlie them are laid bare.

Catherine Belsey emphasizes that we cannot practice literature without theory when she says in *Critical Practice*: "there is no practice without theory, however much that theory is suppressed, unformulated or perceived as 'obvious.' What we do when we read, however 'natural' it seems, presupposes a whole theoretical discourse, even if unspoken, about language and about meaning, about the relationships between meaning and the world, meaning and people, and finally about people themselves and their place in the world" (4).

Belsey sees that our "natural" processes must be demystified so as to reveal the theoretical discourse that underpins them. Gerald Prince emphasizes that theory can help explain our seemingly commonsensical and intuitive interpretive statements and literary judgments:

> every description or interpretation of a work develops in terms of certain points of reference, certain assumptions and expectations, certain questions to ask and goals to reach, some of which take the name of common sense, intuition, and good taste. What theory can do is provide us with explicit and systematically related reference points, validate or explain this assumption and that expectation, demonstrate the relevance or irrelevance of some questions and some goals. (38)

Theory is indispensable because it illuminates our literary conversations, clarifies our impressions and judgments.

Robert Scholes goes so far as to contend that "we cannot teach literature; we can only teach reading, interpretation, or criticism" (12). If this is so, then teachers of literature are actually teachers of literary theory, and their subject is as much the reading strategies their students employ as the literary text under consideration. Teachers of literature on all levels should have a dual allegiance—to their students as interpreters of the texts they are discussing as well as to the texts themselves—and they should build into their course structures mechanisms for enabling students to become aware of their own interpretive strategies and the strategies of others.[1] Mariolina Salvatori makes this point in "Reading and Writing a Text: Correlations between Reading and Writing" when she says, "literature ought to be taught as a way of exploring, understanding, and reflecting on the strategies by which readers—all readers—generate meanings in the act of reading" (659).

But how do we introduce theory to preprofessional undergraduates who do not plan to enter the English profession? What theoretical texts would be useful to them, and how should they be approached? The Department of Humanities at Michigan Tech provides an ideal laboratory for exploring such questions since we have very few English majors and virtually no students who go on to pursue graduate study in English. Our situation has allowed us the freedom to create alternative structures, to reverse traditional hierarchies.

One manifestation of this reversal is the existence within the department of a course designed to bring together two fields of inquiry, literary studies and composition studies, that are usually taught independently of one another. "Literature and Composition" is an upper-level undergraduate course that graduate students in our M.S. program in rhetoric and technical communication may take for credit toward their degree.

When I was assigned the course, I saw it as an opportunity to investigate the nature of the interpretive process, a process that is composed of the subprocesses of reading and writing. An examination of reader-response theory, especially the theory of David Bleich and Louise Rosenblatt, I hoped, would prepare students for their subsequent reading of literature, reading that would, presumably, take place outside the context of the academy. I assumed, though, that a better understanding of both the reading process and the writing process would also be of value to students planning to make communication their profession or to students who would eventually find their way into managerial positions in industry. An important aim of the course, therefore, was to make students self-conscious about their own interpretive processes.

Course texts were both literary and theoretical. We read one novel, Alice Walker's *The Color Purple*, and short stories and poetry from Mary Anne Ferguson's *Images of Women in Literature*. To attempt to understand the processes of reading about literature, we read David Bleich's *Read-*

ings and Feelings and Louise Rosenblatt's *Literature as Exploration*. The composition theory we read included essays from Charles Cooper and Lee Odell's *Research on Composing: Points of Departure* and more recent articles from journals such as *College Composition and Communication* and *College English* by authors such as Linda Flower, Nancy Sommers, and Anthony Petrosky.

Throughout the quarter we read short stories or poems from the Ferguson anthology and the Walker novel. The first five weeks were devoted to reading theory—three weeks to Bleich and two to Rosenblatt. Weeks six, seven, and eight were devoted to composition theory. Students kept journals in which they recorded their responses to their reading, an indispensable activity in a course focusing on response. Students also wrote two formal papers. The first assignment, an essay of 3-4 pages, asked students to analyze one of the stories in the Ferguson anthology for other class members to clarify an unresolved issue raised in class. The second assignment, an essay of 5-6 pages, was as follows:

> Analyze the reading and writing processes employed by two class members in their preparation of Essay # 1. Examine their journal entries, drafts, and revisions. Also, interview them. In your discussion, be sure to refer to the theories of reading and writing we have studied this quarter. Do the processes you have discovered support the theories or refute them? You should aim, in this paper, to inform class members of the results of your inquiry into the reading/writing process and to attempt to resolve issues raised in class regarding that process.

The final paper was due in week nine, and the last several class sessions were devoted to presentations of students' findings.

My aim in structuring the course was to create an interpretive community of readers and writers who had a shared purpose, an exploration of the interpretive process. The term *interpretive community*, of course, originated with Stanley Fish and suggests that language users derive their interpretive strategies from their affiliations with the communities to which they belong. In his "Is There a Text in This Class?" Fish argues that "sentences emerge only in situations" (9) and that those situations or contexts provide practices, purposes, and goals that enable communication to take place. Individual interpreters belong to interpretive communities and so have shared assumptions and shared interpretive strategies. These strategies constrain so that a limited number of meanings are possible for any utterance.

The term *interpretive community* is especially well suited to the pedagogical context I want to describe, since it suggests that teachers and students share an experience and learn a common vocabulary as they interact in the classroom. Teachers and learners engage in an active process of interpretation as they construct meaning communally, collectively, by reading common materials, sharing and negotiating interpretations, and attempting to create knowledge.

Fish does not explore the pedagogical implications of his position. He emphasizes the ways in which interpretations result from the embedded structures, the social relationships that are already in place. His main concern is the movement from affiliation with an interpretive community to the achievement of an interpretation. My primary concern, though, is with the development of interpretive powers that will allow for the production of negotiable interpretations. How do we enable interaction and hence insure that students will develop interpretive strategies that will allow them to comprehend the texts they encounter? For me, an interpretive community represents a solution to a problem rather than a description of a reality. It represents a place where learning is enhanced, where ideas are shared and negotiated.

Sociolinguistic theories of language development are helpful in explaining why interpretive communities are conducive to learning. Such theories suggest that language is acquired through social interaction. Children learn to speak by talking to adults in such a way that their mutual concerns are respected. Interpersonal collaboration allows the child to build a working model of reality and hence to gain some control over her world. As Gordon Wells explains in his essay "Becoming a Communicator,"

> language as experienced by the developing child occurs in a context of interaction, where the child's communication partner both modifies the input to the child in response to the understanding that he manifests, and provides feedback on the way in which his own attempts to communicate are interpreted. From the beginning, therefore, language is experienced as a means of communication with significant others who, although they do not deliberately "teach," actively mediate between the child, their shared situation, and the formal language system. (77)

Children learn to speak by interacting with a more mature communicator who provides feedback through a process of mediation. Language acquisition is not biologically determined; nor is it an innate developmental process. Rather, it occurs through conversation, through social interaction.

The view that language development results from social interaction is, unfortunately, by no means the reigning paradigm in the fields of reading theory and composition theory. Although sociolinguists have been exploring the relationship between language and social context for the past fifteen years or more, reading and writing researchers and theorists have been emphasizing the cognitive processes involved in the development of language abilities. They have been operating within a cognitive paradigm rather than a contextual one. Only recently have we begun to explore the implications for reading and writing of the work of sociolinguistic researchers and theorists.

Harste, Woodward, and Burke clarify this distinction between a cognitive approach to language learning and a contextual or "transactional"[2] one in their important article, "Examining Our Assumptions: A Transactional View of Literacy and Learning." According to Harste, Woodward, and Burke, a contextual model sees the learner and the environment as interacting in a dialogic way. The cognitive view, in contrast, sees the learner as acting upon the environment, and activity that takes place in the mind of the learner is critical. Readers and writers are individual minds thinking. For cognitivists, the task of the theorist and the researcher is to identify the seemingly universal processes that take place within individual minds.

Descriptions of the reading and writing processes that derive from a cognitive model provide a limited conception of the nature of the interaction between reader or writer and text; there would appear to be little outside these entities. The "classic" texts in both fields tend to ignore the importance of the social context in which language takes place. Kenneth Goodman, for instance, one of our most enlightened reading researchers and theorists, nevertheless defines reading, in an early essay, as "A psycholinguistic process by which the reader (a language user) reconstructs, as best he can, a message which has been encoded by a writer in a graphic display" (22). Goodman's reader is singular, isolated—and male. Reading would appear to take place in a cultural vacuum. The definition says nothing about the context within which reading takes place, and the reader is unaffiliated, unmotivated by communal purposes and goals.

Models of the writing process also tend to reflect a cognitive view of language behavior. Janet Emig in "Hand, Eye, Brain: Some 'Basics' in the Writing Process," for instance, finds that the writing process is produced by organic structures that interact—including the hand, the eye, and the brain. Emig's other work, especially *The Composing Processes of Twelfth Graders*, does take social context into consideration in discussing the composing process. In "Hand, Eye, Brain," though, it would appear that writing is a mechanical process and that writers are biological rather than social beings. Donald Murray's definition of writing also reflects the cognitive model, though in a much more subtle way. In his important essay, "Internal Revision: A Process of Discovery,"

Murray says, "The most accurate definition of writing, I believe, is that it is the process of using language to discover meaning in experience and to communicate it"(86). The process of discovery takes the form of prevision, vision, and revision. The writer observes, remembers, explores experience, stakes out a territory to explore, and then reads what has been written and confirms, alters, or develops it, usually through many drafts. According to Murray, "Eventually a meaning is developed which can be communicated to a reader" (87). Once again, the process would appear to be somewhat mechanistic. Murray says of writers, "They discover what they have to say by relating pieces of specific information to other bits of information and use words to symbolize and connect that information" (93). Murray's model does not entirely ignore social context. He suggests, for instance, that we need to examine the environment in which a writer writes in addition to writers' drafts, revisions, tools, habits, and schedules. And surely he is correct in saying that the function of memory in the composing process is an important area of investigation. But he does not emphasize that memory functions within a social context or that it is activated by social needs and goals.

The pedagogical practices that arise out of a cognitive model of the composing process reflect this emphasis on the isolated individual. Students need to "brainstorm," to write freely, thereby releasing from the mind material that is stored in memory. They are encouraged to record their private responses in journals and to reword their drafts until they discover their true meaning.

If we see the reader or writer as situated in a social context, though, we develop a different model of language processing. Emphasis is placed on the transaction between the language user and the environment; the mind interacts with other minds and thereby becomes motivated to develop linguistic facility. Readers or writers are never alone, never thinkers relying solely upon their own resources; they are sociological rather than biological beings; often they are students who are connected in important ways to teachers and to other students.

The "contextual" view of language learning is articulated well by Marilyn Cooper in "The Ecology of Writing." For Cooper, the cognitive model projects an unfortunate ideal image: "the solitary author who works alone in the privacy of his own mind" (365). She calls, instead, for a model that recognizes that "writing is an activity through which a person is continually engaged with a variety of socially constituted systems" (367). Cooper reminds us that the cognitive view is still the dominant paradigm and calls for the development of new theories that locate writing and reading in their social contexts.[3]

A contextual approach to the teaching of reading and writing, then, makes use of the context of the classroom to motivate language development. If journals are used, they are public rather than private. If brainstorming is used, it is aimed at serving a collective purpose. Students write for each other. The discoveries they make that lead them toward a reenvisioning of their drafts arise out of social interaction. Classrooms become interpretive communities where language users read, write, and speak in order to accomplish a common goal.[4]

In the Literature and Composition course I selected texts, designed class activities, and structured paper topics so as to maximize interaction among students. The readings were unified around the theme of the effects of gender conditioning upon behavior. The group was small, eight students, so it was quite easy to create an informal atmosphere where interaction could take place. Class sessions were often spent sharing responses to the texts and using those responses to test the theory we had read and to arrive at a negotiable interpretation of the literature under consideration. As we progressed to a consideration of composition theory, students were preparing essay two and so examined drafts and revisions in addition to response statements. Theory was always tested against actual reading and writing.

In teaching Literature and Composition, I was in the somewhat awkward position of attempting to implement a structure rooted in my belief that language is a social process and that language development takes place through social interaction, while teaching texts that more closely reflect a cognitive view of language learning. Although Bleich concludes *Readings and Feelings* with a discussion of group response to texts, he speaks most frequently in this book as if readers were individual minds confronting single texts. He describes his approach, for instance, as a "subjective" one, suggesting a private, unalterable consciousness. Rosenblatt's language, too, in *Literature as Exploration*, suggests a singular reader confronting a single text. She says, for instance, "The reader must remain faithful to the text" (11); "The literary work exists in the live circuit set up between reader and text" (25); "The reader infuses intellectual and emotional meanings into the pattern of verbal symbols, and those symbols channel his thoughts and feelings" (25). The composition theory we read had a similar emphasis. We studied the Emig and Murray articles mentioned earlier, in addition to ones by Flower, Sommers, and others. These writers, too, tend to focus upon the isolated writer drawing upon cognitive schemata.

When possible, therefore, I tried to point out the limitations of the cognitive view of language processing and to suggest ways in which a contextual model was latent in the materials we were reading. This was especially appropriate in our discussion of Bleich since he no longer uses the term *subjective* as he did in *Readings and Feelings* and *Subjective Criticism*, but instead describes reader-text interaction as an "intersubjective" process. In a more recent work, for instance, the title of which, "Intersubjective Reading," seems to stand as a revision of the title of his major work, *Subjective Criticism*, Bleich points out the limitations of a view of reading that considers only readers and texts and argues that two elements heretofore neglected in reading theory, affect and dialogue, should become central (417). His new terminology actually represents a shift in emphasis rather than a new departure. In *Subjective Criticism*, for instance, he stresses that an object is circumscribed and delimited by a subject's motives. The observer perceives to answer the question, "What do I want to know?" (41). Often this motivation stems from interpersonal interaction. Helen Keller's acquisition of language abilities through her recognition of w-a-t-e-r as a symbol referring to the liquid coming from the spout of a pump was precipitated by interaction with Anne Sullivan, her teacher. The breakthrough was motivated largely by Keller's need to overcome her social isolation.

For Bleich, the classroom context produces similar results. Students, in interacting with the teacher and with each other, form a community where motivation to create new knowledge is high. Bleich's classroom, then, is a context that is conducive to fruitful exchange. Students are stimulated (sometimes provoked) to become actively engaged in meaning-making. Bleich's *Readings and Feelings* and *Subjective Criticism* call for the creation of contexts that are more conducive to student involvement in literature than the traditional classroom. Bleich argues convincingly that students will only read meaningfully if teachers create classroom environments where they will be motivated to do so, and so Bleich's work can be seen as a call for new contexts within which literature can be examined.

Rosenblatt's approach is transactional rather than subjective. For her, reading involves interaction between reader and text. Meaning is neither found, as in the objective model, nor made, as in the subjective model; rather, it is experienced in a unique fusion of subject and object, perceiver and that which is perceived. There are latent contextual elements in Rosenblatt's work as well. Although Rosenblatt does not stress that this fusion must take place within a particular context, she does recognize that readers read for different purposes. In doing so, she implicitly acknowledges that reading is situation-dependent. She sees that we read either to experience and appreciate a work ("aesthetic reading") or to make use of it in some way ("efferent reading"). According to Rosenblatt, students are too often encouraged to read efferently rather than aesthetically, and so the potentially powerful experience of reading becomes a limiting exercise. Rosenblatt argues that teachers should encourage students to enjoy literature, to read it aesthetically (8).[5]

The interaction that took place in Literature and Composition was designed to enhance students' abilities to read literature and to understand their own interpretive processes and the interpretive processes of others. I attempted to create conversations in which students could express themselves freely but also receive feedback from other classmates and from me. During one class session, for instance, we analyzed two student responses to Adrienne Rich's poem, "Aunt Jennifer's Tigers":

> Aunt Jennifer's tigers prance across a screen,
> Bright denizens of a world of green.
> They do not fear the men beneath the tree;
> They pace in sleek chivalric certainty.
>
> Aunt Jennifer's fingers fluttering through her wool
> Find even the ivory needle hard to pull.
> The massive weight of Uncle's wedding band
> Sits heavily upon Aunt Jennifer's hand.
>
> When Aunt is dead, her terrified hands will lie
> Still ringed with ordeals she was mastered by.
> The tigers in the panel that she made
> Will go on prancing, proud and unafraid.

The two responses were significantly different. John's reads as follows:

> I liked this poem, but I'm not sure I can explain in a short time why. There is a lot going on in here; heavy use of symbolism, very regimented rhythm, and vivid imagery. I like the double meaning of "ring" used, in lines 7 & 10.
>
> Even though the vocabulary is large, the poem seems as if it were written by a child, or more probably, from a childhood memory. What makes the poem so powerful is the imagery of the prancing tigers juxtaposed with the downtrodden woman. (Note colors of tigers in line 2, "bright topaz . . . green . . ." and the total lack of colors in Aunt Jennifer's description.) The tigers, even though inanimate, have taken on more life than Aunt Jennifer.
>
> It is surprising, at least to me, that a three stanza poem can deal with so many different things. In the first stanza alone, I can see hints of at least two or three themes. Drawing them out, however, would probably be a lengthy process.
>
> Apparently the author of this poem is only showing up a very small fragment of her observations of her Aunt and Uncle. The rest remains

buried. The third stanza only deals briefly with what must be a lengthy period of spouse abuse, either emotional, physical, or both.

We decided that John focuses upon the poem as object, as literary creation, mentioning the author's use of symbolism, rhythm, and vivid imagery. He develops his response by referring to specific details from the text, the colors of the tigers, for example. But a consideration of the themes of the poem does not occur until paragraph three, and here he essentially defers discussion for a later time. Not until the last sentence of paragraph four do we get a brief discussion of a theme of the poem, spouse abuse. Mary, in contrast, focused almost exclusively on the meaning of the poem. There is little sense that the poem was an object created by an author.

> This poem seems to be very anti-marriage and anti-male. The tigers Aunt Jennifer knits are not afraid of men but the wedding band holds Aunt Jennifer back from what she wants. I don't quite understand the last stanza. It is kind of a feeling of hope. Aunt Jennifer may not be able to be equal but what she creates can be equal and unafraid. It looks back (the poem) to the time of our grandparents. In the first stanza, "men" really stuck out. I had to read the poem two times before I understood what was happening. I don't understand the "terrified hands" part. In the second line it sounds like she dealt with or "mastered" whatever her problems were. Through all her work and hardship, she created something that could stand up to men.

> > fingers fluttering—terrified hands chivalric
> > massive weight of Uncle's wedding band—ringed
> > with ordeals
> > She didn't realize what she was creating.

In this session, we "negotiated" responses by examining two closely. The discussion of the poem itself took place within the context of readers' responses to it and of the theory we had been reading. We decided that Mary's response was Bleichian in that Bleich encourages his students to respond emotionally to the works they are reading. It was also an example of Rosenblatt's "aesthetic" response in that Mary was clearly living through the events of the poem, experiencing it fully. John, in contrast, was employing New Critical analytical techniques, techniques that both Bleich and Rosenblatt discourage students from using in their initial responses to texts.

After discussing the differences in the two responses, we focused on ways in which these differences might be explained, in part at least, by the different genders of the respondents. I observed that our findings correspond in some ways to the findings of David Bleich in his essay,

"Gender Interests in Reading and Language." According to Bleich, when reading fiction, males tend to focus attention on the author in their responses and to treat texts as if they were objects. Females, in contrast, tend to participate in the action of a work and to identify with the characters, male and female alike. Curiously, though, the statements do not correspond to Bleich's finding that in responding to lyric poetry, males and females both tend to identify with the situation described by the poem, to place themselves within it.

The session provided the group with a common purpose—a comparison of the two response statements to learn more about the interpretive strategies of the two students and about the interpretive process itself. Journal entries were shared publicly and stimulated conversation that led to negotiated knowledge. The two responses were not considered merely as manifestations of individual differences but as indications of differences that result from affiliation with social groups.

The final paper necessitated interaction and encouraged students, once again, to examine their own interpretive processes. This time, though, they were looking not only at responses but also at drafts that grew out of those responses and at revisions that grew out of their drafts. Through the processes of reading, writing, and talking, they were making discoveries about the process of interpretation, about the literary texts that were being read and written about, and about the reading and writing theories they were asked to integrate into their papers.

The assignment stimulated conversation. Initially students brainstormed in their journals and shared ideas about possible topics. They then paired up, exchanged materials, and received feedback from classmates and from me on drafts of their papers. They also had an opportunity to share their finished products with others in the form of a ten-minute oral report during the last class session.

The following final essay, which has been condensed somewhat, embodies the dialogic process that led up to it. It was written by a mature student, a strong feminist, who began a degree in our scientific and technical communication program after having completed a B.A. in social sciences at Michigan Tech. Dianna has been an active member of the local NOW chapter for the past ten years and has been reading feminist literature for as long. The format she employs in her paper is an indication that she is not a traditional student of the humanities.

Dianna decided early on that she would compare her essay on Irwin Shaw's "The Girls in Their Summer Dresses" with that of Mary. Dianna had difficulty finding a basis for comparison, though, and her early drafts lacked focus. She was quite willing to share her early attempts with the entire class, and so she received a considerable amount of feedback from classmates and from me. After examining several drafts, we suggested that she focus on the ways in which two different ideological filters affected both the reading and the writing processes. The result reflects the collaborative process that produced it. It also reflects Dianna's struggle to bring multiple perspectives together—that of an earlier self (producer of essay one), Mary, Shaw, and the theorists we read in class—into a coherent essay.

Introduction

In this paper I will compare and contrast the reading responses and writing processes of Mary and myself. I will also examine how our individual experiences and ideologies influence our reading and writing.

Mary, a young woman in the process of developing her own value system and examining ideologies, was more open to the influence of the text and her own response to it than I was. As an older, more mature student with a well-developed ideology and personal value system, I was less open to learning from the text or even to learning more about my response to it.

Reader and Text

As a young, single woman, Mary is attracted to this story about a relationship; it reflects her concerns and interests. Because she comes to the story motivated to explore romantic relationships, she is more likely to gain valuable insights into the text than she would if the text were less relevant to her interests.

I chose to write about this story because I too was attracted to the subject matter—a troubled marriage and the roles of the participants. Because this theme interested me, I was motivated to examine the text more closely to arrive at a deeper understanding of the dynamics involved.

According to Rosenblatt, matching the reader's interest with the text is crucial to the successful interaction between the two. Bleich, on the other hand, negates the importance of matching readers' interests with texts, since he sees any piece of literature functioning equally well to elicit reader response.

Group Discussion

In the group discussion when Mary compared her reactions to others', she discovered that the majority blamed Frances' insecurities for the problem. Mary agreed with the minority view which blamed Michael's behavior for the problem. The minority opinion influenced her to criticize Michael even more harshly than she had done in her initial response.

The group discussion did not change my initial perception that Michael's view of women allowed him to relate to them sexually as a class, without having to deal with them as individuals. Since Michael's sexist attitude is so familiar to me, there was little chance that a new insight which I had not already considered would evolve from the discussion. The majority opinion, which blamed the victim, is an attitude that I have encountered often. I was concerned, although not surprised, that so many of the female students bought into it.

Learning from the Text

Mary's examination of Michael and Frances's relationship led her to clarify her own view of marriage by helping her understand what constitutes a good relationship. By focusing on the individuals in the story and then applying her insights onto society as a whole, Mary used the text to increase her understanding of the complexity of human behaviors and emotions. She took the insights gained from analyzing Michael and Frances's experiences and applied them to her own life—their experiences became hers.

In this sense, Mary's response supports Rosenblatt's theory that literature can enhance readers' lives by expanding their experiences and understanding. Rosenblatt sees literature as a social product, a reflection of society which incorporates individuals' interactions. Mary, to the extent that she identified the problems associated with caring for a "woman-lover" like Michael, saw this story in the context of a society where some men objectify women, and some women acquiesce in their own objectification.

To the extent that I incorporated social science principals into my reading response, I also followed Rosenblatt's model; however, my familiarity with these principals limits my exposure to totally new insights. As a social science student, I have studied the basic social concepts that Rosenblatt believes are so essential for deeper literary insight. Because I have already incorporated this knowledge into my experience, I do not often find entirely new insights in literature. Instead, I may recognize a new slant on an old variation.

The Writing Process

Mary's writing process closely paralleled Murray's model. To begin with, she chose her topic based on her interest in the story. Because she saw Michael as the villain, she believed that her clear perception of this story would enable her to avoid the risk of backing herself into a corner while trying to defend a point about which she was less certain.

Mary spent little time on the prevision stage. Prior to writing, she re-read her journal entry and the story, underlining passages that supported her view that Michael's behavior caused problems in his relationship with Frances.

Her first draft resembled Flower's "writer-based prose"—expressing initial thoughts to clarify reactions without concentrating on the structure of the writing. This approach allowed her the freedom to generate information and alternatives before limiting her focus at this early stage in the writing process.

Mary spent the least time on the task she least liked—the external revision stage. At this point, she had exhausted her creative energies on developing her thesis. The polishing up stage seemed anti-climactic.

My writing process was different from Mary's. First of all, I spent a lot of time in the prevision stage, developing ideas in my head before putting them down on paper. Second, I did not enjoy the writing process as much as Mary because, from the beginning, I was focused on the end-product. I felt anxious because I did not know exactly what I was going to say.

I differed from Murray's approach in the amount of attention and interest I invested in the external revision stage. I usually allow an extra day to polish my work. I enjoy adding these finishing touches. Part of the reason for my focus on this part of the writing process may be due to the fact that I have been trained to be so product-oriented that I know that success at this stage will affect my grade.

Learning through Writing

Murray stresses the importance of writers protecting their innocence. Mary did this by entering the writing process with an open mind. She did not formulate a clear intent before beginning her paper; she merely began by writing about the failing relationship.

Another indication of Mary's openness to discovering through writing was her relaxed approach to the writing task. She was not focused on the product; instead, she wrote to record and explore her ideas in "writer-based prose."

Unlike Mary, I was not open to allowing my thoughts to reveal themselves in the writing process. I concentrated on thinking up my ideas before I began to write. I tried to write my final paper in the first draft.

Mary began writing her paper with the idea that Michael was cruel and that his relationship with Frances was bad. Through her writing, she recognized what was for her the point of the story: modern relationships are threatened by the objectification of women, and women themselves must refuse to cooperate with this attitude.

Like Mary, I also discovered my thesis through writing: Michael used his objectification of women to avoid entering into a deeper, more meaningful relationship with a particular woman—Frances. In this sense, my writing was consistent with Murray's theory that "writers use language as a tool of exploration to see beyond what they know." However, if I had approached the writing process like Mary did, as a free-write, I might have achieved more insights. Unfortunately, since I was so product-oriented, this expectation excluded, to some extent, my receptiveness to additional insights revealed through the writing process.

My first draft was "reader-based"; I wrote directly to my audience, without first clarifying my thoughts on paper. One of the reasons that I have so much trouble facing my writing tasks is because I try to skip the "writer-based" stage by writing initially in "reader-based prose." Not only is this difficult to do, but it also limits my ability to learn what I have to say through the writing process.

Changing Perceptions

Although Mary's initial dislike of Michael continued throughout her analysis of the story, she developed a better understanding of what evoked her negative reaction. Her initial response was that Michael was cruel. By the final draft, she also blamed Frances for her part in their superficial relationship because she allowed herself to be treated as an object.

In the conclusion of her paper, Mary reflects Rosenblatt's belief in the social implications of literature and their power to change readers. Mary concludes that the author has presented an example of modern relationships where "men look at women as objects and women accept this view." The implication is that if readers do not like this view, they should examine their own attitudes toward male and female roles. By rejecting this narrow view of relationships, people can arrive at a more equitable perception of the possibilities for men and women together.

Since I have formulated a strong value system and adopted a feminist ideology, I am less inclined to radically change my perceptions. I do not necessarily focus on literature to help me form opinions; instead, I use it as a measure of my own reality. I am less inclined to change my opinions. I analyze contrary views in the context of my value system. By doing this, I may reach a deeper insight into the faulty premise of other opposing views, especially those based on a sexist view of reality.

Instead of changing my own perceptions through writing, as Mary did, I attempted to change the perceptions of my readers through my writing. I based my persuasive argument on a combination of "pathos" (appealing to the reader's sense of justice and fair play) and "logos" (appealing to the reader's sense of logic).

My writing processes reflected the classical rhetoric approach. This theory identifies the "invention" stage as the most important part of the composing process. Before writing, I consciously reviewed the points that I would use to defend my position. As I wrote, I included these points and new ones that occurred to me during the writing process.

Because my intent was to influence my audience, not to simply report on my own observations, I concentrated on my style and delivery. I did not want my readers to question my argument based on a sloppy, in-articulate presentation, nor did I want them to drift too far from my intended point. I wanted to direct their reaction through the controlled use of language.

Conclusion

Through an examination of Mary's and my reading responses and writing processes, I discovered a marked difference related to our ages and life experiences. As a younger, developing personality, Mary seemed more open to discovering her voice through reading and writing. As an older, more developed personality, I was less open to discovering my voice through reading and writing; instead, I used these processes to further develop my evolved ideology.

My commitment to feminism and my interest in identifying and re-sisting sexist ideology leads me to question and evaluate texts to discover how they are influenced by and reflective of sexism. This focus motivates me to place individuals and events in the context of society, rather than to consider them individually.

Mary is in the process of exploring and developing her value system, and is, therefore, more open to examining texts to discover a variety of life options. In reading literature, she focuses on the specifics as examples of different possibilities. Unlike me, she has not concentrated her at-tention on any particular ideology to the exclusion of others. Over time, she will align herself with a group or groups that reflect her chosen values, and then she may concentrate on developing, testing, and de-fending her position as I have done.

These two case studies seem to suggest the following:

Bleich's theory that readers' personalities affect their reading re-sponses is most evident in mature readers who have strongly aligned themselves with a particular ideology or value system and are mo-tivated to test and develop this perspective rather than to seek new insights.

Rosenblatt's theory that literature serves as a vehicle for learning is most evident in developing readers who are experimenting with different ideologies and value systems to discover their own prefer-ences.

Dianna's essay reflects the pedagogical structure that produced it. It is informal in tone and assumes an audience of class participants — people who know Mary and have read the Shaw story and the theory she refers to. She is continuing the conversation begun in class and the dialogue begun in her own mind as she listened to the positions of others and read the assigned material.

Her essay reveals the powerful influence that Linda Flower's "Writer-Based Prose: A Cognitive Basis for Problems in Writing" had upon her. Flower made her realize that she had not been allowing herself to engage in writer-based writing because she had been too product-oriented. When Dianna read Flower's essay, about midway through the quarter and after she had written essay one but before writing essay two, she commented in her journal:

I am very enthusiastic about this article. For me, this is the most interesting and most useful material covered so far. I appreciate getting specific information on the writing process. I only wish that I had known about this when I first began taking classes.

The idea of writing a journal-like entry to get one's thoughts down on paper, without focusing on the final product, is a great idea. From now on, I will begin all my papers by using writer-based prose. I look forward to enjoying the writing process more. Without having to worry about the product at the early writing stages, I think that I will be able to access more insights and suffer a lot less anxiety.

The idea of transforming writer-based prose into reader-based prose was clear. For me, breaking down the writing process into more manageable units according to a formula makes the writing task more manageable and less threatening.

I had never really thought about how what evolves from one's journal-type writing is in a narrative form, and that what one needs to do with this information is to re-organize this according to the intended purpose of the piece.

I feel cheated—to have been deprived of this information in all my writing to date. I never thought of using writing as a medium for thinking.

I especially liked the part about the limitations of one's short-term memory. This makes so much sense to me. How can one hope to construct a complex thesis by trying to juggle and hold all one's thoughts in one's mind at the same time. Obviously, if writers can unload their thoughts on paper, they will free up their mind to receive/produce new thoughts. Once on paper, the writer's thoughts can be compared, evaluated, re-arranged, and altered. Re-reading one's original draft can in itself stimulate new thoughts.

When I think of all the lost possibilities in my writing due to my starting out the writing process with a pre-conceived idea of what I was going to say, it annoys me. Without being open to new insights, I'm sure I missed the point repeatedly in my own prose. I was doomed to failure by starting out all my writing from the reader-based mode. I can think of many instances where I never considered alternatives to my initially defined thesis, focused as I was on establishing my premise prior to beginning my writing.

I have been procrastinating about a paper due next week. I was uncertain about exactly what I would say, how I would begin, what I should focus on. Now it doesn't matter, as a matter of fact it is better, that I don't limit my vision to a preconceived thesis based on a small amount of information. With the pressure off to produce a particular product, I can simply concentrate my efforts on writing down my thoughts and discovering where they take me.

Dianna realized that in preparing essay one, and in her writing generally, she did not allow her writing to develop on its own. She was too impatient for a polished essay. Mary's drafts seemed to evolve in a way that her own did not, suggesting that Mary was learning from her own text as well as from the feedback she was receiving in class. In contrast, her own drafts remained relatively static; she was not learning from her evolving text. This central insight led to others — that her reading process, too, was attenuated and rigid. She tended to impose meaning on a text rather than to interact with it. Mary, in contrast, was more open to the possible meanings of the text and to the interpretations of others. Dianna recognized that these two different reading strategies, her own and Mary's, in some ways paralleled the strategies described by Bleich and Rosenblatt. Bleich's reader is empowered to impose meaning on a text, but Bleich does not emphasize that the reader learns from the text; Rosenblatt's reader, in contrast, "transacts" with the text and so learns from it.

Dianna applied these insights in the writing of her final paper. She self-consciously employed reader-based writing as she prepared her drafts, allowing her writing process to direct itself. She also was extremely receptive to her classmates' suggestions for revision. The theory she read allowed her to transform her reading and writing processes. The final paper, though, is a curious blend of the informal and the formal, an indication, perhaps, that she is still having difficulty letting go of her product-oriented approach. The forms she learned in her technical writing courses have a powerful hold on her.

Dianna's final paper is not simply an exploration of the ways in which her cognitive processes differ from Mary's. During one of the class critique sessions we suggested that she try to relate her findings to her interpretive filter, her feminist ideology. Was there a relationship between the interpretive strategies she employed and her identification with the feminist movement? We were encouraging her to see herself as a member of a group rather than an isolated individual. The resulting insight, that her feminism is a limitation as well as a strength, was a revelation to her. She had not previously recognized the extent to which her feminist gestalt was restricting as well as liberating. The paper will allow her, perhaps, to develop a more mature perspective, one that recognizes the complexity of the ideology she embraces.[6]

Literature and Composition did not "cover" a literary period or a large number of literary texts and would probably do little to prepare students for the Graduate Record Exam in English literature. As far as I know, however, none of the students who took the course plans to pursue graduate study in English; most will probably become technical writers in industry. I would hope they will continue to read literature, though, and that their reading will be self-reflexive. Certainly Rosenblatt has given them enough good reasons for their doing so. She says in *Literature as Exploration* that literature provides an emotional outlet (36), that it provides an objective presentation of our problems (41), that it helps develop an ability to understand and sympathize with others (40), and that it allows for the possibility of compensating for lacks or failures through identification with characters who possess qualities other than our own (40). I would hope, too, that students came away from the course with an appreciation for differences in interpretation and for the possibility of negotiating difference through interaction with others. An observation by one of the students in her final evaluation of the course suggests that this may have been the case. She said, "I looked forward to seeing how others responded to the literature. It was very interesting and somewhat surprising to see the variety of responses. I guess I had thought that there was an official/correct interpretation. It is liberating to know that, as long as one is true to the content of the text, many different responses are possible."

I suspect that, by the end of the quarter, all of the students enrolled in the course shared this insight. If we didn't always agree about which theory was the most compelling explanation of the reading or writing process, we did all recognize that the process of interpreting a literary text is highly complex and that there is no textual object that we can discuss as if it were independent of our interpretive filters. This awareness should serve students well when they recognize that, for the rest of their lives, they will be attempting to interpret their experience, a rich variety of pre-texts and texts, and to negotiate those interpretations with others. Their success—indeed their survival—will depend upon their ability to make those interpretations prevail.[7]

NOTES

1. Louise Rosenblatt emphasizes this dual allegiance in *Literature as Exploration*. She says, for instance, "The teacher realistically concerned with helping his students to develop a vital sense of literature cannot, then, keep his eyes focused only on the literary materials he is seeking to make available. He must also understand the personalities who are to experience this literature. He must be ready to face the fact that the student's reactions will inevitably be in terms of his own temperament and background" (51).

2. Harste, Woodward, and Burke use the term *transactional* rather than *contextual*, a term they derive from the work of Louise Rosenblatt. As far as I am concerned, the terms are synonymous.

3. Cooper distinguishes her "ecological" model from the contextual models of theorists such as Kenneth Burke, who perceive context as unique, unconnected with other situations. Cooper, in contrast, sees context as encompassing

more than the individual writer and her immediate context. She says, "An ecologist explores how writers interact to form systems: all the characteristics of any individual writer or piece of writing both determine and are determined by the characteristics of all the other writers and writings in the system" (368). The contextual model I am describing here is compatible with Cooper's ecological model.

4. Kathleen McCormick has developed a useful contextual pedagogy, encouraging students, in their responses, to focus on issues from "cultural, historical, phenomenological, and structuralist approaches" (837). The approach I am describing here more closely resembles that described by John Clifford in "A Response Pedagogy for Noncanonical Literature." He says, "Why not teach a text by disclosing and teasing out the implications of the swirling complexity of one's own reading and that of the class. Certainly not to valorize one response over another, but to uncover multiplicity, to highlight surprising possibilities, to study together the molding influence of prior assumptions and expectations" (55).

5. The work of composition researcher and theorist James Britton is an interesting hybrid. His emphasis on "expressive" writing has romantic and individualistic overtones. At the same time, he has been strongly influenced by sociolinguists such as M. A. K. Halliday and stresses again and again in his work the importance of talk in the learning process.

6. I might add that in some ways Dianna overstates the case. Mary's writing process, while less rigid than Dianna's, was also less successful in leading to an acceptable final product, a clear, confident, and convincing discussion of the story. Mary revised extensively because she had little direction; her receptivity, her openness to the prompts of her own evolving text, were liabilities as well as strengths. Ultimately, Dianna's analysis of the Shaw story was considerably more coherent than Mary's.

7. Here I am intentionally echoing Jane Tompkins's resonant conclusion to "An Introduction to Reader-Response Criticism," "when discourse is responsible for reality and not merely a reflection of it, then whose discourse prevails makes all the difference" (xxv). In the contextual model I am developing here, though, discourse interacts with reality rather than is responsible for it.

WORKS CITED

"ADE Study of the English Curriculum." *MLA Newsletter* 18 (Summer 1986): 18-19.

Belsey, Catherine. *Critical Practice.* New York: Methuen, 1980.

Bleich, David. "Gender Interests in Reading and Language." In *Gender and Reading: Essays on Readers, Texts, and Contexts.* Ed. Elizabeth A. Flynn and Patrocinio P. Schweickart. Baltimore: Johns Hopkins University Press, 1986. 234-66.

———. "Intersubjective Reading." *New Literary History* 17 (Spring 1986): 401-21.

———. *Readings and Feelings: An Introduction to Subjective Criticism.* Urbana, Ill.: NCTE, 1975.

————. *Subjective Criticism*. Baltimore: Johns Hopkins University Press, 1978.

Britton, James, Tony Burgess, Nancy Martin, Alex McLeod, and Harold Rosen. *The Development of Language Abilities (11-18)*. London: Macmillan Education, 1975.

Clifford, John. "A Response Pedagogy for Noncanonical Literature." *Reader* no. 15 (Spring 1986): 48-61.

Cooper, Marilyn M. "The Ecology of Writing." *College English* 48 (April 1986): 364-75.

de Man, Paul. "The Resistance to Theory." *Yale French Studies* 63 (1982): 3-20.

Emig, Janet. "Hand, Eye, Brain: Some 'Basics' in the Writing Process." In *Research on Composing: Points of Departure*. Ed. Charles R. Cooper and Lee Odell. Urbana, Ill.: NCTE, 1978. 59-73.

Fish, Stanley. "Is There a Text in This Class?" In *Is There a Text in This Class?: The Authority of Interpretive Communities*. Cambridge: Harvard University Press, 1980. 303-21.

Flower, Linda. "Writer-Based Prose: A Cognitive Basis for Problems in Writing." *College English* 41 (Sept. 1979): 19-37.

Goodman, Kenneth S. "Psycholinguistic Universals in the Reading Process." In *Psycholinguistics and Reading*. Ed. Frank Smith. New York: Holt, Rinehart and Winston, 1973. 21-27.

Harste, Jerome C., Virginia A. Woodward, and Carolyn L. Burke. "Examining Our Assumptions: A Transactional View of Literacy and Learning." *Research in the Teaching of English* 18 (1984): 84-108.

McCormick, Kathleen. "Theory in the Reader: Bleich, Holland, and Beyond." *College English* 47 (1985): 836-50.

Murray, Donald M. "Internal Revision: A Process of Discovery." In *Research on Composing: Points of Departure*. Ed. Charles R. Cooper and Lee Odell. Urbana, Ill.: NCTE, 1978. 85-103.

Prince, Gerald. "Literary Theory and the Undergraduate Curriculum." In *Profession 84*. New York: MLA, 1984. 37-40.

Rosenblatt, Louise. *Literature as Exploration*. New York: Appleton-Century-Crofts, 1937; rpt., New York: Noble, 1968.

————. *The Reader, the Text, the Poem: The Transactional Theory of the Literary Work*. Carbondale: Southern Illinois University Press, 1978.

Salvatori, Mariolina. "Reading and Writing a Text: Correlations between Reading and Writing Patterns." *College English* 45 (Nov. 1983): 657-66.

Scholes, Robert. *Textual Power: Literary Theory and the Teaching of English*. New Haven: Yale University Press, 1985.

Sommers, Nancy. "Revision Strategies of Student Writers as Experienced Adult Writers." *College Composition and Communication* 31 (Dec. 1980): 378-88.

Tompkins, Jane P. "An Introduction to Reader-Response Criticism." In *Reader-Response Criticism: From Formalism to Post-Structuralism*. Ed. Jane P. Tompkins. Baltimore: Johns Hopkins University Press, 1980. ix-xxvi.

Wells, Gordon. "Becoming a Communicator." In *Learning through Interaction: The Study of Language Development*. Ed. Gordon Wells. Cambridge: Cambridge University Press, 1981. 73-115.

PART FOUR

Teaching Reorientations

Bringing about Critical Awareness through History in General Education Literature Courses

Let me start with an example. One of my most sincere but silent freshmen uncharacteristically spoke up as class discussion strayed to the United States' Latin American policy. He was, he declared, willing to fight and die to protect freedom, citing atrocities by right-wing rebels as one reason for his decision. He assumed that right-wing rebels must be communists, since only communists could commit atrocities. He was not alone. Over 50 percent of those in the class supporting our policy did not know the difference between right- and left-wing rebels.

My example—and all teachers of general education courses have their own—indicates that the problem with American culture is not— as Christopher Lasch would tell us—narcissism but amnesia. The two are, however, related. Cultural amnesia leads to temporal narcissism, a failure to have a critical view on the present because of an inability to conceive of any but contemporary ways of constructing reality. Clearly, one of the goals of general education literature courses should be to increase students' critical capacity by having students read works that will expand their narrow sense of the world. And yet widespread cultural amnesia makes that goal difficult to achieve.

Victims of our culture's amnesia, students have difficulty establishing a dialogue with a work of literature that will lead to expanded understanding because of an inability to encounter the otherness of a text from the past. To be sure, students have as much or more difficulty with contemporary works, but this difficulty is part of my point. We need historical analysis because without it we can have no understanding of the present. With no perspective on the present, a culture relinquishes whatever chance it has for shaping the future. Students' alienation from history confines them to a series of fragmented, directionless presents.

Of course, this lack of historical awareness is not the fault of general education literature courses, and to think that changing the way we teach literature will drastically alter the historical conditions that have contributed to it would be naïve. Furthermore, it seems logical to argue that students' historical awareness is the responsibility of history departments, not literature departments. Much of this essay will try to demonstrate that such compartmentalizing of knowledge is a major part of our problem, which is not to say that different departments should not have different tasks. Old-fashioned as I might seem, I will continue to argue that literature should be the primary focus of general education literature courses. We don't need to dissolve disciplines; we need to establish shared responsibilities and coherent connections between them. My reason for stressing historical analysis in literature courses is twofold: students cannot read closely and critically without it, and the critical reading of literature is an ideal activity to increase historical awareness. Thus, it worries me that, rather than combat the historical conditions causing cultural amnesia, many of our existing approaches to teaching literature, especially general education courses, succumb to them. It further worries me to hear advocates of theoretical reform of the curriculum take as an object of attack what some participants at the April 1987 Conference on Doctoral Study in Wayzata, Minnesota, called the dominant, yet discredited, "historical" model of literary education.

Such attacks are misguided because they are historically inaccurate, proof that even up-to-date theorists are not immune to cultural amnesia. For instance, some of the same theorists who attack the historical model also speak of a New Critical hegemony in literary education. Have they forgotten that over fifty years ago the New Critics launched their own attack against what they felt was a discredited historical model? We can't have both a New Critical hegemony and the persistence of a historical model. In fact, we have had neither.

To be sure, the New Critics had a powerful influence on the shape of literary education, and in my own historical account I will try to offer institutional reasons for it. One is that when they attacked historians in the 1930s and 1940s they did so for good reason. Much of what passed as historical analysis involved little more than surrounding a work with a set of historical facts. Indeed, by the 1960s many historians (who never completely disappeared from the scene) were willing to agree with Robert B. Heilman that they " 'asked for' the revolt they got" (38). But that revolt was not limited to New Critics. For instance, one of the most devastating blows against historians was struck by

R. S. Crane of the Chicago school in his 1935 essay "History versus Criticism in the Study of Literature."

The success that New Critics and others had in attacking the old-fashioned historical model makes it clear that it is a mistake to call our present model of literary education historical. Nonetheless, it would also be a mistake to call it critical or theoretical. As Gerald Graff has cogently argued, the dominant model is not historical, critical, or theoretical. Instead, it is a makeshift compromise that operates according to the coverage principle. The coverage principle responds to changes in the study of literature by merely adding a new field of study to the curriculum without any attempt at integration. Graff specifically warns theorists that, unless the coverage principle is challenged, theory will become no more than the latest field tacked on to the curriculum. If theorists really want theory to be integrated into the curriculum, Graff argues, they need to resist the tendency to have it become the new field to be covered by highlighting the implied theoretical assumptions of all educators. In Graff's model theory would serve a function similar to the one that Northrop Frye advocated for criticism thirty years ago: it would unify a curriculum and it would get members of the profession talking to one another again as a corporate body. But if Frye's attempt to use archetypal criticism to break down "barriers between methods" is a product of the consensus politics of the 1950s insofar as Frye claims to attack "no methods of criticism, once that subject has been defined" (341), Graff's role for theory is a product of the 1980s insofar as he claims that the only possible consensus today is one in which we agree to disagree.

Unfortunately, Graff's label has been used by others to describe the "historical" model that tries to cover all literary periods. That Graff himself does not use his label as a description of the historical is clear from his defense of historical analysis. Indeed, to me, it is naïve to believe that the solution to our problems lies in replacing an outmoded "historical" model with an up-to-date "theoretical" one. Instead, the truly innovative model will be the one that makes connections between existing fields. Rather than respond to a new field by adding it pluralistically to the curriculum we need to establish dialectical tensions. Far from discrediting the historical, such a curriculum would help to redefine it. To avoid attempting that redefinition by incorrectly blaming present problems on a historical model would be to repeat a mistake made in our recent past. As Graff puts it, in reducing "history to something so ancillary that readers were better off without it," opponents of the historical were unable to see that "the remedy for bad historical teaching of literature might be *better* historical teaching" (*Professing* 179).

Of course, not everyone would agree with Graff and me that better historical teaching should be our first priority. In an essay on graduate education, one of the most intelligent writers on theory and pedagogy, Robert Scholes, emphasizes "the philosophical naïveté that besets all Americans." Not to provide a program that counters that naïveté, he argues, is to deprive our graduate students of the ability "to perform a seriously critical act," an inability that renders them incapable of "critical evaluation" and thus makes them less efficient teachers of reading and writing (41).

Although I agree with Scholes about both Americans' philosophical naïveté and our failure to teach critical skills, I still maintain my stress on historical analysis. Why I do should help to clarify my position. I would start by pointing out that although Scholes disagrees with the New Critics' narrow definition of literature, his emphasis on training in critical skills has important affinities with them. A major complaint that the New Critics leveled against literary historians was their failure to perform critical evaluation. Granted, Scholes would fault the New Critics' narrow focus on evaluating a work's formal properties. But Scholes' own emphasis on the critical evaluation of texts is more narrow than Frye's vision of criticism as "an ethical instrument, participating in the work of civilization" by freeing the mind from "compulsions of habit, indoctrination, and prejudice" and by making social action "purposeful by enlightening its aims" (348-49).

Unlike many new theorists (Scholes not included), who in their enlightened state confidently proclaim that no criticism is free from indoctrination and prejudice, I do not regard Frye's goals for criticism as an ideologically blind product of liberal humanism. To pursue the Nietzschean half-truth that disinterested critical inquiry is impossible is disastrous for education. Certainly, no inquiry is completely disinterested. But Bacon equated knowledge and power for good reason. Knowledge of the world gives human beings the critical perspective that they need in order to have limited control over their destiny in the world. So long as humanity hopes to wrest a realm of freedom out of necessity, it is necessary to have the clearest possible knowledge of our situation in the world. To state my point as a paradox: it is in humanity's interest to retain a notion of disinterested critical inquiry. Historical knowledge is essential for training the critical faculty for two reasons. First, it helps us to understand the historical forces that have partly determined our situation in the world; and, second, it offers a critical perspective on that situation.

Thus, my response to Scholes is that critical thinking is impossible without a historical sense trained by reading works from the past. For instance, Scholes urges that "for our own good as teachers and for the sake of the future of our world, we must learn to engage in critical dialogue not only with Jacques Derrida but with such as Jürgen Habermas" (42). Arguably, however, the most important works by each, *Grammatology* and *Knowledge and Human Interests*, are historical works. How are we to engage these two philosophers critically without engaging the historical tradition that they engage? Or when Scholes tells us that "we spend far too much time shepherding graduate students through text after literary text—works they ought to be able to read on their own—and not enough time helping them master the discourses they need to position literary texts for effective critical scrutiny" (42), doesn't he risk lapsing into a philosophical naïveté of his own—one that Derrida is at pains to correct—that somehow the reading of literary texts is automatic, whereas the reading of philosophical texts needs training?

Because with Walter Benjamin I believe that a "work's being in time and its being understood are only two sides of one and the same condition" (289), I will continue to stress the need for historical analysis. Further, I would argue that it is needed most by the general student population that takes general education courses. In order to think critically about an issue that could directly affect his life, my student who confused right- and left-wing rebels does not initially need a lesson in deconstruction—for him right and left have always already been deconstructed. Instead, he needs a lesson in history, for as Antonio Gramsci once pointed out, even the terms *east* and *west*—*right* and *left*—have significance only within history. Freed in general education courses from any pretense at covering a discipline, we can concentrate our efforts on creating a critical awareness in our students by discovering the intricate connections between literature and history.

Of course, making a case for the necessity of historical analysis is not the same as suggesting how it can be accomplished, and I do not want to underestimate the difficulties involved. How does one teach historically in an ahistorical culture? That question leads us on a circular investigation from which there seems no escape; for what seems to be the most obvious solution—add a little history to our instruction of literary texts—is itself a symptom of our problem. Students will read literature historically only when they are historically aware. To think of history as some *thing* that we can add to literary texts is the very opposite of historical awareness. Yet how can our students, raised in a culture that suppresses historical awareness, develop it unless we expose them to some history in our classroom?

How difficult it is to answer that question is indicated by one of the most highly publicized recent efforts to solve it. In *Cultural Literacy* E. D. Hirsch bases his argument on one of the founding assumptions of any historical criticism: a work cannot be understood in isolation. But his most popular effort to solve cultural illiteracy — to teach a list of facts — contradicts his major premise, for what guarantee do we have that students will understand those facts unless we provide a context for them?

The problem with Hirsch's solution highlights one of the major difficulties with any truly historical analysis. If every work is part of an intricately interconnected network of historical forces, where can our analysis stop, which is another way of asking where can it begin? To be sure, this is not a new dilemma; Henry Adams faced it when he speculated that "all opinion founded on fact must be error, because the facts can never be complete, and their relations must be always infinite" (410). The dilemma is not new, but it does help to explain why our solution to it has been to avoid it by separating literature from history or by neglecting the historical in our attempts to develop a critical sense.

The answer, however, is to neither avoid nor escape the dilemma of historical analysis, since as historical subjects we are inevitably caught in history's intricate web. Instead, we need to try to understand our dilemma historically. For those intent on more genuine historical teaching a good place to start is with the recognition that it is, after all, historically true that in our culture historical knowledge is no longer considered an essential element of the study of literature or the training of critical skills. Why, we need to know, is this so, and how has it affected the way we teach?

The split between history and literature as well as that between history and criticism coincided with a changed notion of the humanities in this country. Since the reason that almost all undergraduates take a general education literature course is to fulfill their humanities requirement, we need to have some understanding of that change. We can trace it by examining two movements that started in the first half of this century: James Harvey Robinson's New History and New Criticism. That comparison is not intended to supplant more ambitious work that has linked the rise of New Criticism to Cold War politics and an altered student population after World War II. But it does assume that those interested in the split between literature and history would be wise to examine what was happening in history departments as well as literature departments.

Our present ahistorical approach to literature can in part be attributed to the increased specialization of knowledge in the late nineteenth century and its institutionalization in the twentieth. For Robinson the rise of disciplinary specialization was an exciting development. In *The New History* (1912) he was especially interested in the newly established professional social sciences. Robinson felt that histories written in the nineteenth century were too narrowly political, telling the story of great leaders and wars while neglecting other areas of human life. He demanded that historians draw on the social sciences to give a fuller account of change, an account that covered economic, psychological, and social life as well as political life. He wanted more inclusive histories that told the lives of all humankind, not just an elite few. Recognizing the potential of the new disciplines to fragment knowledge, Robinson saw history as the discipline that could draw from them all. To the objection that if, as he urged, each discipline would adopt a historical model of knowledge there would be no need for the discipline of history, Robinson replied that the task of history is to unite these separate histories.

Robinson's view of history as a synthesizing discipline is similar to that of Henry Adams, who in a letter circulated to professors of history argued that "the only channel wide enough" to coordinate and contain the current of twentieth-century multiplicity "is, and ought to be, the department of history" (518). Yet Adams, who today is read chiefly in English departments, had an important difference from Robinson. As Adams wrote William James, his *Education* interested him chiefly as a literary experiment, which William's brother Henry would best understand. In contrast, Robinson, uneasy about history's long subserviency to moral philosophy and literature, stressed history's need to break from both. The historian, he argued, "is at liberty to use his scientific imagination, which is quite different from a literary imagination" (52). Robinson's attempt to achieve scientific status by allying history with the social sciences can be read symptomatically as marking the beginning of a changed relationship between history and other humanistic disciplines.

The sheer volume of material defining and justifying the humanities once caused David Daiches, an Englishman, to observe that a strenuous defense of the humanities goes on all the time in America (153-55). Members of humanities divisions might well respond that such defenses are necessary because the humanities are valued so little in our practical, business-oriented culture. If we did not speak up, the humanities might be funded out of existence in favor of accounting and computer studies programs. But while America has long been a business-oriented society, it was not until after World War I that references to "the humanities" as such started to appear so frequently. Defined as "those subjects which represent the culture of the past," the humanities at that time were intricately linked to historical understanding (Higham 13). But by the 1940s the definition of the humanities had changed. The emphasis on their "rich heritage" was replaced by an emphasis on the critical value to be achieved from their "liberating" knowledge of "choice, preference, taste." As one apologist put it, "The element common to the humanities is their common concern with values." Key words became "spiritual," "moral," "humanizing," "valuation," "design for living," and "broad vision" (Higham 20-21), words often found in the writings of the New Critics.

There are a number of reasons why historical knowledge was no longer considered an essential element of a humanist's critical faculty. I want to emphasize an institutional one. The older definition of the humanities as cultural heritage developed when the major institutional question in American universities was whether higher education should be predominantly literary and ethical or chiefly specialized and scientific. The compromise was to make a split. Science explained the existing world; the humanities preserved our heritage. But, as we have already seen, during the late nineteenth and early twentieth centuries the newly developed social sciences complicated that compromise. American universities responded to the rise of these new disciplines by creating a three-part division of knowledge: the natural sciences, the social sciences, and the humanities. Within this new version of the trivium, history departments have a split identity, sometimes belonging with the social sciences, sometimes with the humanities. We can see how history's changed status subverted the historical orientation of the humanities by looking at what Robinson hoped to accomplish by allying history with the social sciences.

Robinson's distrust of the literary imagination grew out of an Aristotelian notion of literature. In the *Poetics* Aristotle argued that poetry was superior to philosophy and history because it combined the concreteness of history with the universality of philosophy. For Robinson the literary attempt to shape the past to illustrate timeless truths continued history's subordination to moral philosophy. The past, he argued, did not illustrate timeless truths, which is not to say that he saw no value in studying it. Quite the contrary.

For Robinson the past was not a repository of eternal values, but a constant illustration of the one great historical truth: change. Historical study yields usable truths, but they are usable only because they help us to understand how the past became the present. If the task for Leopold von Ranke was to tell *wie es eigentlich gewesen war,* for Robinson it was to tell *wie es eigentlich geworden ist;* not how it really was, but how it came to be. Influenced by pragmatism and what George Santayana called "that strange pragmatic reduction of yesterday to tomorrow" (686), Robinson wanted his New History to serve the present by helping us establish a new future. Its value did not arise from the humanistic task of preserving a heritage but from the scientific one of explaining the existing world.

If the New History's attempted emancipation from literature and moral philosophy was at odds with the established goal of humanistic education, it seemed necessary to establish a critical perspective on the present. Within a generation, however, its critical function was seriously compromised when admissions of historical relativism replaced claims of scientific objectivity. The transformation of New History into historical relativism is a complicated story, but we can get a sense of it by juxtaposing two statements by one of Robinson's allies, his onetime colleague and collaborator Charles A. Beard. In *An Economic Interpretation of the Constitution of the United States* (1913) Beard confidently proclaimed that the superiority of his method lay in its use of economics to distinguish between "remote and proximate causes" (4). Writing in 1936 he provides a concise illustration of how his former scientific confidence had turned to relativism. Asking after the causes of America's entry into World War I, he responds, "A search for the causes of America's entry into [World War I] leads into the causes of the war, into all the history that lies beyond 1914, and into the very nature of the universe of which the history is a part; that is, unless we arbitrarily decide to cut the web and begin at some place that pleases us" (*Discussion* 79). As today's antifoundational thinkers know all too well, history's intricate web seems to destabilize all critical positions within it.

Thus, it is no accident that New Critics, who arose at the same time that relativism dominated history departments, sought a basis for both moral values and criticism outside of history. Indeed, a critical perspective on a world of flux increasingly dominated by relativism, science, technology, and commerce seemed to depend on timeless, humanistic values. If it seemed ironic that the New History's effort to be a science soon led to relativism, from a New Critical perspective it made perfect sense. Once the study of history severed itself from the goal of moral philosophy, relativism was inevitable. Nonetheless, if historians like Robinson no longer saw the past itself as a repository of eternal values, they could still be sought in monuments from the past that existed in a separate temporal realm apart from historical flux. They could, that is, unless literary historians, as New Critics felt they did, also succumbed to relativism by insisting that aesthetic value changed over time. Condemning literary historians' relativism, Cleanth Brooks declared that "the Humanities are in their present plight largely because their teachers have more and more ceased to raise normative questions, have refrained from evaluation. In their anxiety to avoid meaningless 'emoting', in their desire to be objective and scientific, the proponents of the Humanities have tended to give up any claim to making a peculiar and special contribution." If the humanities are to endure, he argues, "they must be themselves—and that means, among other things, frankly accepting the burden of making normative judgments" (235).

So far I have emphasized the differences between New History and New Criticism to describe a change in the goal of humanistic education. It is important, however, to recognize that their differences developed from some shared assumptions. Not only did both accept a split between literature and science, they also agreed about an Aristotelian notion of literature. But if Robinson rejected the timeless universality that Aristotle attributed to literature, the New Critics embraced it and used it to argue that literature, not history, was the discipline that could combat the fragmentation of the modern world. Whereas other disciplines confined themselves to specialized types of knowledge, literature's special quality was that it resisted the fragmentation accompanying specialization. Literature, we were told, is organic and whole. Engaging the entire person, its special qualities are accessible to everyone—not just specialists. In fact, literature's claim to universality and nonspecialization is what helps justify requiring all undergraduates to take a course in it. The special knowledge it brings transcends major, class, race, gender. In short, literature humanizes. Since the special knowledge of literature humanizes in and of itself, there is no need to supplement it with knowledge from other disciplines. To do so is to risk reducing its unity and wholeness to a narrow, more specialized knowledge. This includes history. If Robinson wanted to free history from literature because the literary imagination would make history subordinate to moral philosophy, New Critics wanted to keep literature separate from history because history would obscure the universal truths dramatized in great works of literature.

This split left us with two different goals for teaching general education literature courses. On the one hand, we try to teach students the reading skills they need to gain access to the humanizing knowledge contained in the literary work; on the other, we try to make them read the greatest works of literature, since these contain the fullest expression of the human condition. The first goal leads to courses such as "Introduction to Fiction" or "Introduction to Poetry and Drama"; the second, to "Masterpiece" courses. Organized to emphasize the techniques peculiar to literature—point of view, plot, atmosphere, imagery, and so on—the first very often completely ignores historical considerations in selecting works to read. The second often seems to consider history because frequently works are organized in chronological order, but that chronological ordering is only superficially historical. Works are chosen because of their intrinsic merit, their value as autonomous works of art. Although a teacher is not forbidden from doing so, relating each work to its historical situation is not necessary because each stands on its own. The humanizing experience comes in the reading of individual works, not in relating one work to something outside of itself.

From this overly simplified sketch of the assumptions underlying the organization of many introductory courses, a contradiction becomes apparent. The notion of a piece of literature as an organic, autonomous whole that combats the fragmentation of the modern world can easily lead to teaching practices that contribute to the fragmentation our students experience in their lives; a fragmentation confirmed in their educational experience. At the same time sophomores take a general studies literature course, they might also take economics, biology, math, and accounting. There is nothing, not even the literature course, that connects the knowledge they gain from these different courses. For although literature is supposed to offer unified knowledge, its special brand of knowledge has been defined against the other types of knowledge they are exposed to. Whereas Robinson tried to combat the fragmentation of knowledge by using history to unite the various disciplines, New Critics tried to combat it by excluding other disciplines. Furthermore, because each work students read in a literature course is an organic whole that stands on its own, there is really no reason why they should relate one work to another taught in the same course. As they read one work, then another, then another, each separate and unique, each reading can too easily contribute to their sense of education as a set of fragmented, unrelated experiences in which wholeness and unity are to be found only in temporary, self-enclosed moments.

My (too symmetrical) comparison between New History and New Criticism emphasizes that the separation of literature and history cannot be blamed on literary critics alone—especially one school of critics. But if my brief history reminds us that historians share some of the responsibility for the separation, it also gives a different perspective on the New Critics' powerful argument that a historical approach would assimilate literature to another discipline and thereby destroy students' appreciation of literature's special humanistic qualities. As noble as the New Critics' defense of the humanistic value of literature sounds, we need to remember that one reason their assumptions about literature became institutionalized was that they coincided with institutional needs. Indeed, it is instructive to consider some of their eloquent defenses of the humanistic value of literature as simultaneous defenses of institutional turf. For instance, one of Cleanth Brooks's biggest fears was that literature will be parceled out "among the cultural historians and sociologists, respectively" (234). If teachers of the humanities "are to be merely cultural historians, they must not be surprised if they are quietly relegated to a comparatively obscure corner of the history division. If one man's taste is really as good as another's, and they can pretend to offer nothing more than a neutral and objective commentary on tastes, they must expect to be treated as sociologists, though not as a very important kind of sociologist" (235). If the choice is between buying Brooks's definition of the humanities or becoming an unimportant member of the history or sociology department, there is no choice.

Of course, the point of this essay is that there is a choice and that it is to be found by countering the spirit of the age more successfully than did the New Critics. What I propose is that we learn from New History, but correct its mistake of separating history and literature by starting to think of a historically based study of literature as a discipline that can relate separate realms of knowledge. Rather than retreat to literature as the last outpost of humanism in a dehumanized world, we might start using literature to combat the fragmentation our students sense by making connections with other human activities they experience.

But how, given the difficulties I have suggested, can I believe in the possibility of integrating literature and history? After all, despite the seeming novelty of today's new historicism, calls for historical analysis did not suddenly arise in the 1980. In the '60s *College English* printed a number of essays arguing for historical teaching. In 1969 Roy Harvey Pearce collected essays under the title *Historicism Once More* and in 1972 Wesley Morris published *Toward a New Historicism*. If a new historicism was not institutionalized pedagogically then, why might it be today?

It has a chance, even if a slim one, because historical conditions are different. For one, a "theoretical" revolution has occurred in literary studies. In November 1962 Pearce, just back from a Fulbright in France, chided the profession for its provincialism by asking, "Who among us reads, or reads those who read, Curtius or Lukács or Ingarden or Alonso or Castro or Bachelard—to drop just a few names?" ("Literature" 371). Today we would drop a different set of names, but few would accuse the profession of not paying attention to theorists.

One of the most important effects of new theory has been to challenge the very notion of the literary. Advocating a new historicism in response to New Criticism, Pearce and Morris did not substantially question New Critical boundaries, such as extrinsic/intrinsic. Instead, they argued that a work's relation to history enhances its intrinsic value. Today such boundaries have been blurred and the Aristotelian notion that works of literature are organic wholes is under attack. Rather than emphasize the ability of art to order a seemingly formless world, we focus on a text's gaps and aporias, on its ability to defamiliarize.

To some this changed notion of literature might seem to mitigate against connecting literature and history. For instance, Hayden White's popular attempts to bridge the two disciplines depend on the Aristotelian definition. According to White, "In point of fact [an interesting metaphor], history—the real world as it evolves in time—is made sense of in the same way that the poet or novelist tries to make sense of it, i.e., by endowing what originally appears to be problematic and mysterious with the aspect of a recognizable, because it is familiar, form. It does not matter whether the world is conceived to be real or only imagined; the manner of making sense of it is the same" (98).

It is easy to see why White is more popular with literary critics than historians, since statements like his turn history writing into a subset of literature. But if literary critics are flattered to think that, as one critic puts it, a history of history reveals "the revenge of literature" (Orr), such thoughts do not really increase the historical analysis of literature. Furthermore, as we saw with Robinson, it was precisely an Aristotelian notion of literature that caused many historians to ally themselves with the social sciences. To suggest how a different notion of literature can open literature to historical analysis without making history subservient to it, we can return to Robinson.

Robinson urged the historian to use a scientific rather than literary imagination because for him the "conscientious historian has come to realize that he cannot aspire to be a good story-teller for the simple reason that, if he tells no more than he has good reason for believing to be true, his tale is usually very fragmentary and vague. Fiction and drama are perfectly free to conceive and adjust detail so as to meet the demands of art, but the historian should always be conscious of the rigid limitations placed upon him" (51). The "literary" historian is too prone to "yield to the temptations to ignore yawning chasms of nescience at whose brink heavy-footed History is forced to halt, although Literature is able to transcend them at a leap" (55). Robinson distrusts the literary imagination because the Aristotelian notion of literature conflicts with the concept of reality that governs his historical inquiry. According to Hans Blumenberg, a thinker who deserves mention when theorists drop a few names, Aristotelian mimesis depends on the belief in a closed cosmos, in which nothing new or unfamiliar is allowed to become real. The task of the artist is to imitate a reality that may be obscured but is, nonetheless, preexisting and unchanging, or as White puts it, to endow "what originally appears to be problematic and mysterious with the aspect of a recognizable, because it is familiar, form."[1] Appropriate to ancient and medieval times, this reality concept was challenged in the Renaissance by the reality concept of an open context that legitimizes the element of surprise and unfamiliarity. Essential to this reality concept is a different notion of temporality, for it "always looks forward to a future that might contain elements which could shatter previous consistency and so render previous 'realities' unreal" (33). How important this reality concept is for Robinson's New History is illustrated by Blumenberg's argument that "the change in the concept of reality removes the dubiousness from what is new, and so *terra incognita*, or the *mundas novos*, becomes possible and effective as a *stimulus* to human activity; if one might phrase the process as a paradox, surprise is something to be expected" (33n).

Clearly an Aristotelian notion of literature is incompatible with the reality concept of an open context in which the imposition of a familiar form on the unfamiliar would be to obscure reality, not to reveal it. So long as literary critics share Robinson's Aristotelian beliefs about literature, literary and scientific historians seem doomed to occupy separate kingdoms. Indeed, Blumenberg's account helps to explain why a group of predominantly conservative Southern agrarians would adhere to an aesthetic aligned with belief in a closed world, an aesthetic that stressed literature's spatiality at the expense of its temporality. Without a sense of institutional history it is harder to explain how these conservative beliefs acquired so much control in disciplines known as the liberal arts, especially because literary works at the time often challenged a closed concept of reality. For instance, not many years before Robinson accused literature of transcending "yawning chasms of nescience" at a leap, Herman Melville had written: "Truth uncompromisingly told will always have its ragged edges" (130). Furthermore, if literary modernism often betrayed a nostalgia for a closed world, it also demystified notions of imitation. In fact, as Blumenberg notes, much literature since the Renaissance, including the entire genre of the novel, depends on the reality concept of an open context. It has become fashionable to associate recent theories of literature with postmodernism, but it might be more accurate to say that literary theory is finally responding to a modern concept of reality.

A different notion of the literary allows us to connect literature and history, not by arguing that historians, poets, and novelists alike make the unfamiliar familiar, but by challenging a reflection theory of art.[2] No longer seen as occupying a timeless space of order where it can reflect an already existing truth obscured by the unstable, fluctuating world of history, literature is seen as participating in a world that is no more closed than the boundaries separating art and history. Such a notion of the literary makes it impossible to understand a work apart from the historical reality into which its ragged edges disappear. Rather than transcend yawning chasms of nescience at a leap, literature confronts us with gaps in our knowledge, and thus, as Blumenberg puts it, works as a *"stimulus* to human activity,'' activity that will help to create a new future.

Part of that activity for teachers should be to create institutional opportunities for the integration of literature and history. Recent trends in literary theory suggest the direction that such institutional change might take. It is not an accident that many of the most influential ideas in contemporary theory come from fields other than literature. Too long restricted by disciplinary boundaries, the study and teaching of literature has been vitalized by ideas drawn from linguistics, philosophy, psychology, and anthropology. To be sure, not all borrowings have led explicitly to historical analysis. Nonetheless, it is significant that most of the prominent figures in other fields come from Europe.

As we have seen, American universities responded to disciplinary specialization by creating a division between the humanities, the social sciences, and the natural sciences. In Europe, however, the social sciences have more often been linked with the humanities to constitute the human as opposed to the natural sciences. Whereas the European human sciences help to foster interdisciplinary analysis, the American division fosters the disciplinary rivalry that caused New Critics to oppose humanistic knowledge to that pursued in the social sciences. As John Higham observes, "Americans have designed for themselves a somewhat distinctive map of high culture, on which social sciences and humanities appear as rival confederations disputing territory they jointly occupy'' (10).

The failure of that institutional division to meet the historical needs of some of our students is illustrated by changes occurring outside literature departments at the same time that Pearce and Morris were unsuccessfully attempting to establish a new historicism within them. In the late 1960s, women and ethnic groups vocally demanded increased representation in American society. In the university these groups challenged the institutionally defined role of literature courses. The reason why is easy to find. More than other groups in American society, ethnic groups and women experienced the failure of traditional humanities courses to live up to their name. Speaking eloquently in the name of the personal liberation provided by reading great literature, defenders of the humanities seemed to have established a canon that excluded literature written by a large segment of humanity. Significantly, it is precisely these excluded groups who have most self-consciously countered the general tendency of American culture to lapse into amnesia by rethinking and reconstructing our relation to the past. Institutionally this led to interdisciplinary programs of women's and ethnic studies that have helped to highlight the social and historical function of literature.

Clearly, the felt need of women and ethnic groups to rethink our relation to the past is one of the most important preconditions for new historical analysis in teaching literature, and I might easily have started my essay by stressing that need. But I did not for an important reason.[3] As essential as it is to stress the exclusion of ethnic groups and women brought about by our established approaches to literature, the very obviousness of their exclusion can lead to confusion. Because members of these groups have challenged traditional approaches, it might appear that the new stress on history is ideologically and conveniently weighted to speak for their interests. I started with the condition of general cultural amnesia and then traced how the institutional division of knowledge helps perpetuate that amnesia to stress that traditional approaches exclude much more than literature of interest to particular groups. Their exclusions are of method as well as content. Insofar as those methodological exclusions fail to counter our students' alienation from history, they serve to marginalize all students by contributing to their sense of isolated fragmentation.

It is for this reason that I have stressed the link between historical and interdisciplinary analysis. If like Robinson's New History the analysis of literature opens itself to other disciplines, the criteria used to establish literary evidence are altered. To draw on evidence that New Critics labeled extrinsic—evidence from social and economic history as well as intellectual history—is to produce a different notion of what constitutes a history of literature. By interweaving evidence previously compartmentalized, these new histories open up teaching possibilities that can help to combat the fragmentation that our educational system helps to perpetuate.

The fragmentation of knowledge that our students experience is so ingrained within the institutional structure of our universities, which in turn is so vitally linked to our culture's social structure, that it would take a radical restructuring of our society to combat fully students' lack of historical consciousness, and we need to be wary about simple or unrealistic solutions. For instance, when Terry Eagleton condemns literature departments for being part of the ideological state apparatus and then urges a move to rhetorical or cultural studies, I have to wonder what would exempt those programs from the same fate. Furthermore, if English departments cannot cover their own discipline, how do we expect to organize a department that covers everything? Rather than flatter ourselves by thinking that we can singlehandedly take on the educator's burden, we need to make it clear that we cannot act alone. Without a doubt a university should train students to read "all kinds of texts in all kinds of discourses and media" (Scholes 42), but the responsibility for establishing a textual curriculum should not rest with one department. Such a curriculum needs to be developed through interdepartmental cooperation. Instead of cutting down the amount of literature that students read in our courses to make way for the reading of other kinds of texts (students, especially nonmajors, already read too few works that we call literary), we need to make sure that they read other texts closely in other courses. When members of other departments chide us—as they often do—by asking why students can't write, we should ask them why students don't know politics, philosophy, or economics.

The point of that question is twofold. First, although the institutionalization of disciplinary specialization has had negative educational consequences, specialization itself is not the problem. Disciplinary specialization arose in response to a historical need that has not gone away: a complex society demands specialized forms of knowledge (Haskell). Specialized forms of knowledge produce specialized discourses that require special training to learn how to read them. Students need to specialize, but they also need to be able to make connections between specialized forms of knowledge to have an understanding of their place in history.

And so I come to the second point of my question. Teachers of literature cannot act alone, but they can take the lead in training students to interrelate knowledge. The historical analysis available to us today makes an introductory literature course an ideal place for such training to occur. To those who would argue that such a course would ignore the special quality that distinguishes literature from other modes of discourse, I would respond that at this particular historical moment the special quality of literature is that it enables such analysis. Certainly students' appreciation of literature will be enhanced if it helps them to make connections between their isolated studies of a complex world. To those who would argue that my emphasis on literature continues to treat it as a privileged mode of discourse, I would respond that so long as literature continues so amply to repay such analysis it has earned that privileged status.

Once we accept the goal of general education courses in literature as helping students to connect different realms of knowledge rather than to introduce them to yet one more isolated realm of knowledge, some practical, if not revolutionary, possibilities present themselves. My suggestions are sketchy and require elaboration and adjustment to local circumstances, but they are a start.

One simple suggestion is to interrelate the holy trinity of humanities, social science, and natural science requirements by pairing courses. Exactly what should be paired depends on available personnel and personalities, but I could imagine students simultaneously taking a social science course on the family as an institution and a humanities course on the family in literature; a course on the history of science could be paired with a course on metaphor and narrative as modes of knowledge. If links between the three divisions prove institutionally unfeasible, at least literature and history courses should be coordinated, as they sometimes are at smaller schools. Students can be required to take world literature in conjunction with world civilization or American literature in conjunction with American history.

Another option would be to copy the success of writing-across-the-curriculum programs by adopting literature-across-the-curriculum programs. Literature can connect with almost any discipline offered at the university: law, science, economics, and so on. A business major who wrestles with *Merchant of Venice* and *Death of a Salesman* may have a different perspective on the role of commerce in the present world, just as the English major in such a course might develop a different perspective on literature's connections to business and be forced to master the discourse of business departments.

As minor as these institutional changes are, they are bound to be resisted. With all of my talk about the restrictions of disciplinary boundaries, most of us still teach in institutional settings where those boundaries are, if anything, more solid as budgetary cuts force departments—especially humanities departments—to protect their institutional turf.

Recognizing that the production and reception of literature always takes place under the pressure of historical constraints, historical analysis offers some practical suggestions on how to deal with such dilemmas. Rather than ignore those constraints, we can use them as a teaching principle. By reflecting on what we are doing and the constraints that arise from that activity, we can raise important historical questions that evolve from our students' and our concrete situations.

The most obvious constraint our students confront is the requirement that they take a general studies literature course in the first place. The least we can do (and it continues to surprise me how often this is not done) is explain to them the institutional—and social—reasons for their humanities requirement. An answer to that question requires reflection upon the function of literature at the present time, a reflection impossible without comparison to its function at other historical moments.

Another constraint a college situation imposes on reading is a required syllabus. Sharing with students the criteria of selection and organization of the syllabus would help to combat any sense they might have that works are randomly chosen and unrelated. One of the most important questions to ask is whether the organization of the syllabus is designed to increase students' historical awareness. As I have already suggested, the typical chronological ordering is not necessarily historical. In courses organized chronologically the temptation is to teach according to a teleological narrative of emergence, the kind of narrative that structured most nineteenth-century histories and eventually led to the demise of old-fashioned historicism, insofar as we use that term in its precise sense of designating a mode of historiography practiced most often by German-trained scholars (Iggers). Although narratives of linear progress have been attacked by Nietzsche, Benjamin, and Foucault, educators have not been very innovative at coming up with alternatives for literary education. One reason for the persistence of such narratives is that it is difficult to conceive of a successful course without a *telos*. The very notion of education, or, in German, *Bildung*, is intricately related to a narrative of development. But perhaps we can best achieve our goal of developing students' historical awareness by disrupting chronological order.

Such disruptions should not be random, but self-conscious juxtapositions that stress historical difference. We might, for instance, start with *Billy Budd* and then move to *Antigone* to historicize what some consider to be the universal conflict between the desire for individual rights and the need for social order. As similar as the conflicts in the two works seem, there is an important historical difference.

In *Antigone,* as in *Billy Budd,* natural law is pitted against humanmade law, and an individual, aligned with natural law, threatens to disrupt social order. Only a modern misreading, however, would identify Antigone's appeal to natural law as an appeal for individual rights. Antigone defies humanmade law, not in the name of individual freedom, but in the name of a social group—the family—and its right to bury its dead. No more believing in the possibility of individual freedom outside society than Socrates, Antigone still has a concept of nature and natural law. The natural state for her is, however, not prior to society, but already social, inhabited by social groups, like the family. It is these natural groups, not individuals, who have natural rights. The play's conflict does not illustrate a timeless conflict between natural individuals and society; instead it registers an important historical transformation as rule of Greek society transferred from established families to a new form of state.

To historicize the conflict in this way is to problematize the popular narrative in which Western democracies emerged out of ancient Greece, for ironically the form of the state against which Antigone struggles is similar to the version of the state that we celebrate as the precursor to modern democracy. Challenging family privilege, it asserted the equal rights of all citizens (not individuals). Creon's inaugural address even echoes concepts and phrases from the speeches of Pericles. Those echoes do not keep Creon from being a tyrant. Nonetheless, although we have turned Antigone into a symbol of the courageous individual resisting the tyranny of the state, we should remember that our modern version of the conflict between the individual and society—even our modern version of a tyrant—would be unthinkable without the rise of the Greek concept of a society comprised of individuals equal in the eyes of the state. Whereas that concept of society is compatible with modern notions of a social contract in which nature consists of individuals with inalienable rights, it is incompatible with Antigone's notion of a socialized nature in which rights belong to groups, not individuals. To juxtapose *Billy Budd* and *Antigone* in this way is not only to see how modern notions of the state emerged from Greece but also to see the cost of that emergence, for where in our system of justice, we need to ask our students, do we have a place for group as opposed to individual rights?

A historically organized course is not directed backward in time; instead, it puts the past in dialectical relation to the present. Because reading a work from the past always takes place within a historical moment that we call the present, a work's moment of reception is a vital part of its historical existence. Thus, efforts lumped under the label of reader-response criticism that use literature to articulate students' beliefs can be an important aid in historical analysis. But our task is not just to have students articulate beliefs. They also need to put those beliefs at risk by developing a critical perspective on them. A popular way of trying to develop that critical perspective is to use the classroom as an interpretive community and through discussion to draw out different and conflicting student responses. The limitation of that otherwise valuable method should be clear. It virtually guarantees that truly different past ways of constructing reality will be excluded. To read works from the past and to analyze their moments of production as well as reception is to introduce a critical perspective impossible to draw out of students lodged in the present.

Of course, there is nothing new about seeking a critical perspective on the present in works from the past, so I need to distinguish my analysis from two of the most common attempts to do so. Part of the New Critics' program, the first finds a standard for evaluation in enduring works from the past because they are said to contain timeless truths. Thus, the critical perspective that they provide is not within history but transcends it. Influenced by Robinson's New History, the second stresses the role of a usable past. The notion of a usable past places works within history, but a progressive history emerging into the present. Common to these two different approaches is a belief that works from the past are relevant to the present because of identity, not difference. On the one hand, past works contain truths that apply equally well to the present and the past. On the other, they are usable insofar as they are part of a tradition leading to the present.

Clearly these defenders of tradition are very different from critics who stress a work's moment of reception at the expense of its moment of production. Nonetheless, in their stress on identity they too close off aspects of the past. In contrast, the historical analysis that I am advocating establishes a dialectical relation between a work's identity with the present and its difference from it. Its identity allows us in the present to relate to it. Its difference provides a critical perspective on the present. Historical analysis does not rest content with recovering the preexisting meaning of a work or with drawing out present responses to it. Instead, its dialectical process brings a new perspective into existence. It is precisely through respecting a work's temporal otherness that we make it most relevant to our present.

Unfortunately, even our current concern with otherness can deprive students of that new perspective. At the university where I last taught, most instructors in the general education course in literature and society include women and ethnic writers along with white males. And yet, one semester four out of five sections had included only works written in the United States in the last fifty years. If we decide to narrow our focus to United States society and literature, exploration of the complexity of life in a multiethnic culture is clearly an important goal. But wouldn't including Frederick Douglass, Harriet Jacobs, or Anne Bradstreet keep students who probably will take no other literature courses from having a time-bound perspective on issues of race and gender? In efforts to make general education courses relevant, we too often deny a historical perspective to those most in need of it.

To be sure, we need not move to the past to get a sense of cultural otherness. Students' critical perspective on their place in history can be increased by complementing my emphasis on temporal otherness with third-world or postcolonial literature. For instance, the juxtaposition of *Billy Budd* and *Antigone* would be both enriched and complicated if we then turned to *Things Fall Apart* or *Burger's Daughter*, and certainly my student who confused right- and left-wing rebels would have a different perspective if he read *100 Years of Solitude*. But even the terms *third-world* and *postcolonial* demand historical explanation.

Having started with questions about the historical organization of a course, I have inevitably raised the question of the choice of works. It is not the purpose of this essay to enter into that debate other than to suggest, as I already have, that sometimes efforts to open the canon can also close it. Nonetheless, I do want to emphasize that, in sharing with our students the criteria of selection and organization of the syllabus, we are forced to raise questions like those of the canon and the status of narratives of emergence that are so important in today's theoretical debates. As Graff has argued, because such debates have an effect on how students are taught, it makes no sense to protect students from them.

Even so, I don't want to turn an introductory course into a course on "theory." Our awareness that all reading takes place within a system of constraints should not lead to a situation in which we spend more time discussing those constraints than reading. When New Critics advocated close readings of texts, they responded to a real historical need. Students still need to develop a sensitivity to the nuances of a work's language, its patterns of imagery and metaphor, and its structures. Although historical teaching demands that we use some class time to introduce historical material that cannot be generated by class discussion, it does not abandon close readings to talk generally about "history." Instead, it reads closely to achieve a fuller historical awareness.[4] In teaching an individual work we can often start as we have before, but we cannot stop where we have. Just when we used to conclude by tying the threads of a text together and demonstrating its organic unity, we need to take the time to unwind a loose thread to open it to its historical situation. To do so is to alter what it means to read closely, which should alter how we teach close reading.

For an example I will look at Shakespeare's "Sonnet 87." I choose a short poem intentionally because lyrics seem least likely to lend themselves to historical analysis.

> Farewell, thou art too dear for my possessing,
> And like enough thou know'st thy estimate.
> The charter of thy worth gives thee releasing;
> My bonds in thee are all determinate.
> For how do I hold thee but by thy granting,
> And for that riches where is my deserving?
> The cause of this fair gift in me is wanting,
> And so my patent back again is swerving.
> Thyself thou gav'st, thy own worth then not knowing,
> Or me, to whom thou gav'st it, else mistaking;
> So thy great gift, upon misprision growing,
> Comes home again, on better judgment making.
>   Thus have I had thee as a dream doth flatter,
>   In sleep a king, but waking no such matter.

A love poem relying heavily on legal terminology—"estimate," "charter," "releasing" (with the pun on lease), "bonds," "determinate," "granting," "patent," "judgment"—this sonnet can sensitize students to different types of diction. It also illustrates how the Shakespearean sonnet form lends itself to a reversal or change of tone in the final couplet. Drawing upon these two formal elements, we can remark on how both help the poet to accomplish a very difficult task in the highly emotional moment of the breakup of a love affair: they allow him to praise his beloved and also to maintain his self-worth. On the one hand, the legal language distances the poet emotionally; on the other, when contrasted with the language of the couplet, it convinces the reader of the poet's emotional involvement. For while the couplet compares the affair to a dream, the legal language confirms its actuality. Read this way, the poem can be said to transcend time and speak to anyone who has experienced or can imagine experiencing the breakup of a love affair.

To historicize the poem is to let it speak more poignantly to students. One of the commonplaces of Renaissance studies is that the Renaissance coincided with the discovery of the modern interiority of self. As Anne Ferry has argued, one amazing aspect of the sonnets is Shakespeare's ability to express inner feeling at a historical moment when our modern vocabulary for the inner self was lacking. What Ferry does not note is that the "private" language of the inner self develops simultaneously with a public language of the law. This co-occurrence happens because the notion of an autonomous, independent self capable of private interior feelings is in part the result of the legal definition of self developing in the Renaissance as feudal social relations transformed into capitalist ones—in other words, as the very notion of possession changed. In feudalism the self is not constituted as an independent, autonomous subject; instead, mutually dependent human beings are connected in hierarchical relationships of servitude and mastery. Under capitalism humans are constituted as independent agents who freely enter into contractual relations. In describing his relation to the lover in the legal language of contract, the poet implies his status as a free agent capable of freely entering into and out of human relations. Thus, we can better understand how Shakespeare's use of legal language allows him to maintain his self-worth while heaping praise on his beloved. At the same time we can detect a nostalgia for a different relationship not so freely entered into and dissolved. For in the poet's flattering dream in the couplet he reverts to the language of feudal relations—"In sleep a king"—implying that bonds cannot be broken. The cost of that eternal bond, however, is a relationship of subservience and mastery. To conclude, the play between the poem's amorous subject and its legal language, between the first twelve lines and the couplet, is one between different historical concepts of social relations, concepts in severe tension in Shakespeare's England, a tension that persists today, as even our postindustrial society retains residual elements of feudal relations. In fact, I can guarantee that students will share the tension the poem dramatizes between the contractual and eternal notion of a love relationship. Reading the poem historically they will be in a better position to understand the historical forces leading to the tension they feel between the desire for freedom and commitment in love. They will also be better able to understand the costs involved in both desires as well as some of the reasons contractual relations have increasingly dominated the world in which they live.

I acknowledge that I am demanding a lot from general education teachers. In addition to knowing literary works we will have to be familiar with the history of various ages and have the ingenuity to relate the two. The demands such analysis places on us present real problems. Certainly one reason why other forms of analysis seem to have a better chance of institutionalization in this country is that they do not make similar demands. For instance, even though there are widespread calls that we abandon the New Critics' narrow notion of literature and teach a wide range of discourses, most of the analyses that present themselves as alternatives do not substantially alter the framework it established. The major skill they demand is one New Critics demanded—a close, critical reading of texts. My point is that we cannot read closely unless we read historically and that close reading can alter our sense of history. If historical analysis is to be institutionalized, the false opposition between close and historical readings needs to be overcome.

In this essay I have tried to avoid the popular practice of singling out the New Critics for blame, but I also want to avoid the equally common practice of overstating the debt we owe to them for teaching us how to read closely: after all, they were not the first to read closely. Some old-fashioned philologists would spend an entire semester reading only a hundred lines, tracing the history of each word and grammatical formation. To be sure, the New Critics developed important reading skills neglected by philologists, but they in turn neglected skills students need to read closely. Thus, I disagree with Jonathan Culler when he blames New Critics for our present problems in criticism, but praises their influence on teaching, going so far as to call the New Critics' "commitment to the autonomy of the literary text, a fundamental article of faith with positive consequences for the teaching of literature" (4). Culler reconciles this seeming contradiction by arguing, "But what is good for literary education is not necessarily good for the study of literature in general, and those very aspects of New Criticism which assured its success in schools and universities determined its eventual limitations as a program for literary criticism" (4). On the contrary, I argue that what is good for the study of literature in general is good for literary education. Why should we deprive our students of the insights our study of literature has to offer?

The danger in teaching and studying literature is not, as so many fear, that historical analysis will subordinate the special qualities of literature to another discipline, thus turning teachers of literature into second-rate historians who have abandoned their role as teachers of the humanities. Instead, it is that in demarcating a special territory for literary studies we save literature as an academic institution at the cost of reducing it to a specialized discourse related only extrinsically to human society and history. Indeed, not to study and teach historically is to deny students the very possibility of reading critically. Emphasizing our failure to teach critical evaluation, Scholes asks, "How many of you would trust your undergraduates—or even your graduate students, even your colleagues—to tell you why one text is better than another?"

(42). Historical analysis of literature does not stop with the judgment of texts. Instead, it teaches a critical process by which we judge the very conditions of our judgments. A product of the past, forever capable of reproduction in the present, literature can help bring into existence a historical consciousness that reflects upon and judges our present situation, a reflection and judgment necessary if students are to help determine what sort of future they will have.[5]

NOTES

1. Like Robinson, White's Aristotelian notion of literature comes into conflict with his view of reality, which does not assume a closed cosmos. Maintaining formalist views of literature and what could be called anarchistic views of historical reality, White inevitably feels that literary form imposes itself on historical reality. He refuses to entertain the possibility that literature, as a part of reality, also has the capacity to bring new forms into existence.

2. Stephen Greenblatt makes an important distinction when he says that literature is a "register of historical complexity" (5). Unlike a reflection, a register does not occupy a position outside of history to imitate it. Instead, it is part of the very historical complexity that it records. Nonetheless, Greenblatt still adheres to a mimetic model. A way to retain literature's capacity to represent without lapsing into a mimetic model is suggested in Wolfgang Iser's recent work. Unfortunately, much criticism calling itself historical continues to operate according to a reflection model.

3. This is not to argue that Ethnic Studies and Women's Studies departments are the answer. There are many problems associated with their establishment, not the least of which is that women and minorities have now become the object of study for one more specialized discipline. Furthermore, some feminist analysis is notoriously ahistorical while much interdisciplinary historical analysis continues to subscribe to a naïve reflection model of literature.

Considering the American Studies movement would complicate my account. Nonetheless, it can be seen in similar terms. According to Robert Spiller, "The development of a method for American Studies is bound up with the effort to resolve the dilemma posed by the dualism which separates social facts from aesthetic values." This dualism could be transcended by a "dynamic cooperation" between historical and aesthetic studies (20, 21).

4. See Fredric Jameson's claim that the answer for a historical critic is not to turn "away from the formalizing kinds of criticism to something else, but rather of going all the way through them so completely that we come out the other side" (32).

5. A much shorter and different version of this essay appeared as "The Historical Necessity for—and Difficulties with—New Historical Analysis in Introductory Literature Courses" in *College English* (Sept. 1987): 509-21. Copyright 1987 by the National Council of Teachers of English. Reprinted with permission. I began formulating my ideas for an Institute on Contemporary

Criticism and Introductory Literature courses in June 1985. I thank the participants for their criticism. Most of all I thank my previous students for keeping me aware of their felt historical needs.

Since that essay appeared Howard Horwitz seems to have read my argument to be that the critical awareness I speak of will somehow *necessarily* " 'help' us and our students 'shape the direction of the future.' " He then refutes such causal thinking with, "It is not clear to me that instruction in the constructedness of subjectivity, the constructedness of history, and the indignities of history need evoke in students activism rather than cynicism and decadence" (820n58). But I never make a necessary causal link between the pedagogy I am advocating and activism (Horwitz's word, not mine). Instead, as I hope the reader will agree, I am quite cautious about claiming any particular affect. As I wrote in that essay and this one, it would be naïve to think that "changing the way we teach will drastically alter the historical conditions" that have led to our students' lack of historical consciousness. What I do argue is that rather than succumb to these conditions, we should try to combat them in our teaching. I also argue—and this is debatable—that a historical consciousness is a necessary condition *if* "students are to help determine what sort of future they will have." Horwitz, it seems, confuses necessary conditions for sufficient ones and attributes a causal argument to me that I never make. Perhaps both Scholes and I are wrong. Maybe we need instruction in logic before either philosophy or history. We might also need instruction in the use of quotations. Horwitz jars my phrase "shape the direction of the future" out of context and thus ignores the caution with which I use it. The original context speaks of a "cultural amnesia" that "has left us with no perspective on the present, thus *making it more difficult than ever* to shape the direction of the future" (510, emphasis added).

WORKS CITED

Adams, Henry. *The Education of Henry Adams.* Boston: Houghton Mifflin, 1973.

Beard, Charles A. *The Discussion of Human Affairs.* New York: Macmillan, 1936.

———. *An Economic Interpretation of the Constitution of the United States.* New York: Macmillan, 1913.

Benjamin, Walter. "Literaturgeschichte und Literaturwissenschaft." In *Gesammelte Schriften,* 5 vols. Frankfurt a.M.: Suhrkamp, 1972, vol. 3.

Blumenberg, Hans. "The Concept of Reality and the Possibility of the Novel." In *New Perspectives in German Literary Criticism.* Ed. Richard E. Amacher and Victor Lange. Princeton: Princeton University Press, 1979.

Brooks, Cleanth. "Criticism, History, and Critical Relativism." In *The Well Wrought Urn.* New York: Harcourt, 1947. 215-47.

Crane, R. S. "History versus Criticism in the University Study of Literature." *English Journal* 24 (1935): 645-67.

Culler, Jonathan. *The Pursuit of Signs.* Ithaca: Cornell University Press, 1981.

Daiches, David. *English Literature.* Englewood Cliffs, N.J.: Prentice-Hall, 1964.

Denham, Robert, ed. Draft of "Summary of Reports from the Discussion Groups at the Conference on Doctoral Study," Spring Hill Center, Wayzata, Minn., 2-5 April 1987.

Eagleton, Terry. *Literary Theory: An Introduction*. Minneapolis: University of Minnesota Press, 1983.

Ferry, Anne. *The "Inward" Language: Sonnets of Wyatt, Sidney, Shakespeare, Donne*. Chicago: University of Chicago Press, 1983.

Frye, Northrop. *The Anatomy of Criticism*. Princeton: Princeton University Press, 1957.

Graff, Gerald. *Professing Literature: An Institutional History*. Chicago: University of Chicago Press, 1987.

———. "Taking Coverage in Coverage." *Profession 86*. New York: Modern Language Association, 1986. 41-45.

Greenblatt, Stephen. *Renaissance Self-Fashioning*. Chicago: University of Chicago Press, 1980.

Haskell, Thomas L. *The Emergence of Professional Social Science*. Urbana: University of Illinois Press, 1977.

Heilman, Robert B. "History and Criticism: Psychological and Pedagogical Notes." *College English* 27 (1965): 32-38.

Higham, John. "The Schism in American Scholarship." In *Writing American History: Essays on Modern Scholarship*. Bloomington: Indiana University Press, 1970. 3-24.

Hirsch, E. D. *Cultural Literacy*. Boston: Houghton Mifflin, 1987.

Horwitz, Howard. " 'I Can't Remember': Skepticism, Synthetic Histories, Critical Action." *South Atlantic Quarterly* 87, no. 4 (Fall 1988): 787-820.

Iggers, Georg C. *The German Conception of History*. Middletown, Conn.: Wesleyan University Press, 1968.

Iser, Wolfgang. "Feigning in Fiction." In *Identity of the Literary Text*. Ed. Mario J. Valdés and Owen Miller. Toronto: University of Toronto Press, 1985. 204-28.

———. "Fictionalizing Acts." *Amerikastudien* 31 (1986): 5-15.

Jameson, Fredric. "Criticism in History." In *The Weapons of Criticism*. Ed. Norman Rudich. Palo Alto: Ramparts, 1976: 31-50.

Lasch, Christopher. *The Culture of Narcissism: American Life in an Age of Diminishing Expectations*. New York: Norton, 1978.

Melville, Herman. *Billy Budd, Sailor (An Inside Narrative)*. Indianapolis: Bobbs-Merrill, 1975.

Morris, Wesley. *Toward a New Historicism*. Princeton: Princeton University Press, 1972.

Orr, Linda. "The Revenge of Literature: A History of History." *New Literary History* 18 (1986): 1-23.

Pearce, Roy Harvey. *Historicism Once More*. Princeton: Princeton University Press, 1969.

———. "Literature, History, and Humanism: An Americanist's Dilemma." *College English* 24 (1963): 364-72.

Robinson, James Harvey. *New History: Essays Illustrating the Modern Historical Outlook.* New York: Macmillan, 1912.

Santayana, George. "Dewey's Naturalistic Metaphysics." *Journal of Philosophy* 22 (1925).

Scholes, Robert. "Some Problems in Current Graduate Programs in English." *Profession 87.* New York: Modern Language Association, 1987. 40-42.

Shakespeare, William. "Sonnet 87." In *Shakespeare, the Complete Works.* Ed. G. B. Harrison. New York: Harcourt, 1948.

Spiller, Robert. "Value and Method in American Studies: The Literary versus the Social Approach." *Jahrbuch für Amerikastudien* 4 (1959): 20-25.

Thomas, Brook. "The Historical Necessity for—and Difficulties with—New Historical Analysis in Introductory Literature Courses." *College English* 49 (Sept. 87): 509-21.

White, Hayden. *The Tropics of Discourse.* Baltimore: Johns Hopkins University Press, 1978.

ROBERT CON DAVIS

A Manifesto for Oppositional Pedagogy: Freire, Bourdieu, Merod, and Graff

> English literature is only chatter about Shelley.
>
> E. A. Freeman

> An epoch is characterized by a complex of ideas, concepts, hopes, doubts, values, and challenges in dialectical interaction with their opposites, striving toward plenitude.
>
> Paulo Freire

> Those who argue that the humanities have become disablingly incoherent seem to me right, but many of them fail to see that coherence can no longer be grounded on some restored consensus, whether it be traditional "basics," revolutionary ideological critique, or something else.
>
> Gerald Graff

> The question here . . . is what position intellectuals can occupy if they are to carry out a transformative and not a reproductive, legitimating role in society.
>
> Jim Merod

In the late 1960s and early 1970s a number of Western theorists from different disciplines—most prominently Michel Foucault and Noam Chomsky—seemed as a group to leap the boundaries of academic inquiry through their politically provocative critiques of culture and social practices. Much of that critique is ongoing and has produced a body of "oppositional" thought that deliberately challenges dominant cultural and political orders with ideologically subversive schemes and practices—in education, literary criticism, politics, economics, psychoanalysis (as an institution), gender relations, and other areas. This oppositional criticism draws from contemporary semiotic, deconstructive, and Marxist theory but also, though less obviously, from a tradition of oppositional "logic" first theorized by Aristotle as a kind of algorithm of interpretive relations.

An exemplary instance of this thought is oppositional pedagogy—the attempt by Paulo Freire, Pierre Bourdieu, and many others to theorize but also to initiate radical social change through pedagogy, through what students are taught and how they are taught it. These include attempts to theorize the function and impact of pedagogy in society, especially the interaction of schools and universities with other social institutions. This is a particularly urgent task in light of the belief, as Louis Althusser advances, that education occupies the *"dominant position"* as the implementer of state ideology in modern Western societies (152). Since the 1960s, this urgency has characterized the oppositional promise of ideologically motivated change for an institution that is widely believed by the political left, as Althusser shows, to be resistant to such change on the grounds of its ties to the state. Those on the right, by contrast, hold education to be a value-free, fundamentally nonpolitical practice. From this angle the oppositional pedagogue is seen as one exploiting a privileged position to satisfy ulterior (political) motives: the teacher-as-political-deviant.

Traditionally assigned a conservative function and operating within prescribed boundaries, the political pedagogue, in fact, exemplifies the dilemma of the oppositional critic in general as one dependent on the social function of bourgeois institutions and yet committed to far-reaching change within and beyond them. Oppositional pedagogues, in other words, "play a fundamental role in producing the dominant culture," as Henry Giroux, David Shumway, Paul Smith, and James Sosnoski point out, but are committed nonetheless to offer "students forms of oppositional discourse . . . at odds with the hegemonic role of the university" (480)—the dilemma of oppositional pedagogy being precisely that of trying to destroy and reconstitute an activity even while performing it.

Amidst this activity of oppositionalism, an implicit but powerful manifesto for pedagogy has evolved, perhaps the only thorough and consistent critique of conventional educational practices to emerge in the last twenty-five years. Theorists are divided, though, on the crucial question of precisely how change takes place *within* existing institutions and also how it can be initiated. In *The Politics of Letters* (1987), for instance, Richard Ohmann writes that we "can [already] take satisfaction" over institutional changes effected in curriculum and administration by radical students and teachers since the 1960s, particularly the "renewal of American marxism" in the academy (130). Giroux and his colleagues find the opposite to be true as they describe post-1960 compromise and collaboration, institutional denaturing, in the once subversive programs of interdisciplinary study in higher education. Accordingly, Ohmann believes, rather optimistically, that change has been and can be initiated from within, whereas Giroux et al. believe that change in American education has emanated, and can only emanate, from outside the dominant discourse. The roles of conflict (opposition) and change in the production of ideology are at the heart of the oppositional critique of education. At issue is not only an interpretation of institutional history since 1960 but a struggle to reshape and define pedagogy in relation to radical theory.

In what follows I will examine the seven specific tenets of oppositional pedagogy's implicit manifesto to argue that, as Paulo Freire, Jim Merod, and Gerald Graff show, oppositionalism must be viewed in an interactive, dialogic relationship with existing institutions and has no existence "outside" of the dominant discourse. We will see, further, that the formidable difficulties uncovered by oppositional theorists in education, while not intractable, require a rethinking of "pedagogy" as a radical practice, its function and what it can achieve. What Freud described as the "impossibility" of education as a practice is explained by the oppositional critics by reference to its intrinsically ideological and dynamic nature—by the impossibility of separating it from political practices and what Althusser calls the "ideological State apparatus," the mechanism that produces the dominant ideology in culture (152). I want to argue that it is precisely the work of the oppositional pedagogue to provide the interface and, therein, close the gap between dominant and competing discourses that hold out the possibilities of cultural revolution and change.

The Tenets of Oppositional Pedagogy

The recent impetus for an oppositional pedagogy comes from two sources—third-world attempts to reject foreign domination in education and radical attempts to rethink the nature of social change in France after the May 1968 student/worker uprisings. The book that made the case for revolutionary teaching in third-world countries and the basis for a manifesto of oppositional pedagogy is Paulo Freire's well-known *Pedagogy of the Oppressed* (1968). This book espoused a case for a dissenting pedagogy based on political involvement by those who do not want merely to interpret but to change education—and culture. Freire's theory of how teachers will be involved in social revolution gives both a critique of pedagogy and a general plan to change third-world education in light of three principles, which in essence constitute the first three tenets of the oppositional manifesto.

Tenet 1

Freire first looks at the way school curriculum and institutional practices have indirectly collaborated with objectionable governments and social systems, set themselves up as "free" and then, say, in "civics" lessons, advance the prevailing ideology of oppression. To counter this practice, he advocates the development of what he calls "*conscientizacao*," the "ability to perceive social, political, and economic contradictions" in society and culture—what I will call "discourse awareness" (*Oppressed* 19). Discerning the implications of "contradiction" as class conflict for Freire, moreover, is the process but also the ultimate aim of education. This awareness must then lead to an actual theory of class conflict, for "without [such] a revolutionary theory" of class, as Freire quotes Lenin, "there can be no revolutionary movement," and without a movement or revolutionary moment there is no impetus to "theory"—hence the importance of "discourse awareness" as the basis of education.

Tenet 2

His second principle regards the active participation of students as the oppressed struggling in their own liberation. The "oppressed" person, he says, "must be among the developers of this [revolutionary] pedagogy" (39), by which he means that the oppressed must become active in the tasks usually reserved for teachers and administrators. An increase in their participation reduces their alienation, the real goal of liberation and the "revolutionary" aim of oppositional pedagogy. Once active in their education, as Freire argues, students will not allow pedagogical decisions to be made by others—administrators and "experts" not themselves subject to the teaching they supervise. Rather, students must actively produce knowledge even about what will be taught and who will teach.

Tenet 3

Tenet 2 also points toward the scope of change needed for a lasting effect. Freire stipulates that the "historical task [or responsibility] of the oppressed [is] to liberate themselves *and* their oppressors" (28, emphasis added). Education has been transformed only when the relations of education most broadly are reconstituted. Whereas in traditional instruction—as Giroux, Shumway, Smith, and Sosnoski describe—"experts in a discipline impart to apprentices the received knowledge about a particular subject matter" (481), the active subject/teacher imparting knowledge to passive students, in revolutionary pedagogy students and teachers exchange and alternate their roles. In this way, as Freire points out, students are liberated from the role in which they are "alienated like the slave in the Hegelian dialectic" (*Oppressed* 59), and the teachers, too, are liberated from the equally alienating "master" role—a change allowing "both parties to construe themselves as agents in the process of their own cultural formation" (Giroux et al. 482).

Whereas Freire concentrates on the revolutionary moment of "*conscientizacao,*" or awakening, in a third-world setting, Pierre Bourdieu and Jean-Claude Passeron in *Reproduction in Education, Society, and Culture* (1970) attempt to theorize the mechanism that generates contradictions as education reproduces state—"official"—ideology. Bourdieu and Passeron's analysis is the premier example of a theoretical effort to understand cultural practices in the wake of a general failure to do so in the midst of the French student/worker "revolution" of May 1968. The urgency of Bourdieu's work, in particular, therefore, is not aimed at initiating "discourse awareness" so much as reaffirming an advanced ideological critique that was severely threatened in the aftermath and failure of the 1968 revolution. That is, whereas Freire's analysis is an urgent call to action, Bourdieu's is a reflective and theoretical speculation on ideology *as a function* within the structure of the class system and as a specific practice that reproduces the state. Bourdieu wants to focus precisely on how education advances state values and, further, how the oppositional critic—speaking within the dominant discourse but committed to speaking "beyond" it—is inevitably caught in Epimenides's liar's paradox and says, "what I am telling you is a lie" (12).

Tenet 4

Bourdieu's primary contribution to the manifesto of oppositional pedagogy is to show the operation of the liar's paradox in discourse itself and that we will understand education as an institution, as a cultural practice, only as—as Freire points out—we focus on the contradictions of discourse. This is not an easy task with an encompassing cultural practice such as education, whose power and legitimacy derive from its manipulation of powerful symbolic forms quite apart from its expressed intent. Education officially promotes "truth" and "open inquiry" as universal and unchanging values, but, as Bourdieu warns, "every power which manages to impose meanings . . . as legitimate by concealing the power relations which are the basis of its force, adds its own specifically symbolic force to those power relations" (vi). A case in point is that "anyone who teaches" will "be treated [by students] as a father" (19), and the school or academy itself will therein draw to itself a grand version of this transferential, symbolic authority and become the institutional "one who is supposed to know." (Freud and Lacan, of course, speak of this process at great length.) Such symbolic (specular) authority inevitably poses in the guise of universal values and, in so doing, masks the functional aim in the promotion of state ideology.

Tenet 5

Specifically hidden by education's symbolic authority, as Bourdieu argues, is the replication and continuance of the class system. In an analysis of the "educational career and its system of determinations," Bourdieu shows how the starting point of an "initial class membership" is renegotiated and "retranslated" through an educational network that finally assigns "eventual class membership" (256-57), a process governed at each step by ideological determinations such as "relation to class origin," "relation to language and culture (manners)," "capital of social connections," and so on (257). Bourdieu's detailed mapping of this process shows the importance of "hiddenness" in cultural discourse and the exercise of "symbolic violence" so that the "arbitrariness of [educational] content" is "never seen in its full truth" (11), the effectiveness of pedagogy (what Bourdieu calls the "pedagogic effect"), in fact, being predicated on the difference between the claims of education and the enunciation, or functional effect, of pedagogical discourse.

Often referring to these precepts of a "revolutionary" pedagogy, oppositional critics since 1968 have extended Freire's and Bourdieu's analyses to specifics in the teaching of reading and writing, history, business, law, and other areas.[1] In *Criticism and Social Change* (1983), for instance, Frank Lentricchia cites John Dewey and Kenneth Burke — both of whom foreshadow Freire and Bourdieu — to reintroduce the distinction between "education as a function of society" and "society as a function of education" — views, Lentricchia notes bluntly, "dividing the world between those who like it and those who do not" (1). In the former view, education is seen as having an inculcating function in society — as a kind of training, or askesis, in the rigor of reinvesting an already constituted community with ever new validity and authority. In the latter view, education is projected as an ongoing and somewhat perverse activity responding to society as it emerges and evolves, education being an index of social changes and fundamentally "oppositional" (evolving in opposition to what came before) in its service to continual revolution.

Here the concept of critique — again Freire's "discourse awareness"—is largely Marxist, emphasizing class struggle, ideological discourse, and the economic basis of social organization. Any pedagogical event (e.g., teaching a class, choosing texts, etc.) is ideological in that it serves certain interests and not others. Evolutionism could be taught at one historical moment, and that choice and the rejected alternatives it entails (biblical creationism and Native American creation stories, etc.) then constitute a semiotic system governed by standards reflecting dominant cultural values expressed as ideology. Such a critique theorizes the functional value of pedagogy's contributions to ideology at particular moments of cultural life.

Tenet 6

Even the identity and subjective make-up of students are the products of discourses that to a degree *create* the student. The "discourse awareness" that enables such distinctions Stanley Aronowitz and Henry Giroux call "critical literacy"—education as the analytical connection between "knowledge" and "power" (*Education under Siege* 132), between the material force of a historical moment and the "understood," or theorized, event. For such a critique, there is a specific "pedagogical value" to opposition—as Aronowitz and Giroux argue—"in the connections it makes between structure and human agency" (107), what we readily know and are free to act on and what we resist knowing. In this way, ideological resistance, or blockage, is a crucial indicator of the direction critique can and should take at any one moment.

In other words, the critical-literate student also discovers him- or herself as a subject in the fact of the ideological connections forged, as Aronowitz and Giroux say, between "culture and the process of self-formation" (107)—the cumulative history of the connections made between personal agency and social structure. "Self" is literally the sedimented layers—the history—of previous connections to "human agency," between information and necessity, cognition and performance, and is an aspect—in this way—of the critique of "knowledge" and "power."

Tenet 7

Oppositional pedagogy should also attempt, as Jim Merod argues, to account for its own institutional placement as an agent of change and to show an "understanding of the institutional context within which students and teachers do their work—from which they can see their work as interpreters to be situated with concrete social and political consequences" (151). On this basis, Merod criticizes Fredric Jameson's readings of literary texts for the way they articulate ideology in narrative but are "unavailable [to show] the passage from interpretive theory to the making of a body of critical intellectuals who know where they work, what they work for, and how they mean to achieve regenerative social goals" (18) (see especially Jameson's *The Political Unconscious*). Teachers and critics, as Merod argues, interpret literary texts, but they also need to take the measure of their own "insertion" within "the divisions of labor that continue to define our economic and social world" (19), which means theorizing the political and social context of their work as teachers and intellectuals—accounting for the social impact of their labor and what they want to achieve. They cannot, as Merod accuses Jameson of doing, leave "the creation of a critical [and pedagogical] community to one side as a later, more revolutionary moment of theory" (18).

But if Jameson errs by taking for granted the institutional context of intellectual work, oppositional critics trying to situate their work politically must also contend with the resistance to generating a critique of education and working toward radical change from within an institution. The critique advanced by members of the Group for Research on the Institutionalization and Professionalization of Literary Study (GRIP), Henry Giroux, David Shumway, Paul Smith, and James Sosnoski is a case in point. In "The Need for Cultural Studies: Resisting Intellectuals and Oppositional Public Spheres," Giroux et al. advocate the rise of cultural studies as an oppositional practice within American society. They reason that the proliferation since the 1960s of interdisciplinary programs in American universities (women's studies, African-American studies, American studies, etc.) was initially a practice conceived to counter and displace reigning ideologies that govern the exercise of power in American life—"both the enabling and constraining dimensions of culture" (473). The cultural critique emanating from such enterprises, they argue, is needed "to identify the fissures in the ideologies of the dominant culture" (473). These new programs "succeeded" gradually through being "institutionalized" as permanent departments and inevitably began to harmonize more with institutional expectations concerning the social problems they isolated and the conclusions they drew. Finally, in the 1980s most of these programs have been denatured, institutionally assimilated to the point where they have lost their oppositional force and have no critique to advance.

Giroux et al. believe that this failure mandates a whole new oppositional strategy. Whereas oppositional critics generally imagine their work as situated within institutions, Giroux et al. reject any exchange between critics and the institutions they wish to supplant or change. For them, the possibility of assimilation and ideological contamination dictates the removal of intellectual work completely out of existing institutions. Giroux et al. argue that needed, rather, are "new" cultural studies institutes that avoid the pitfalls of existing organizations. These virtual noninstitutes will start on fresh (noncontaminated) ground, transcend professional compromises, and generally avoid the ideological boundaries that limit programs in the universities.

These utopian speculations, however, demonstrably shed little light on pedagogical work done within the academy, and to that extent they are disappointing as an attempt to situate the work of cultural criticism. Jameson may avoid institutional questions in his concern with narrative texts, but Giroux et al., with a quite different approach, are too little interested (at least in the critique I refer to) in the context of work being done within schools or the academy and, like Jameson, fail to explain "what [intellectuals] work for, and how they mean to achieve regenerative social goals" (Merod 18). Giroux et al. avoid the resistance of textual and institutional practice too well, are too eager in their utopianism, and disappear into the future (fictive) institutes they have projected as pedagogical ideals.

Neither Jameson nor Giroux et al., in short, illuminates the logic of cultural opposition, the system of intellectual work, that connects (and disconnects) them to the institutional site of their own intellectual labor. In the absence of a critique of oppositionalism's logic, oppositional pedagogy remains ineffectual—a source of observations about teaching and social change but not a program for the liberation of students and teachers from a counterproductive (master/slave) scenario. A radical critique of oppositional pedagogy, fundamentally redefining student-teacher relationships, would necessarilly cast pedagogy as an institutional and not a utopian or isolated practice.

The Situated Critique of Pedagogy

In a recent book Gerald Graff provides a good instance of Tenet 7 in action. He gives an institutional critique for one discipline, English studies, and readily advances our understanding of oppositional pedagogy as a cultural force. In *Professing Literature: An Institutional History* (1987), Graff describes the institutional discourse that has taken place in America since 1828 as "English" has become a profession—both a department in universities and colleges and a body of "expert" professional knowledge. He shows how American universities at first imitated German models in the teaching of philology and language and then gradually developed an "English" curriculum with the advent of the English major and graduate education at Johns Hopkins University,

Indiana University, Cornell, and Princeton. His "history" is an account of intensified professionalization and the developing role of "expertise" in the American academy, the movement of the university away from clerical training and the study of ancient languages and toward scientific and critical inquiry within well-demarcated professional boundaries. He relates the history of how American universities have achieved the social prestige and cultural impact they have today.

Graff's complex historical account identifies four pedagogical positions that influence each other within the American academy. He recounts these positions as ideologically opposed to each other, that is, how their "history" constitutes an ideological discourse in American education based on what oppositional theorists show to be the "logic" of opposition. The most pervasive, and still influential, position Graff calls professional "humanism," by which he means the belief that there is a "truth" of human affairs to be found in the systematic inquiry into classical and Anglo-American literature. Once the English department in America became a professional guild toward the end of the nineteenth century, professional humanism became the guiding orientation of "field-coverage" as departmental organization. As Graff explains, "the literature department adopted the assumption that it would consider itself respectably staffed once it had amassed instructors competent to 'cover' a more or less balanced spread of literary periods and genres, with a scattering of themes and special topics" (7). This organizational format even now "seems so innocuous as to be hardly worth looking at" (7), and yet it expresses a "faith that exposure to a more or less balanced array of periods, genres, and themes would add up in the mind of the student to an appreciation of humanism and the cultural tradition" (9). Underlying this humanistic enterprise is the belief that *"literature teaches itself"* (9–10), and, thus, there is little perceived need to discuss the adequacy of the "field-coverage" scheme or theoretical issues related to it because, as Graff concludes, such a system fosters "the illusion . . . that nobody [has] a theory" (9).

Directly related to professional humanism was another nineteenth-century approach to literary study that can be called amateur appreciation developed in the "classical college." This approach originally was articulated when the college mission was preparation for professional study, "Christian leadership and the ministry" as well as medicine and law (20). Originally centered on the study of Greek and Latin so as "to inspire the student with the nobility of . . . cultural heritage" (28), this "liberal studies" education facilitated "gentle breeding," "appreciation," and "acculturation for 'the cultivated gentleman'" (20). This education often focused on classical grammar, and teachers promised that Greek literature's wisdom "would somehow rub off on students through contact with linguistic [and grammatical] technicalities" (35).

This "amateur" approach is little evident today as professed curriculum, but it exists as a residue in many English departments and is the personal commitment of many professors, especially those who disapprove of the entire direction of modern literary studies, including its emphasis on research and publication, and who still imagine returning to a fantasized "innocent"—or at least not so professionally involved—appreciation of literature based on the natural and pure love of words. Allan Bloom's recent *The Closing of the American Mind*, for example, promotes the shaping of mind through an amateur's close reading of classical texts, and almost every English or modern language department has one or two adherents to this approach.

The third approach is that of scientific and rigorous methodology, which Graff traces to the nineteenth-century "German-trained cadre of scholarly 'investigators' who promoted the idea of scientific research and the philological study of the modern languages" (55). Beginning with nineteenth-century philology, the new academic professional was an expert working from rigorous discovery models and aiming to increase the knowledge store, this professional's loyalties going, as Graff says, "to his 'field' rather than to the classroom dedication that had made the older type of college teacher seem a mere schoolmaster" (62).

The new humanities professional soon became diversified in literary and historical scholarship and other closely related areas not specifically philological. Eventually, with the rise of New Criticism in the 1930s, the new "scientific" approach carried over to speculative concerns within literary criticism. This development conflicted from the start with research-based (historical and linguistic) activities, a conflict that continues today as theory versus scholarship and theory versus humanism. Through its rational principles, its pragmatic and teachable methods, and the demonstrable results it achieved, New Criticism of this period continued the move toward professional expertise and away from the "appreciation"-based or even humanistic concerns of the earlier approaches.

The fourth approach is the attempt to see "English" as a kind of cultural studies. Graff actually enacts this option himself by reading the discourse of English as a cultural phenomenon, situated within an ideological matrix, that has been evolving since the early nineteenth century. In other words, he identifies pedagogical practices and the way they have caused "English" to become a professional entity in the academy. Moreover, he examines the impact of these practices on the university work environment and on the cultural areas they interact with. His concern is always to identify the ideological transformations at work as the English department as we know it comes into being. The institutional and cultural impact identified with each approach shapes "English," his analysis accounting for what has happened in culture so that "English" takes a particular shape as a discipline. He also focuses on the connections Aronowitz and Giroux make between power and knowledge, between "English" as a cultural force and as a body of knowledge.

The "Logic" of Opposition

In his critique of the discourse of the American English department Graff has adopted the procedures of the oppositional critic. He does this by positioning his own critique as a practice in relation to other real and unrealized practices, that is, within a specific work environment. Graff's own analysis thus fits within the professional discourse he has discussed, within the ideological logic of pedagogical practices. In fact, his is precisely the practice of oppositional pedagogy that Jim Merod called for, the beginning of liberation for the oppressed—in this case, the intellectually oppressed—that Freire called for in education generally.

Most "oppositional" about Graff's work, though, is the nature of his critique, the way in which he attempts to map the "logic" of ideology in the practices of pedagogical discourse. The oppositional tradition I associate with him—traceable to the pre-Socratics and Aristotle, and moving through Marx, Antonio Gramsci, Robert Blanche, A. J. Greimas, Edward Said, and Fredric Jameson—formulates specific strategies for thinking about what it means for ideas to oppose each other, how change occurs in cultural relations, and when opposition becomes appropriated by its "opposition" (for a discussion of this mechanism, see my "Theorizing Opposition"). This tradition, in short, speculates on cultural conflict and how to interpret it in specific settings.

The oppositional critics that Graff follows, moreover, often assume a common foundation for language and politics. They assume the existence of a four-part algorithm that governs the possibilities for change in any cultural practice. In Aristotle's own practice in *On Interpretation*—the prototype of A. J. Greimas's "semiotic square" and the model behind Jameson's oppositional critique in *The Political Unconscious*—the attempt to theorize opposition shows that interpretive possibilities move along the particular lines of ideology and not others. Oppositional critics believe that if this were not so, political change could not be accounted for, would not be marked within the cultural text. That is, without the control of the oppositional metaphor, knowable differences would be lost in chance iterations and would not be formulable as ideologically significant. "There can be no knowledge," as Aristotle warns in the *Posterior Analytics*, "of that which [exists or comes to be] by chance" (42). Aristotle sees opposition, as do Baudrillard and Greimas, too, as embodying the very possibility of rational analysis and of what could be termed "intelligibility" in reading the world text.

Graff's discourse and manner of reading belong in this tradition. For example, the classical oppositional square (see Aristotle's *On Interpretation* and Greimas and Rastier's "The Interaction of Semiotic Constraints") creates a representation of ideology on two levels of opposition that together form a discourse. The first level couples propositions that form a "contrary" relationship, as in Graff's opposition of professional humanism/amateurish "appreciation." These terms oppose each other to establish a range of difference. Their "opposition" semanticists call "contrary," as in the association of "black" and "green"; their association forms a set and a range of differences, such as professional humanism in relation to an amateur's appreciation.

On the second (subaltern) level of opposition, a third term indicates the specific hierarchy, the ideology, by which meanings are organized within the range of reference defined by the first level. The third term, by being a specific case or rule, in effect, "interprets" the first level and precisely "describes the 'nature' of the category upon which the [first-level] binary opposition is inscribed" (Schleifer 54). In Graff's example of professional humanism/amateurish "appreciation," the third term is "scientific research"—rational inquiry as the designation of power governing the humanism/appreciation opposition. Scientific investigation signifies ideology in this oppositional discourse and "situates" the first level of reference, interprets and limits it, by signifying the hierarchy that organizes it. The third term, in this way, inscribes a set of values positioned as a particular pattern in the square's hierarchy.

The fourth term of this ideological reading is "oppositional pedagogy"—liberation of the educationally oppressed. "Oppositional pedagogy" opposes and negates "amateur's appreciation," has a "contrary" relation to "scientific research," and gives final (negative) expression to the professional humanism this discourse began with. In summary, the first-level terms signal the coexistence of "contrary" possibilities; the third position articulates values inherent in the square, and the fourth term is a potential resituating of this discourse—what Jacques Lacan calls, in a similar context, a resituated "subjectivity" or subject position, a new "moi." The fourth term, in other words, fore-grounds an "other" potentiality, an "other" within discourse, made possible by the play of difference between the initial terms humanism/appreciation on the first level. The fourth term actually marks a new authority that will emanate from or be repressed in this discourse. The discourse of Graff's humanism/appreciation opposition can be projected as follows:

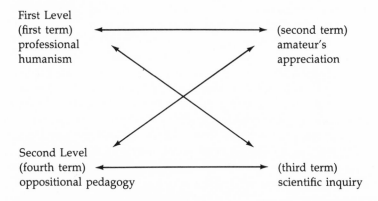

First Level
(first term)   (second term)
professional   amateur's
humanism   appreciation

Second Level
(fourth term)   (third term)
oppositional pedagogy   scientific inquiry

All of these relationships are established by an oppositional tie, of one kind or another, to the first term. The fourth term, however, "closes" the square by articulating a possibility effaced, or repressed, in the square's articulation and, in so doing, goes "beyond" the square by recognizing the possibility of a new pedagogy. Oppositional pedagogy comes into the square as the instance of what was suppressed all along through the insistence on various formal oppositions. The square, then, implicitly advances the fourth term as the completion but also as the potential destruction—the oppositional "other"—of its own logic.

As a historical phenomenon this critique shows "oppositional ped-agogy" to be a specific proposition rupturing the historical fabric of pedagogical discourse, a "rupture" that has left its trace but is not yet representable as a specific practice. This is Freire's conception, too, of the "pedagogy of the oppressed" as being, at this historical moment, within the articulations of the dominant bourgeois discourse (what Jameson calls the "political unconscious"), but "without a discourse" and, at the same time, an emergent pedagogical practice. "Oppositional pedagogy" is a historical event, thus, that the logic of bourgeois ideology helps to generate *and* at the same time suppresses, the power of op-positional pedagogy persisting on the margins of discourse as the scan-dal of the "political pedagogue." Accordingly, the potential of teaching as simultaneously a neutral *and* subversive activity is at the heart of Graff's critique of the American English department.

In Graff's reading of the humanism/appreciation opposition, each term of the discourse further defines an ideological hierarchy and maps the institutional and cultural text. This discourse of ideological reading, the progressive articulation of oppositional systems, has the effect of rendering cultural discourses intelligible by submitting "all the differences to . . . the principle of contrariety, which in turn becomes the pivot-point for relating, organizing, and systematizing differences"—in other words, an ideologizing of pedagogy (Anton 86). The result is a situated pedagogical discourse, or a representation of one, inscribed by the square's four terms, either as representing "positions" or values.

What we are viewing in Graff's method of critique, as with Jameson, Said, Greimas, and the oppositional critics generally, is an ideological approach to the problematic of teaching. Ideology, in this view, is an "effect" of discourse produced within a system of differences that are continually subject to reordering and transformation within that system, the momentum of which is driven by history. The irruption of oppositionalism in pedagogical discourse, therefore, is a disruptive cultural event, a virtual subversion and a manifestation of "history"—the diachronic emergence of the unthought and the initially unintelligible.

Of course I am not claiming that Graff literally follows Aristotle to generate the oppositions of pedagogical discourse; he may not even associate Aristotle with this critique as I do. He has grasped, however, as Aristotle, Gramsci, Greimas, and Jameson also believe, that the relations of opposition map a logic of resistance within the cultural text, the "logic" of ideology. To the extent that Graff locates the resistances of the oppositions he examines, he is testing the possibilities of ideology and moving toward something previously unthought. In this specific sense—regarding the potential of ideological critique—Graff's reading of pedagogical discourse is oppositional, that is to say, ideological.

The Manifesto

The logic of opposition here points out, among other things, that the move "outside" of educational institutions and the dominant discourse is problematic, in a sense impossible. As I interpret him, Graff demonstrates that oppositionalism occurs within a cultural discourse that includes dominant practices, the dominant and alternative practices responding to each other in a series of ruptures and resistances. In an important sense the oppositional critique depends on the dominant, hegemonic practices it opposes and the resistances that separate them. As Graff's analysis shows, to an important degree the opposition within discourse indeed can escape the confines of the dominant ideology, but while doing so it does not escape culture and the logic, and resistances, of ideology. Although the GRIP critics, for instance, urge radical pedagogues to flee established institutions and avoid official assimilation and recognition, the clean escape from the dominant discourse does not exist—in theory or practice. Graff's critique and the very logic of opposition, as I have presented them, demonstrate as much and argue, in fact, that there is no escaping ideology, which is precisely the interplay and hierarchicalizing power of discourse—an expression of cultural function and value. There is no ideological "outside"—no cultural escape route or area of the culture free of ideological resistance and force.

Clearly discernible in the oppositional critique I have been discussing are Freire's three principles—"conscientizacao," self-liberation of the oppressed, and radical change (alteration of the entire system), but also there is the general argument for recognizing the ideological nature of teaching. That is, by situating educational practices oppositionally, and by deciphering pedagogical practice as an ideological discourse within culture, Graff identifies social contradictions to the strategic end of improving conditions for new teaching practices. Graff's is a critique, in other words, calculated to lead not just to theoretical interpretation, but to radical change. Thus, unlike the GRIP theorists, he positions radical change as originating from within the academy in the practice of those oppressed by—or "involved with" or "responsible to"—the academy.

By describing what has hitherto been only implicit as a manifesto of oppositional pedagogy, I am not claiming that Freire's and Bourdieu's authority underwrites radical pedagogy through the late 1980s, or that Graff's practice, for example, merely elaborates the earlier ones—or that oppositional pedagogy would not have emerged without Freire and Bourdieu, and so on. But I am advancing that in the implicit manifesto of oppositional pedagogy is a strong critique of contemporary education and the beginnings of a program for radical change. This manifesto also provides a perspective on how change takes place and how it is positioned within culture.

Moreover, the cultural critique of pedagogical practices, which Freire, Bourdieu, and Merod call for and which Graff enacts, points out aspects of pedagogy that can only be seen or grasped as practices. In the case of the English department in America, we see that teaching takes a variety of forms within a cultural set of ideological options. There is, in sum, no such thing as "pedagogy," a transcendental practice for the appropriation and dissemination of "truth" existing outside of history and socially derived conditions, but there is the practice of what has actually been taught. In short, oppositionalism shows that pedagogy does not exist neutrally or ideally. It is not a fixed entity but a social practice and a cultural construct, a dynamic and unfinished (hence "impossible" to fix) activity—an enactment-as-practice of ideology in culture.

The implicit manifesto of oppositional pedagogy, finally, presents seven tenets that are calculated to suggest strategies for resisting the seductions of ideology in contemporary culture,[2] the most powerful strategy being to effect a fundamental reconception of what teaching is. Henceforth, in light of the oppositional manifesto, as it begins to have an impact, teaching cannot be taken as a value-free or ideologically innocent activity because knowledge itself is inherently political.[3] Pedagogy is an inherently political practice, and the manifesto of oppositional pedagogy shows the necessity, moreover, to understand teaching fundamentally as a situated cultural practice whose effects are learning only insofar as "learning" itself is seen in ideological terms—as having a political impact. All knowledge, in other words, does something to someone, benefits and oppresses, empowers some and deprives others—exists, in short, as a dimension of work with an effect in the world.

The implicit manifesto of oppositional pedagogy attempts to reverse the traditional, fixed hierarchy of teacher over student, active agent over passive receptacle—oppressor and oppressed—and critique that hierarchy. This critique follows from Freire's "discourse awareness" and the perception of social contradictions and then builds a new conception of education, in reference not to utopia but to actual instances of teaching, teaching situations and the critical connections to be made between knowledge and power. In this oppositional style, for example, Graff presents actual (institutional) approaches to teaching—professional humanism, scientific inquiry, etc.—in the dialogue of ideological relations. He situates himself, moreover, within that discourse as he articulates the relations of knowledge and power, the ideological understanding of cultural practice and the institutional force of "English" in America.

The revolutionary pedagogue, in other words, plays student and teacher and learns/teaches in a creative oppositional exchange with his or her culture. In the actual practice of situating teaching within culture, oppositionalism demonstrates that its aim is not merely to interpret pedagogy but, through critical practice, to change it strategically. It is in this sense that the insights of oppositionalism have become a manifesto for a new teaching and a source of radical practices whose influences are now being disseminated in the academy.

Finally, in the spirit of oppositionalism, I provide a last cautionary note about not taking any version of revolutionary teaching as an ideal or fixed practice, itself the new commonsense grounding for education. As we regard contemporary culture and pedagogy, we must not "fail to see," as Graff reminds us, that "coherence can no longer be grounded on some restored consensus, whether it be traditional 'basics,' revolutionary ideological critique, or something else" (15). Oppositional discourse is, after all, only the name and a representation for the ruptures and changes that eventually may shape the practices for which we as yet have no models. It is a genuine paradox of cultural discourse that these practices gradually take shape as a kind of access to the future—an access to that which is already being "opposed" even before it can be made known or teachable.

NOTES

1. See especially Ivan Illich's *Deschooling Society* (1971), Richard Ohmann's *English in America* (1976), and Michael W. Apple's *Cultural and Economic Reproduction in Education* (1982) and (edited with Lois Weis) *Ideology and Practice in Schooling* (1983). Other works have continued to focus the radical critique of education in line with broad political and social concerns—such works as David W. Livingstone's *Class Ideologies and Educational Futures* (1983), Paulo Freire's *The Politics of Education* (1985), Stanley Aronowitz and Henry A. Giroux's *Education under Siege* (1985), and Ohmann's *Politics of Letters* (1987). Some of the most recent works emphasize pedagogy as influenced by contemporary literary and cultural theory and discuss cultural "critique" as the project to understand pedagogy broadly within a cultural frame, volumes such as William Cain's *The Crisis in Criticism* (1984), G. Douglas Atkins and Michael L. Johnson's collection *Writing and Reading Differently* (1985), Gerald Graff's *Professing Literature* (1987), and Jim Merod's *The Political Responsibility of the Critic* (1987).

2. On the seduction of contemporary ideologies, see Ira Shor's *Culture Wars: School and Society in the Conservative Restoration, 1969-1984* (1986). Shor argues that the authority of official educational institutions in America was severely challenged and damaged in the social turmoil of the 1960s. "Official" attempts to restore authority after the 1960s, he argues, fall into three phases. From 1971 to 1975 there was a tremendous governmental advocacy of vocational issues and career aims. From 1975 to 1982 there was much concern, in spite of considerable evidence to the contrary, over poor "language" competence and a "literacy crisis." From 1982 on there has been a demand for "discipline" in education, renewed "academic" preparation, technological sophistication,

and the pursuit of "excellence." Shor contends that in each case the apparent educational "concern" masked an attempt to reestablish institutional authority lost in the 1960s and blatant moves toward conservative politics. It is the aim of Shor's book to work through the "seduction" of these "official" stances by means of a critique of American education. In his foreword to Shor's book, Paulo Freire focuses on exactly these recent seductions of ideology.

3. Along the same line, Jane Gallop, for instance, reminds us that the term *pedagogy* carries with it specific ideological freight as—as reflected in the word's etymology—the "teaching of boys." She asserts that pedagogy at base is male instruction as a metonymic connection to male social privilege (118), and within this comment is an insight that also sheds light, by the way, on the connection made frequently by de Sade, Dickens, and others of pedagogue and pederast— hence the universal fear, as I mentioned earlier, of the teacher-as-political- deviant. By dismantling pedagogy as a universal and timeless institution, Freire, Merod, and Graff unsettle the fixity of pedagogy as a singular concept and deconstruct the implicit maleness, the fixity, Gallop speaks of—the ideological freight at the heart of "pedagogy" as traditionally conceived in Western culture. Barbara Johnson makes a similar challenge to pedagogy by questioning the Western repression of "feminism" in teaching—the absence, in other words, of girls in the boys' school (182). She points out that the connection often exists between the flight from traditional pedagogy and the advent of a "de- viant" practice—in Molière's phrase—"*L'Ecole des femmes*" (165), a girls' school, a practice ideologically in opposition to the traditional male orientation of schooling. Barbara Guetti, similarly, identifies traditional pedagogy as a "male" teaching in the sense of being an unalterable practice that represses femininity, a scenario she shows to be borne out in Choderlos de Laclos's *De l'education des femmes*.

WORKS CITED

Althusser, Louis. "Ideology and Ideological State Apparatuses." In *Lenin and Philosophy and Other Essays*. Trans. Ben Brewster. New York: Monthly Re- view Press, 1971.

Anton, John Peter. *Aristotle's Theory of Contrariety*. London: Routledge and Kegan Paul, 1957.

Apple, Michael W. *Cultural and Economic Reproduction in Education*. London: Routledge and Kegan Paul, 1982.

Apple, Michael W., and Lois Weis, eds. *Ideology and Practice in Schooling*. Philadelphia: Temple University Press, 1983.

Aristotle. *On Interpretation*. Trans. Jean T. Oesterle. Milwaukee: Marquette University Press, 1962.

——. *Posterior Analytics*. Trans. Hippocrates G. Apostle. Grinnell, Ia.: Per- ipatetic Press, 1981.

Aronowitz, Stanley, and Henry A. Giroux. *Education under Siege*. South Hadley, Mass.: Bergin and Garvey, 1985.

Atkins, G. Douglas, and Michael L. Johnson, eds. *Writing and Reading Differently.* Lawrence: University Press of Kansas, 1985.

Bloom, Allan. *The Closing of the American Mind.* New York: Simon and Schuster, 1987.

Bourdieu, Pierre, and Jean-Claude Passeron. *Reproduction in Education, Society and Culture.* Trans. Richard Nice. London: Sage Publications, 1977.

Cain, William E. *The Crisis in Criticism.* Baltimore: Johns Hopkins University Press, 1984.

Davis, Robert Con. "Theorizing Opposition: Aristotle, Greimas, Jameson, and Said." *L'Esprit Createur* 27, no. 2 (1987): 5-18.

Freire, Paulo. *Pedagogy of the Oppressed.* Trans. Myra Berman Ramos. New York: Continuum, 1982.

———. *The Politics of Education.* Trans. Donaldo Macedo. South Hadley, Mass.: Bergin and Garvey, 1985.

Gallop, Jane. "The Immoral Teachers." *Yale French Studies* 63 (1982): 117-28.

Giroux, Henry, David Shumway, Paul Smith, and James Sosnoski. "The Need for Cultural Studies: Resisting Intellectual and Oppositional Public Spheres." *Dalhousie Review* 64, no. 2 (Summer 1984): 472-86.

Graff, Gerald. *Professing Literature: An Institutional History.* Chicago: University of Chicago Press, 1987.

Greimas, A. J., and François Rastier. "The Interaction of Semiotic Constraints." *Yale French Studies* 41 (1968): 86-105.

Guetti, Barbara. "The Old Regime and the Feminist Revolution: Laclos' *De l'education des femmes.*" *Yale French Studies* 63 (1982): 139-62.

Illich, Ivan. *Deschooling Society.* New York: Harper and Row, 1971.

Jameson, Fredric. *The Political Unconscious.* Ithaca: Cornell University Press, 1981.

Johnson, Barbara. "Teaching Ignorance: *L'Ecole des femmes.*" *Yale French Studies* 63 (1982): 165-82.

Lentricchia, Frank. *Criticism and Social Change.* Chicago: University of Chicago Press, 1983.

Livingstone, David W. *Class Ideologies and Educational Futures.* Sussex, England: Falmer Press, 1983.

Merod, Jim. *The Political Responsibility of the Critic.* Ithaca: Cornell University Press, 1987.

Ohmann, Richard. *English in America: A Radical View of the Profession.* New York: Oxford University Press, 1976.

———. *The Politics of Letters.* Middletown, Conn.: Wesleyan University Press, 1987.

Schleifer, Ronald. *A. J. Greimas and the Nature of Meaning.* Lincoln: University of Nebraska Press, 1987.

Shor, Ira. *Culture Wars: School and Society in the Conservative Restoration, 1969-1984.* Boston: Routledge and Kegan Paul, 1986.

NOTES ON CONTRIBUTORS

NANCY R. COMLEY is associate professor of English and director of composition at Queens College of the City University of New York. She has published numerous articles on the pedagogy of literature and composition and has collaborated with Robert Scholes, Gregory L. Ulmer, and others on *The Practice of Writing* (1985), *Elements of Literature* (1986), *The Fields of Writing* (1987), and *Text Book* (1988).

REED WAY DASENBROCK is associate professor of English at New Mexico State University. He has published widely in scholarly journals and is the author of *The Literary Vorticism of Ezra Pound and Wyndham Lewis: Towards the Condition of Painting* (1985) and the editor of *Redrawing the Lines: Analytic Philosophy, Deconstruction, and Literary Theory* (1989).

ROBERT CON DAVIS is associate professor of English at the University of Oklahoma. He has published widely in contemporary literature. With Ronald Schleifer he edited *Rhetoric and Form: Deconstruction at Yale* (1985) and *Contemporary Literary Criticism* (1989), and with Patrick O'Donnell he edited *Intertextuality and Contemporary American Fiction* (1988).

BARBARA C. EWELL is associate professor of English at Loyola University in New Orleans. She has published widely on Renaissance literature and in women's studies and is the author of *Kate Chopin* (1986).

ELIZABETH A. FLYNN is associate professor of humanities at Michigan Technological University. She is the founding editor of *Reader: Essays in Reader-Oriented Theory, Criticism, and Pedagogy*. She is a co-editor of *Gender and Reading: Essays on Readers, Texts, and Contexts* (1986).

BRUCE HENRICKSEN is professor of English at Loyola University in New Orleans. He has been an editor of *The New Orleans Review* and is the editor of *Murray Krieger and Contemporary Critical Theory* (1986). His articles have appeared in numerous journals, and he is currently writing a book on Joseph Conrad's narrative voices.

GEORGE P. LANDOW is professor of English and art at Brown University. His books include *Approaches to Victorian Autobiography* (1979), *Victorian Types, Victorian Shadows: Biblical Typology and Victorian Literature, Art, and Thought* (1980), *Images in Crisis: Literary Iconology, 1750 to the Present* (1982), *Ruskin* (1985), and *Elegant Jeremiahs: The Sage from Carlyle to Mailer* (1986). His work in humanities computing includes the editing and partial writing of *Context32,* a body of hypermedia documents relating to the Intermedia system at Brown University.

LORI H. LEFKOVITZ is assistant professor at Kenyon College. She has written articles on theory, nineteenth-century literature, and Judaism and feminism. She is the author of *The Character of Beauty in the Victorian Novel* (1987).

THAÏS E. MORGAN is assistant professor of English at Arizona State University. She is currently finishing a translation of Gerard Genette's *Mimologiques*, with a critical introduction. She is working on a book concerning gender and canonicity in mid-Victorian to early modern poetry and is editing a volume on gender issues.

ROBERT SCHOLES is Andrew Mellon Professor of Humanities and professor of English and comparative literature at Brown University. His numerous publications include *Structuralism in Literature* (1974), *Semiotics and Interpretation* (1982), and *Textual Power* (1985), which won the Modern Language Association's Mina P. Shaughnessy Prize. His textbooks include *Text Book* (1988), written with Nancy R. Comley and Gregory L. Ulmer.

R. A. SHOAF is professor of English and coordinator of graduate studies at the University of Florida. He is the author of *Dante, Chaucer, and the Word: Money, Images and References in Late Medieval Poetry* (1982), *The Poem as Green Girdle: "Commercium" in "Sir Gawain and the Green Knight"* (1984), and *Milton, Poet of Duality: A Study of Semiosis in the Poetry and Prose* (1985). He is the founding editor of *Exemplaria: A Journal of Theory in Medieval and Renaissance Studies*.

BROOK THOMAS is professor of English at the University of California at Irvine. He is the author of numerous articles and two books: *James Joyce's* Ulysses: *A Book of Many Happy Returns* (1982) and *Cross-examinations of Law and Literature: Cooper, Hawthorne, Stowe, and Melville* (forthcoming).

GREGORY L. ULMER is professor of English at the University of Florida. His many articles and books include *Applied Grammatology* (1985). He is coauthor, with John P. Leavey, of "GLASsary," the introduction to the English translation of Jacques Derrida's *Glass* (1987). He collaborated with Nancy R. Comley and Robert Scholes in writing *Text Book* (1988).

INDEX

271

91   57

PN
81
.R375
1990

PN
81
.R375/1990
AUTHOR

TITLE
Reorientations

DATE DUE	BORROWER'S NAME

Gramley Library
Salem College
Winston-Salem, NC 27108-

Gramley Library
Salem College
Winston-Salem, NC 27108